Learning from Case Studies in Chaplaincy

University Center
for Chaplaincy Studies

ISBN 978-94-6301-281-2

Eburon Academic Publishers
www.eburon.nl
info@eburon.nl

Cover design: Textcetera, The Hague
Graphic design: Studio Iris, Leende

Learning from Case Studies in Chaplaincy

Towards Practice Based Evidence & Professionalism

Renske Kruizinga, Jacques Körver,
Niels den Toom, Martin Walton, Martijn Stoutjesdijk (eds.)

Eburon
Utrecht 2020

Table of Contents

Chapter 1.

Introduction

Researching Living Human Encounter

Martin Walton

> Why did I
> give you a coat
> when you said
> I feel so cold
> and not
> the sun
> *(De Bruijn, 1992, p. 26)*

The poem above is very brief. Although it begins as a question, it lacks a question mark. In all its succinctness the poem does tell a little story. A feeling was expressed to which another responded by offering a coat. The effect is not reported, but there was apparently some reason to reconsider and to ask why a coat was given and not the sun. That suggests that some other need appeared that could not be addressed by the gift of a coat. That opens up the possibility that "sun" in this case does not just refer to the sun, but is a metaphor for something else. If that be the case, then the utterance of feeling cold may not be a statement about physical temperature. It might refer to some emotional or existential experience. The sun may refer to some offering of warmth or light. Whether the sun will suffice where the coat did not, is left open. The image of sun is so great that it may be a response to an almost endless experience of feeling cold. The story seems to stop there, but more than just a question the poem has become narrative material for further reflection.

We could read this poem as a metaphor for an encounter in chaplaincy care. It then contains, implicitly or explicitly, several characteristics of a case study as they have been developed in recent years in chaplaincy care. A need, feeling cold, is expressed and assessed by another. An intervention is offered in the form of a coat. The outcome, or lack of one, is reason for reassessment and some larger care plan. A possible second intervention is to give a "sun." The encounter is documented in written form and reflection begins. A first matter for consideration is whether the initial assessment and intervention were adequate and what kind of outcome they induced. Consequently, one might ask what led to the reassessment and what might be the expected outcome from the second intervention that is taken into consideration.

We could also read the poem itself as a way of offering recognition for the fact that the experience of "feeling cold" is, for the person who expresses it, too vast to be met by anything less than the sun itself. In that case the poem itself is not just a reflection, but an intervention in the form of offering recognition. Or the poem could express the self-reflection of the chaplain who feels that offering something small like a coat is inadequate and thus expresses the desire to offer more, or who realizes that he or she wants to offer more than can reasonably be given. All these readings of the poem are like different doors to the case, raising questions without question marks. They point to elements of a case study that can aid the imaginary chaplain to further reflect upon the encounter, describe it and turn the poem into a full-fledged case study.

Case studies in chaplaincy care

What is a case study in chaplaincy care? In the Dutch Case Studies Project (CSP), we understand a case study to be an informative and methodical description in which the accompaniment process and the contribution of professional chaplaincy care are demonstrated and argued with the intent of identifying criteria or characteristics of good practices. The inspiration for the project came from the 2011 call by George Fitchett to produce and publish case studies in chaplaincy care for the sake of developing research material (Fitchett 2011). A further impetus was provided by the collections of case studies published by Fitchett and Steve Nolan (Fitchett & Nolan, 2015; Fitchett & Nolan, 2017; Fitchett & Nolan, 2018). Halfway through our four-year project, we saw the number of published and publishable case studies growing. We also saw differences in the way case studies were written; for example, in the descriptive approaches, in the way the relation of practice and theory was addressed and in the concreteness of reported outcomes.

The excitement about the emerging field of case study research along with the concerns about how the research was developing led us to convocate an international case study research conference for the sake of synergy and reflection. The conference "Do we have a case?" on case study research in chaplaincy care was held in February of 2019 in Amsterdam. Host institution was the Dutch University Center for Chaplaincy Studies and its supporting universities, Tilburg School of Catholic Theology and the Protestant Theological University in the Netherlands, in collaboration with the Academic Advisory Board of the Dutch Association of Spiritual

Caregivers. The conference, which was the first of its kind on case study research in chaplaincy care, drew participants from six countries in Europe and from the United States. The volume at hand consists of contributions presented at the conference and includes case studies material, initial findings from case study research, reflections on methodology of the research and observations on the contribution of case study research to the professionalism of chaplains.

Although we speak of an emerging field of research, case studies in chaplaincy care are an old phenomenon. We might find the origin almost a century ago when Anton Boisen (1936/1971) coined the term "living human document." The term may sound objectifying to us today, as if a person could be compared or reduced to a document. The intention, as Charles Gerkin (1984) reiterated in his revival of the term in the 1980s, was, however, subjectifying. The intention was to afford the inner world of a human being the same respect and the same close reading and intensive care as a holy text. The living human document is also a living holy document.

For educational purposes, Boisen began writing case studies and teaching others to do so. Teachers, students and practitioners have since been writing case studies in all sorts of training and educational settings. About twenty five years ago Bonnie Miller-McLemore (1996) commented on the manner in which the term the living human document could be individualized and isolated from context. She proposed the term living human web, in order to emphasize the network of relations in which persons find themselves. As there is no text without a context, so there is no human being without a web of relations and meanings.

In both instances, whether we speak of a document or a web, the focus of the case is on a person, a patient or some recipient of pastoral care, and specifically on the inner world and outward dynamics of the person in question. In training and educational settings there was often a shift of focus, from the living human document, to the way the pastor or chaplain interacted with the living human being in a care relation. The aim was to enable the student or chaplain to further develop his or her pastoral posture and repertoire.

The cases being developed in case study research, presume the living human document, discern the living human web, and even assume a well-developed posture and repertoire on the part of the chaplain. The immediate focus remains, as in educational settings, on the interaction between a chaplain and another person, in what we might call the living human encounter. The broader focus, however, is not on the person in care, not on the personal development of the chaplain, but on the development of the profession of chaplaincy. That means that central to case study research is not just the assessment with regard to a living human document, not just the personal inner development and insight of a living human chaplain, but close attention to the actions and interactions, assessments and considerations, interventions and effects in and of chaplaincy care as a professional practice. What are the effective elements of that care? What are the outcomes?

For the reading of a living human document Gerkin could roughly rely on the analogy of text and reader. Reading a human web and discerning the context requires a more thorough social analysis. Reading the living human chaplain requires critical reflection and introspection. Reading the living human encounter in the context of professional chaplaincy confronts us with an almost exponential growth of complexity that reckons with all the various actors, backgrounds, contexts, settings, existential issues and cultural situations. In order to address the challenge of that complexity two strategies are available, complexity recognition and complexity reduction. The challenge of recognizing and accounting for complexity is addressed by thick description, for example in a narrative approach, or in the use of a format. Complexity reduction is realized by the focus on specific questions that are put to the material. In the simplest form the questions are what a chaplain does, for what reasons and with what effect?

One of the questions often asked is whether a case study with such a focus can adequately describe an instance of chaplaincy care, the living human encounter, the narratives, the mystery of an intimate and dialogical relationship. Can a case study capture the relational dynamics, the transcendent references and the essence of the care process? One way of responding to such questions is by asking another question. Can a chaplain in the spiritual care process really do justice to a person in care, to the living human document and to his web? Can a spiritual assessment or other analysis capture the essence and mystery of the other person and her situation? Can it tell us why the sun should be given rather than a coat? In all cases the answer is clearly "no." For holy things, whether holy documents or holy encounters, are not supposed to be captured. They are to be communicated. They are to be respected and read for the sake of communication on the crucial, critical and practical elements they offer for understanding another person, or for understanding chaplaincy encounters and care. Case study research is not about the essence of things, but about the crucial and constructive elements that support that essence.

Therefore, this book, just like the conference, is in utmost respect and indebtedness dedicated to all those documented and undocumented living, holy, human beings to whom we thank our profession and research.

This volume is composed and offered for publication in gratefulness to all those living human chaplains who share their stories and the stories of others.

Contributions to the present volume

A conference provides a variety of perspectives on a common theme, like different doors that lead into the same or similar houses. The contributions in this volume have been arranged in four overlapping categories. The first section sketches the development of case study research and addresses issues of research methodology. The second section also deals with methodology but moves at the same time towards initial findings with regard to case study research. Section three looks more closely at specific case studies, touches at times on method, but also identifies challenges and critical issues that arose in the exercise of case study research, particularly in research communities of chaplains. The challenges and critical questioning return in the fourth and final section but in relation to the effect that participation in case study research has on the professionalism for chaplains with regard to their practice and professionalism.

For those who wish to read selectively, a brief introduction of the individual chapters follows. Two matters are worthy of emphasis. The collage of doors in this volume is a reflection of the state of the research. It also parallels the research strategy of the CSP in first examining chaplaincy in the breadth, then moving to comparison in order to, in the third place, develop a focus. (Other strategies are possible as in the forthcoming volume of Wirpsa and Pugliese [2020] with case studies on the role of chaplains in medical decision making.) For that reason, it is perhaps better to speak of a state of the development than of a state of the art in case study research. However, significant progress is being made and we think that this volume contributes to that.

A second point has to do with the fact that several of the contributions in this volume have multiple authors. Shared authorship reflects the way research is understood and pursued in the CSP, in research communities of eight to ten chaplains under academic moderation, in the context of a larger project in which about 60 chaplains participate (or have participated). In the CSP a case is only "complete" when it has been described according to the shared format, when its contents have, if possible, been confirmed by others involved in the case and when the research community has offered comment and critical perspectives that are integrated into the case. Even though the original description of the case is from a particular, usually individual, chaplain, the case study is considered to be a shared product.

I. Methodology in case study research

In chapter 2, "The State of the Art in Chaplaincy Research: Needs, Resources and Hopes," George Fitchett locates case studies research and its specific contribution within the recent history of chaplaincy research and offers several suggestions for next steps in cases studies research, with regard to the ways in which case studies can be used in research, a possible focus on rituals and identification of interventions and outcomes.

In chapter 3, "Putting Chaplaincy Research into the Picture. The Dutch Case Studies Project," Jacques Körver introduces the Dutch Case Studies Project by situating it in the context of empirical research on what chaplains actually do and explaining how that research tradition, including Dutch contributions, led to a positive response among Dutch chaplains to participate.

In chapter 4, "Researching Practices. Lessons from Dutch Youth Care," Jan Willem Veerman shares lessons learned from research on youth care in the Netherlands. A "good enough study" is one that uses methods and seeks types of evidence that are appropriate to the stage of research development in the field and that do justice to practice. Veerman orders various levels of evidence and various types of research, including RCT's and case studies, in five levels of a research ladder.

In chapter 5, "Up and Down the Participation Ladder. The Use of Narratives in Collaborative Research," Gaby Jacobs locates working with case studies, particularly in the CSP, on various levels of a participation ladder with which she clarifies various types of collaborative research. Also, she makes a case for the narrative approach taken in the case studies research as a key to unearthing information not available in another way. She ends by pointing to possibilities of broadening the collaboration and expanding the story, or stories, especially by the inclusion of clients of chaplaincy care.

In chapter 6, "The Science of the Particular," Jacques Körver clarifies the development and format of the Dutch Case Studies Project and touches again on the nature of evidence that case studies provide. To that end he illumines several examples from case study descriptions in terms of naturalistic case studies and their characteristics: emic issues arising from the case itself, influence of context, attention to meaning and interpretation, holistic understanding and provision of detailed information.

II. From methodology to initial findings

In chapter 7, "Chaplains' Case Study Research. Building Towards a Theory of Chaplaincy Care?," Steve Nolan looks at the results of case studies in chaplaincy care up until now and identifies five factors that chaplaincy care has in common with psychotherapeutic care: assessment, rapport, active listening, intentional use of self and challenge, and therapeutic attitudes such as positive regard and empathy, and five factors that are specific for chaplaincy care: reference to transcendence, working with beliefs and philosophies, employing ritual, ministry of presence, and

In chapter 8, "Comparing Multiple Case Studies of (Military) Chaplaincy Care. Methodological Issues," Carmen Schuhmann and Theo Pleizier formulate three challenges that arise when multiple case studies are gathered for research: determining what counts as data in relation to singular and multiple cases; sampling with regard to context and focus; and methodological strategies for comparison. They also identify three patterns that were seen in case studies on military chaplaincy: issues of positioning in relation to military institutions, distinguishing the soldier from the human being, and "being known" as a chaplain.

In chapter 9, "Professional Proximity. Seeking a Balance Between Relation and Content in Spiritual Counseling," Myriam Braakhuis notes that the emphasis on relationship, empathy and presence among chaplains runs three risks: lack of courage to confront clients, failure to address existential and spiritual themes and failure to observe relational boundaries. She offers the concept of "professional proximity" as an antidote.

In chapter 10, "Effects of Health Care Chaplaincy. A Qualitative Study with Case Reports," Nika Höfler and Traugott Roser indicate how case studies in the context of a multi-method research project can be used to survey the perspectives of chaplains on their interventions and the resultant changes and how Grounded Theory can be used to analyze the material for the sake of developing theory that is as yet not present.

III. Case studies and critical issues

In chapter 11, "Personal Experiences in Writing a Case Study," Paul Galchutt reflects on how phenomenology and narrative hermeneutics provided him with a framework to write a case study as research. He illustrates key elements of a case study (the point of the case, interdisciplinary context, background and relationship) with a story taken from his work in palliative care.

Chapter 12, "With an Open Mind for the Unexpected," contributed by Reijer de Vries, Marja Went, Martin van Hemert, Soerish Jaggan and Geerhard Kloppenburg, begins with a several case examples from Went of her working with (ambulatory) presence, Biblical stories and womanist theology in a prison setting. The examples illustrate the significance of brief, informal encounters in chaplaincy care and the role of denominational background. In addition, some particularities of prison chaplaincy are identified.

In chapter 13, "Is MacDonald's Freedom?," Tjeerd van de Meer shows how two, at first sight very different, case studies from his work as a youth care chaplain, also have a common theme: the challenges that young people face in dealing with their identity, especially in relation to cultural and social notions on freedom. Getting a young man briefly out of the institution and going to MacDonald's is a metaphor for those issues.

The case study in chapter 14, "Agreement is Agreement? Moral counseling in a Life-Threatening Dilemma," authored by Monique van Hoof, Hanneke Muthert, Jacques Körver and Martin Walton, describes how Van Hoof provided moral counseling to a young woman who was headed toward committing suicide because of a previous agreement with a fellow patient and friend who had done just that. Van Hoof patiently and systematically helps the young woman explore her own perspectives and values, and in doing so ends up offering care to the treatment team as well.

In chapter 15, "You Can Remove a Person from the War, But Not the War from a Person," Gertjan Jorissen, Carmen Schuhmann and Theo Pleizier describe a case of chaplaincy care by Jorissen of a veteran with moral injury from his service in World War II and in the Dutch East Indies in the early 1950s. The case study shows how the chaplain clarifies the "contract" of care, develops themes of love and loneliness, using his expertise as a representative of both the military and religious life.

IV. Case study research and professionalism

In chapter 16, "What Does Participation in the Case Studies Project Mean for One's Professionalism?," Jacqueline Weeda and Hanneke Muthert explore several common ingredients and critical issues that were identified by a case study research community of chaplains in mental health care. Common ingredients include abstinence from judgement, bridging periods of waiting, using rituals and developing imaginative forms. Critical challenges pertain to the nature of proximity and of goal orientation, determining a body of knowledge for chaplaincy and accessing narratives for research.

In chapter 17, "Interdisciplinary Work in Chaplaincy Care," Loes Berkhout shows how participation in a case study research community helped her to distinguish chaplaincy care from the care she previously provided as a psychologist. She locates the difference not in themes so much as in approach. Language and endorsement (representing a transcendent dimension) play a significant role in that.

In chapter 18, "Towards a Distinct Professional Identity. What Chaplains Have Learned in Flanders Case Study Research," Lindsey Desmet shows how chaplains in a case study project in Belgian acquired language in which to communicate with other health care disciplines on interventions and outcomes, allowing them to clarify their distinctive contribution to care.

Chapter 19, "What Are Chaplains Learning by Producing Case Studies?," views the same Flanders case study research project from the perspective of the moderator, Frieda Boeykens. She reports on the learning process of herself as supervisor and on the challenges encountered by the chaplains in moving into a research role: taking a meta-position on one's own work, using a third person perspective, fostering a critical discussion culture and employing theoretical frameworks.

In chapter 20, "Oneself as Another. Combining the Roles of Chaplain and Researcher in the Dutch Case Studies Project," Niels den Toom shares preliminary results from his meta-research on the Case Studies Project in which he interviews chaplains on how participation contributes to their professional practice. From an understanding from the participants as science-practitioners he describes four relations between the roles of chaplain and researcher: resemblance, difference, tension and reinforcement.

In the epilogue, chapter 21, "Developing the Case," the editors of the volume, Jacques Körver, Renske Kruizinga, Niels den Toom and Martin Walton, go knocking on some doors in order to appraise in the various contributions to the volume, draw out significant aspects of the state of development of case study research and point to several issues on methodology (agenda, evidence, comparison, quality control), characterizations of chaplaincy and professionalization.

References

Boisen, A. T. (1936/1971). *The Exploration of the Inner World: A Study of Mental Disorder and Religious Experience*. Philadelphia: University of Pennsylvania Press.

De Bruijn, L. (1992). [no title]. In J. Koehoorn (Ed.), *Wie geen doel heeft kan niet verdwalen* (p. 26). Deventer: Brinkgreven.

Fitchett, G. (2011). Making our case(s). *Journal of Health Care Chaplaincy, 17*(1-2), 3-18.

Fitchett, G., & Nolan, S. (Eds.) (2015). *Spiritual Care in Practice. Case studies in Healthcare Chaplaincy*. London: Jessica Kingsley Publishers.

Fitchett, G., & Nolan, S. (Eds.) (2017). Special Issue: Chaplain Case Study Research. *Health and Social Care Chaplaincy, 5*(2).

Fitchett, G., & Nolan, S. (Eds.) (2018). *Case Studies in Spiritual Care. Healthcare Chaplaincy Assessments, Interventions & Outcomes*. London: Jessica Kingsley Publishers.

Gerkin, C.V. (1984). *The Living Human Document. Revisioning Pastoral Counseling in a Hermeneutic Mode*. Nashville: Abingdon.

Miller-McLemore, B. J. (1996). The Living Human Web: Pastoral Theology at the Turn of the Century. In J. S. Moessner (Ed.), *Through the Eyes of Women: Insights for Pastoral Care* (pp. 9-26). Minneapolis: Fortress Press.

Wirpsa, M. J., & Pugliese, K. (Eds.) (2020). *Chaplains as Partners in Medical Decision Making: Case Studies in Healthcare Chaplaincy*. London: Jessica Kingsley Publishers.

I. Methodology in Case Study Research

Chapter 2.

The State of the Art in Chaplaincy Research
Needs, Resources and Hopes

George Fitchett

Two decades of spiritual care research and scholarship
In this chapter I will review the recent history of chaplaincy research with special attention to chaplaincy case study research.[1] I will also suggest next steps for that research. My thinking about next steps for chaplaincy research is shaped by what has been accomplished in this field, so I begin with a brief summary of those accomplishments and the lessons I take from them. Figure 1 lists some milestones in spiritual care research from the past two decades. This period begins with the first use of the term "evidence-based pastoral care," in 1998 by Canadian spiritual care researchers Tom O'Connor and Elizabeth Meakes. It includes US spiritual care researcher Larry VandeCreek's 1999 warning that chaplains were missing from the growing research and scholarship about religion and health. Several years later Art Lucas initiated the focus on outcome oriented chaplaincy care with his *Discipline for Spiritual Caregiving* (2001; the term "need, resources, and hopes" in the title of this chapter is taken from his work and refers to concepts in his spiritual assessment). Within a few years a growing body of research about, and sometimes by, chaplains suggested VandeCreek's fears might not be realized. By 2008 the research was extensive enough for NHS Scotland to commission Harriet Mowat to undertake her groundbreaking and informative "Scoping Review."

Figure 1. Milestones in research about spiritual care in healthcare

Year	Publication or event	Description
1998	O'Connor & Meakes, "Hope in the midst of challenge: Evidence-based pastoral care"	This article is the first published use of the term "evidence-based pastoral care."
1999	VandeCreek, "Chaplaincy the absent profession"	In this article VandeCreek, a leading US chaplaincy researcher warned that chaplains were missing from the growing research and scholarship about religion and health.

1   This discussion reflects my limitations: I am far more familiar with research in the U.S. than elsewhere in the world and I am only familiar with research about spiritual care in health care contexts.

Year	Publication or event	Description
2001	Lucas, "Introduction to the Discipline for Pastoral Care Giving"	In this essay Lucas introduces chaplains to the idea of outcome-oriented chaplaincy care.
2008	Mowat, "The potential for efficacy of healthcare chaplaincy and spiritual care provision in the NHS (UK): A scoping review of recent research"	One of the first reviews of chaplaincy research.
2012	Cadge, *Paging God: Religion in the Halls of Medicine*	An in-depth look at chaplaincy practice at a US hospital.
2012	Cobb, Puchalski, & Rumbold (Eds.), *Oxford Textbook of Spirituality in Healthcare.*	A collection of essays about religion and health and spiritual care from an international group of authors.
2012	"Spiritual Care and Health: Improving Outcome and Enhancing Wellbeing," international conference in Glasgow sponsored by NHS Scotland	The 2-day conference brought together chaplains, other clinicians, researchers and scholars to hear the latest reports about spiritual care research and develop relationships that supported further collaboration.
2014	Myers & Roberts (Eds.), *An Invitation to Chaplaincy Research: Entering the Process*	A collection of essays to help chaplains understand and get started doing research.
2015	Morgan, "Review of Literature - Spiritual Health Victoria"	A review of over 400 research articles about spiritual care.
2015	Start of Transforming Chaplaincy (Fitchett & Cadge)	Initially a 4-year initiative to advance research literacy among US healthcare chaplains. It has become a center to support research literacy and spiritual care research (www.transformchaplain.org).
2017	Start of European Research Institute for Chaplaincy in Healthcare (ERICH), Leuven, Belgium	A research institute for chaplains to enhance spiritual care practice. ERICH works closely with the European Network of Health Care Chaplaincy (ENHCC) (www.pastoralezorg.be/page/erich/).
2018	Fitchett, White, & Lyndes, *Evidence-based Spiritual Care: A Research Reader*	A collection of 21 articles illustrating the range of recent research about chaplaincy care.
2018	Start of University Center for Chaplaincy Studies (UCGV), Netherlands	A collaboration of the Tilburg School of Catholic Theology and the Protestant Theological University to support research and scholarship about chaplaincy in many sectors (www.ucgv.nl).

A few years later (2012) an international team of editors (Cobb, Puchalski, & Rumbold) brought us a major overview of research and practice with their *Oxford Textbook of Spirituality in Healthcare.* The 2012 conference, "Spiritual Care and Health: Improving Outcome and Enhancing Well-being, International Conference," convened in Glasgow by NHS Scotland provided an important opportunity for spiritual care researchers from around the world to develop relationships that would become the foundation for future collaboration. The year 2012 also saw the publication of sociologist Wendy Cadge's important ethnographic study of chaplains in a US hospital, *Paging God, Religion in the Halls of Medicine*. In addition to its important description of what hospital chaplains do, publication of the book brought Cadge, a scholar with a supportive but critical perspective on the strengths and weaknesses of the profession, to the attention of chaplains and their colleagues.

In the Fall of 2011, HealthCare Chaplaincy in New York City received a three-year grant from the John Templeton Foundation to support research about spiritual care in palliative care. Grants were given for six projects, some of which, such as the Chaplain Taxonomy (Massey et al., 2015), have had an important impact on the profession. Additionally, the project fostered relationships among a group of senior palliative care researchers, spiritual care researchers, other scholars and chaplains that again formed the foundation for future collaborations. A useful introduction to research for chaplains (Myers, 2015) was another product of this project. Researchers continued to keep track of the growing research in the field and in 2015 Australian colleagues at Spiritual Care Victoria (as of 2019 Spiritual Health Association. Ltd) produced a review of over 400 published studies (Morgan, 2015).

Wendy Cadge and I met in 2006 and in 2013 we began working on the proposal that became the Templeton Foundation funded Transforming Chaplaincy project. That 4-year project, launched in 2015, focused on advancing research literacy among US healthcare chaplains most notably by supporting 17 Transforming Chaplaincy Fellows to earn a Master's of Public Health or similar basic research degrees. Meanwhile Scottish colleagues were developing a patient-reported outcome measure of the impact of chaplain care (Snowden & Telfer, 2017). Conducting research with the Scottish PROM (see also chapter 4) has been an initial focus of the European Research Institute for Chaplaincy in Healthcare (ERICH) which was launched with the support of an anonymous donor at an international conference in 2017. The following year the Tilburg School of Catholic Theology and the Protestant Theological University in the Netherlands came together to form the University Center for Chaplaincy Studies (UCGV) which will foster research in spiritual care in many sectors in addition to healthcare. The UCGV works together with several universities in various research projects. These years also saw a growth in research literacy education for chaplains. Members of the Transforming Chaplaincy team published *Evidence-based Spiritual Care: A Research Reader* (Fitchett et al., 2018), a collection of 21 articles about spiritual care research that can serve as a textbook for chaplain research literacy programs.

While this is not a comprehensive review of the past two decades of chaplain research, hopefully it is sufficient to guide us as we ask what lessons can be drawn from these years as we plan for the future. I think three factors have been important in bringing us to the present moment in spiritual care research. The first factor is the commitment to develop a research-informed profession on the part of individual spiritual care providers and organizations with which they were affiliated and, in Europe, practical theologians. This includes chaplaincy researchers and their employers, leaders of professional chaplaincy organizations, and individual chaplains who understand and support the importance of research for the future of the profession and who have worked to develop their own research literacy. The second factor is partnerships. Doing research and advancing research requires teams, people with complementary knowledge and skills and people who bring critical perspectives about our ideas and efforts. These include other chaplains and chaplaincy researchers, and importantly non-chaplaincy research colleagues, non-chaplain advocates of spiritual care and funders. The third factor is the growth in chaplains with the background required to be involved in research. In 1999 when Larry VandeCreek lamented that chaplains were missing from religion and health research there were essentially no chaplains, in the US at least, with advanced education in research. Since then there has been important growth in the number of healthcare chaplains around the world with masters and doctoral level education in research. These chaplains play a critical role in advancing spiritual care research.

The development of chaplain case study research

In the first decade of the period just described, spiritual care research used qualitative and quantitative methods. As I read the two randomized clinical trials (RCTs) of chaplaincy care that had been published during that period (Bay et al., 2008; Iler et al., 2001) I began to wonder if we had the detailed information about chaplain interventions that was needed to support further RCTs of chaplain care. I looked in the literature to see if there were case studies of chaplain care that had such descriptions and was surprised to find there were essentially no published chaplain case studies. (See Fitchett, 2011, for some exceptions to this statement and for additional background to the development of chaplain case studies research described here.) As a result, in 2009 I convened a team of three US oncology chaplains to write case studies about their work. In 2011 we published the first case study (Cooper, 2011).

The case was accompanied by two responses. The first response, from a chaplain with experience in the oncology context (King, 2011), was designed to model how chaplains can use case studies to discuss and debate the strengths and weaknesses of the spiritual care described in the case. The second response to Cooper's case was designed to show how to build the link between case studies and research (Canada, 2011). Specifically, in this response we wanted to do two things: a) to provide a theoretical framework for the spiritual care provided in the case, and b) to describe ways that the changes observed in the case could be measured. In addition, we published my essay about the importance of case studies for chaplaincy research (Fitchett, 2011) and an essay about the ethics of case study research (McCurdy & Fitchett, 2011). The following year a second case study was published (King, 2012), again with two responses (Maddox, 2012; Schlaugh, 2012). Figure 2 shows milestones in the development of chaplain case study research.

Figure 2. Milestones in chaplain case study research

Year	Publication or event	Description
2011	Fitchett , "Making our Case(s)"	Essay that describes the importance of case studies for chaplaincy research and education.
2011	Cooper, "Case study of a chaplain's spiritual care for a patient with advanced metastatic breast cancer"	First published chaplain case study.
2011	McCurdy & Fitchett, "Ethical issues in case study publication: 'Making our case(s)' ethically"	An essay describing the ethical issues that should be considered in publishing a chaplain case study.
2012	King, "Facing fears and counting blessings: a case study of a chaplain's faithful companioning a cancer patient"	Second published case study.
2013	Risk, "Building a new life: A chaplain's theory-based case study of chronic illness"	Third published case study. Describes intentional use of narrative theory to guide spiritual care and includes quantitative assessment of change in patient's depressive symptoms.
2015	"Making the Case on Chaplaincy & Spiritual Care," Conference in in Utrecht, Netherlands	Organized by the Academic Committee of the Dutch Association of Spiritual Caregivers in the Care Sector and hosted by Tilburg School of Catholic Theology, this 3-day conference brought together chaplains, researchers and scholars to consider the important role of case studies for advancing chaplaincy care.
2015	Fitchett & Nolan, *Spiritual Care in Practice*	The first book of chaplain case studies. Contains nine cases describing spiritual care in pediatrics, mental health care and palliative care with critical discussion of cases by chaplains and other healthcare colleagues.

Year	Publication or event	Description
2016	Nolan, "'He needs to talk!': A chaplain's case study of nonreligious spiritual care"	Fourth published case study. Focuses on chaplaincy care for a non-religious hospice patient and his family.
2017	Fitchett & Nolan (Eds.), Special Issue on Chaplain Case Studies, *Health and Social Care Chaplaincy*	This special issue of the journal includes 6 cases from diverse national contexts as well as a description of the case study outline from the Dutch Case Studies Project.
2018	Fitchett & Nolan, *Case Studies in Spiritual Care*	Second book of chaplain case studies. Contains 9 cases including 4 cases illustrating chaplains' use of ritual. Cases are accompanied by critical discussion by chaplains and healthcare colleagues.
2019	"Do we have a case?," International Conference on Case Study Research in Chaplaincy Care Amsterdam	Organized by the University Center for Chaplaincy Studies, this 2-day conference brought together chaplains, researchers and scholars to share experiences with chaplain case studies and hear reports from the Dutch Case Studies Project.
2020	Wirpsa & Pugliese, *Chaplains as Partners in Medical Decision Making: Case Studies in Healthcare Chaplaincy*	Third book of chaplain case studies. All 9 cases in the book describe chaplains addressing complex medical decisions with patients, families, and staff.

As can be seen from Figure 2, to date there have been two books of chaplain case studies each containing 9 cases (Fitchett & Nolan, 2015, 2018) plus one special issue of the journal *Health and Social Care Chaplaincy* which contained 6 cases (Fitchett & Nolan, 2017). Two additional cases have been published in JHCC (Risk, 2013; Nolan, 2016; see Nolan, 2019 for a list of the published cases, including titles and country). Including a case published in Hebrew (Schultz, 2017), to date 29 chaplain case studies have been published. They report spiritual care provided in palliative care, mental health care, pediatrics, care for veterans and other contexts by chaplains from around the globe (15 from the US, 7 from the UK, 2 from Israel, and 1 each from Australia, Canada, Germany, Iceland, and the Netherlands). An additional book of 9 chaplain cases will be published in 2020 (Wirpsa & Pugliese). What is distinctive about this book is that all the cases focus on one topic: chaplains helping patients, families and healthcare colleagues make difficult decisions about treatment.

Dutch colleagues have played an important role in advancing chaplaincy case study research. This began with a 3-day conference convened in 2015 in Utrecht by Martin Walton (Groningen) and Jacques Körver (Tilburg). The conference gathered chaplains and chaplaincy researchers and students from Netherlands, UK and the US to discuss chaplain case study research. Following the conference, the organizers issued a call for

Dutch chaplains working in all sectors of chaplaincy (e.g., healthcare, corrections, the military) to participate in the Case Studies Project (CSP). Currently over 50 Dutch chaplains are meeting in small groups for four years to share case studies about their work. An important focus of their efforts includes linking cases to theories and to best practices. An initial description of the project, as well as one of the cases it produced, was published in the special issue of *Health and Social Care Chaplaincy* (Walton & Körver, 2017; Van Loenen et al., 2017). Additional reports from the project were presented in the 2019 conference, "Do We Have a Case?" and are included in this volume. The 2019 conference also included reports of recent case study research from Belgium and Germany (see this volume).

The rationale for chaplain case studies

In my 2011 essay I describe three reasons why case studies were important for chaplaincy research: 1) to provide a foundation for research about what chaplains do, and especially the effectiveness of chaplaincy care; 2) to support the education of new chaplains and the continuing education of practicing chaplains, and 3) to help educate non-chaplains, including healthcare colleagues, healthcare managers and the general public about who chaplains are and what they do. I will comment on each of these and evaluate where we have come in chaplaincy case study research.

With their detailed description of the patients' (and/or family's) situation, the chaplains' assessment of that situation, the chaplains' intervention, and a description of any changes that occurred as a result of the intervention (outcomes), case studies provide a rich opportunity for research about each of these elements of chaplaincy care. However, to date there have only been three small projects that have examined the published case studies. In the first I looked at the evidence for change in outcomes in the nine cases in the second book of case studies (Fitchett, 2018). I found that in some cases it was unclear, and probably not possible to know, if the chaplains' care had any effect on an observable outcome (e.g., the case of an older woman with progressive dementia). In other cases it was unclear and would require some additional effort to know if the chaplains' care had any effect, perhaps by asking the patient, or family member, to complete an instrument like the Scottish PROM (e.g., the mother of a boy being admitted for psychiatric care). In yet other cases, the chaplains' care appeared to have had a significant effect on an important outcome but the chaplain hardly mentioned it in his analysis of the case (e.g., a mother who was afraid the care team would not follow her wishes regarding care for her unborn child who had Trisomy 13). My conclusion was that in current practice we gather limited evidence about the effects of our care on important outcomes. Additionally, I noted that our training appears to keep us from observing when our care is affecting such outcomes. That is, the emphasis on being present in chaplaincy education has often meant that chaplains in training do not learn to think about or observe the effects of their care on patient outcomes.

Case studies can also be used for research about more specific questions about chaplaincy care. For example, questions have been raised about whether chaplaincy care is as effective in situations where the chaplain's faith tradition differs from the patient or family for whom they are caring (Abu-Ras, 2011; Abu-Ras & Laird, 2011). In the second project I reviewed several cases from the 2018 book to examine this issue. I observed that of the nine cases in the book, three were cases where there was discordance in the chaplain and patient/family religious affiliation, but that this did not seem to interfere with effective spiritual care. Both of these examples of using case studies for research about chaplaincy were preliminary and only meant to be suggestive of how cases studies could be used for research about chaplaincy care.

A third example is Steve Nolan's examination of the published case studies to engage the question of what is central in chaplaincy care (2019 and this volume). Is it the chaplains' relationship with the patient (being present) or is it the effect of that care on important outcomes? Nolan concludes the existing cases suggest this is a false dichotomy; all good spiritual care is concerned with both the process of the care, the relationship, and with the outcomes associated with the care. He also uses the case studies to describe factors that chaplaincy has in common with psychotherapy and factors that are specific to chaplaincy.

Clearly there is an opportunity to use the existing case studies for more research about chaplaincy. That opportunity will expand as more case studies are published and as projects like the Dutch CSP matures. There have been no published reports about the two additional uses of case studies: educating chaplains and educating non-chaplain colleagues. In the US colleagues have mentioned using case studies in their CPE programs. I am also aware of chaplaincy departments that have added discussion of case studies to staff meeting. It will be important to see reports of the effects of these activities on the students and staff chaplains participating in them. It also remains to be seen if sharing case studies with healthcare colleagues, a normative part of the protocol in the Dutch CSP, has any effect on their understanding of what chaplains do and the referrals they make.

To date, the published case studies have been recruited and selected in part to illustrate the diversity of clinical and national contexts in which chaplains work. In their forthcoming book, Wirpsa and Pugliese (2020) show what can be done when there is an intentional effort to examine cases that address one aspect of chaplaincy care, in this case, care related to medical decision-making. Within the nine cases in their book three describe chaplains supporting patients who are making decisions about whether to continue treatment in the face of serious illness, three describe chaplains working with patients and families who together are making similar decisions, and three cases describe chaplains' care in cases where religious beliefs play a central role in the families' decisions about care for a seriously ill loved one. Collecting these cases in one book allows us to see the range of situations where chaplains are playing an important role in medical decision-making. It allows us to examine similarities and differences in this work across patient/family, racial/ethnic background as well as religious affiliation, or absence thereof.

Together, the cases highlight the important role chaplains are playing in these difficult situations. Collecting and publishing the case studies was an intentional element of a larger project designed to explore chaplains' role in medical decision-making (Wirpsa et al., 2019) and illustrates how case studies can be used in mixed methods research, for example complementing and expanding on findings from survey research. Chaplains in training may be hesitant to move beyond providing supportive care in the kinds of complex cases presented in the book. It will be interesting to see if studying cases such as these help novice chaplains play a more active role when patients and families are faced with difficult medical decisions. Similarly, it will be interesting to see if bringing cases such as these to the attention of medical colleagues helps them better understand the role of chaplains in such cases and make earlier referrals to them.

Future directions in chaplain case study research

We have seen some early indications of the rich possibilities of using chaplain case studies for research about chaplaincy care. In this section I will highlight some additional ways that case studies can be used to advance chaplaincy. As I have mentioned, case studies can be used to examine specific issues in chaplaincy, such as the strengths and limitations of interfaith chaplaincy care. One of the cases in the Wirpsa and Pugliese book describes how a white, female, liberal Protestant on-call chaplain initiated a relationship with the family of a black, evangelical Protestant patient who had suffered a devastating stroke (Kirby, 2020). The chaplain was able to facilitate important communication between the medical team and the family that helped them make important decisions about the patient's treatment. Another case in the book describes the work of a

Conservative Jewish chaplain with an ultra-Orthodox Jewish family of a gravely ill patient (Axelrud, 2020). The case illustrates that within major faith traditions there are often important subgroups that may be as challenging for chaplains as care provided across major religious traditions. A collection of case studies that intentionally addressed this issue, or other important issues in chaplaincy care, would be informative for the profession. Here it should be noted that what is important for this and other topics are not just cases reporting chaplaincy practice but critical reflection on the practice, including the chaplains' assessment, interventions, and observations about outcomes.

As the book by Wirpsa and Pugliese (2020) illustrates, case studies can be used to examine chaplaincy care in specific clinical contexts. In addition to examining specific chaplaincy activities, as they do in their book, case studies can be used to examine chaplaincy care with specific clinical populations. For example, while there are some models for spiritual care for older adults and people with dementia (Mackinley & Trevitt, 2007), there is much to be learned about spiritual care for this important segment of the population. There is one published case study that describes chaplaincy care for an older woman with progressive dementia (Goodman & Baron, 2018), but much can be learned from collecting and examining additional cases studies in this population.

Case study research could also focus on specific population sub-groups. One important sub-group for study are people with no religious affiliation, including those who describe themselves as spiritual but not religious. This is a growing segment of the population in the US (Pew Center, 2015) and the majority of the population in some nations including the UK (Sherwood, 2017). Nolan has published a case (2016) describing "non-religious spiritual care" to an older man at the end of his life and his family. Wendy Cadge and Michael Skaggs (2018) and others (Nolan, 2019) have observed that chaplains in all sectors will assume a growing role in providing spiritual care for this segment of the population. Many more case studies about spiritual care with people with no religious affiliation will be important to help us develop best practices in spiritual care for this segment of the population.

Chaplains' longstanding focus on empathic presence with no agenda (Adams, 2018; Lucas, 2001) has meant that many chaplains are uncomfortable with the idea of a chaplain intervention, not to mention examining the impact of their interventions on measurable outcomes. However, chaplains do offer interventions. Sometimes this is the intervention of empathic supportive presence. At other times it is a more intentional protocol such as the Spiritual Care Assessment and Intervention framework developed to provide support for family members of loved ones in an ICU (Torke et al., 2019). Jay Risk has published a case study in which he offers an intervention based on narrative theory in his care for an older man with progressive disability related to Parkinson's Disease (2013). Narrative theory is an interest for many chaplains and it often guides their care. A collection of case studies where chaplains' care was informed by narrative theory would be an interesting way to explore and advance this approach to spiritual care.

In Nolan's model (2019), rituals are one of the specific factors unique to chaplaincy care. In compiling our second book of case studies (Fitchett & Nolan, 2018), Steve Nolan and I did not intentionally set out to focus on rituals in chaplaincy care but ritual was a key element in four of the cases we received, so we decided to publish them together along with critical commentary about the role of ritual in chaplaincy care by Mark Cobb (2018) and Herbert Anderson (2018). Rituals actually play an important role in many more than four of the case studies that have been published. These include some of the cases about medical decision-making in the Wirpsa and Pugliese collection (2020) and in care for patients and/or families with no religious affiliation (e.g., Van Loenen et al., 2017). Other chaplaincy researchers have used qualitative methods to examine the role of ritual and chaplaincy care in specific clinical contexts (e.g., care for parents with perinatal loss; Kelly, 2007; Newitt, 2014). Case studies offer an important opportunity to expand on this research for this and other groups where rituals are part of the care offered by chaplains.

Developing research about chaplaincy interventions must be accompanied by research about the effects of chaplaincy care on important outcomes. This should include research about measurable and chaplaincy-specific outcomes (Damen et al., 2019; Snowden & Telfer, 2017). But case studies can also play an important role in this area. For example, we can begin to learn the language of outcomes by identifying and describing changes that occurred as a result of the chaplains' care in the case studies that have already been published and we can continue to encourage chaplains to comment on changes in outcomes in their analysis of their cases. In some instances, data may be available that permit measurement of changes that occurred for patients in chaplaincy case studies. The case published by Risk is an example of this N=1 method (2013). The patient for whom he provided care was also in a study and completed a validated measure of depression at the time of his referral to Risk and around the time Risk's care for him ended. As Risk reports, there was a clinically significant decrease in the patient's level of depressive symptoms during this interval. As the patient did not receive any other clinical interventions during this period, it is reasonable to infer that the chaplain's care played a role in this improvement. As I have described here, there are several ways that case studies can make an important contribution to an outcome-oriented approach to chaplaincy care.

Finally, I want to suggest that case studies can make an important contribution to building and testing theoretical models to inform chaplaincy care. It has been noted that where chaplaincy education is based on Clinical Pastoral Education (CPE), providing a theoretical foundation for chaplaincy care is often neglected (Little, 2010). One implication of this is that while spiritual care is often focused on helping people rebuild a sense of meaning that has been disrupted by serious illness (Mackinley & Trevitt, 2007; Monod et al., 2010), many chaplains are unfamiliar with important models for religious coping (Pargament, 1997) and the role of religion/spirituality in meaning making (Park, 2013). Chaplaincy care and chaplaincy education could be strengthened by introducing chaplains to these models and by illustrating them with a series of case studies. This approach could be applied to other important theoretical foundations for chaplains' spiritual care, not just for models of meaning-making.

Conclusion

In just a few years we have been introduced to the idea of chaplaincy case studies and seen the publication of more than two dozen cases describing care in diverse clinical and national contexts. We have begun to see the potential of case studies for advancing chaplains' spiritual care through spiritual care research and chaplaincy education. We have also identified the important role that case studies may play in improving non-chaplain healthcare colleagues understanding of chaplains' contributions to care for patients and their loved ones. There are many additional ways that research using chaplaincy case studies can contribute to the profession. We have much to learn from important initiatives such as the Dutch Case Studies Project.

References

Abu-Ras, W. (2011). Chaplaincy and Spiritual Care Services: The Case for Muslim Patients. *Topics in Integrative Health Care, 2*(2), 1-15.

Abu-Ras, W. and Laird, L. (2011). How Muslim and Non-Muslim Chaplains Serve Muslim Patients? Does the Interfaith Chaplaincy Model have Room for Muslims' Experiences? *Journal of Religion and Health, 50,* 46-71.

Adams, K. (2018). Defining and Operationalizing Chaplain Presence: A Review. *Journal of Religion and Health, 18.* Advanced online publication.

Anderson, H. (2018). Critical Response to the Use of Ritual Case Studies – A Pastoral Theologian's Perspective. In G. Fitchett & S. Nolan (Eds.), *Case Studies in Spiritual Care: Healthcare Chaplaincy Assessments, Interventions and Outcomes* (pp. 205-211). London: Jessica Kingsley Publishers.

Axelrud, A. (2020). "If G-d feels Sara should experience a recovery, it will be a great gift. However, if G-d doesn't, my belief system will never change." – Leah, an Orthodox Jew, speaking about G-d's role in her daughter's devastating illness. In M. J. Wirpsa & K. Pugliese (Eds.), *Chaplains as Partners in Medical Decision Making: Case Studies in Healthcare Chaplaincy* (pp. 165-174). London: Jessica Kingsley Publishers.

Bay, P. S., Beckman, D., Trippi, J., Gunderman, R., & Terry, C. (2008). The effect of pastoral care services on anxiety, depression, hope, religious coping, and religious problem-solving styles: A randomized controlled study. *Journal of Religion and Health, 47*(1), 57-69.

Cadge, W. (2012). *Paging God: Religion in the halls of medicine.* Chicago: University of Chicago Press.

Cadge, W., & Skaggs, M. (2018). Chaplaincy? Spiritual Care? Innovation? A Case Statement. Working Paper, Department of Sociology, Brandeis University.

Canada, A. L. (2011). A psychologist's response to the case study: application of theory and measurement. *J Health Care Chaplain, 17*(1-2), 46-54.

Cobb, M. (2018). Critical Response to the Use of Ritual Case Studies – A Chaplain's Perspective. In G. Fitchett, & S. Nolan (Eds.), *Case Studies in Spiritual Care: Healthcare Chaplaincy Assessments, Interventions and Outcomes* (pp. 212-221). London: Jessica Kingsley Publishers.

Cobb, M., Puchalski, C. & Rumbold, B. (Eds.) (2012). *Oxford textbook of spirituality in healthcare.* Oxford: Oxford University Press.

Cooper, R.S. (2011). Case study of a chaplain's spiritual care for a patient with advanced metastatic breast cancer. *Journal of Health Care Chaplaincy 17*(1), 19-37.

Damen, A., Schuhmann, C., Leget, C., & Fitchett, G. (2019). Can Outcome Research Respect the Integrity of Chaplaincy? A Review of Outcome Studies. *Journal of Health Care Chaplaincy.*

Fitchett, G. (2011). Making our case(s). *Journal of Health Care Chaplaincy, 17*(1-2), 3-18.

Fitchett, G. (2018). Afterword: Case Studies and Chaplaincy Research. In G. Fitchett & S. Nolan (Eds.), *Case Studies in Spiritual Care: Healthcare Chaplaincy Assessments, Interventions and Outcomes* (pp. 259-269). London: Jessica Kingsley Publishers.

Fitchett, G., & Nolan, S. (Eds.) (2015). *Spiritual Care in Practice: Case Studies in Healthcare Chaplaincy.* London: Jessica Kingsley Publishers.

Fitchett, G., & Nolan, S. (2017). Guest Editors Special Issue: Chaplain Case Study Research. *Health and Social Care Chaplaincy, 5*(2).

Fitchett, G., & Nolan, S. (Eds.) (2018). *Case Studies in Spiritual Care: Healthcare Chaplaincy Assessments, Interventions and Outcomes.* London: Jessica Kingsley Publishers.

Fitchett, G., White, K. B., & Lyndes, K. (Eds.) (2018). *Evidence-Based Healthcare Chaplaincy: A Research Reader.* London: Jessica Kingsley Publishers.

Goodman, A., & Baron, J. (2018). "For myself and for your people with whom I pray" – Mrs Pearlman, an 82-year-old woman with a terminal diagnosis of advanced Alzheimer's disease. In G. Fitchett & S. Nolan (Eds.), *Case Studies in Spiritual Care: Healthcare Chaplaincy Assessments. Interventions and Outcomes* (pp. 187-204). London: Jessica Kingsley Publishers.

Iler, W. L., Obenshain, D., & Camac, M. (2001). The impact of daily visits from chaplains on patients with chronic obstructive pulmonary disease (COPD): A pilot study. *Chaplaincy Today, 17*(1), 5-11.

Kelly, E. (2007). *Marking Short Lives: Constructing and Sharing Rituals Following Pregnancy Loss.* Oxford: Peter Lang.

King, S. D. (2012). Facing fears and counting blessings: a case study of a chaplain's faithful companioning a cancer patient. *Journal of Health Care Chaplaincy, 18*(1-2), 3-22.

King, S. D. (2011). Touched by an angel: a chaplain's response to the case study's key interventions, styles, and themes/outcomes. *J Health Care Chaplain, 17*(1-2), 38-45.

Kirby, M. (2020). "She's dying from a broken heart" – Mary telling the story of her sister Alma's death. In M. J. Wirpsa & K. Pugliese (Eds.), *Chaplains as Partners in Medical Decision Making: Case Studies in Healthcare Chaplaincy* (pp. 175-184). London: Jessica Kingsley Publishers

Little, N. K. (2010). Clinical Pastoral Education as professional training: Some entrance, curriculum and assessment implications. *Journal of Pastoral Care & Counseling, 64*(3), 1-8.

Lucas, A. M. (2001). Introduction to the Discipline for Pastoral Care Giving. In L. VandeCreek & A. M. Lucas (Eds.), *The Discipline for Pastoral Care Giving* (pp. 1-34). Binghamton: The Haworth Pastoral Press.

MacKinley, E. B., & Trevitt, C. (2007). Spiritual care and ageing in a secular society. *Medical Journal of Australia, 186*(10), S74-S76.

Maddox, R. T. (2012). The Chaplain as Faithful Companion: A Response to King's Case Study. *Journal of Health Care Chaplaincy, 18*(1-2), 33-42.

Massey, K., Barnes, M. J. D., Villines, D., Goldstein, J. D., Pierson, A. L. H., Scherer, C., Vanderlaan, B., & Summerfelt, W. Th. (2015). What do I do? Developing a taxonomy of chaplaincy activities and interventions for spiritual care in intensive care unit palliative care. *BMC Palliative Care, 14*(10). Retrieved September 13, 2018 from: http://www.advocatehealth.com/chaplaincy-research

McCurdy, D. B., & Fitchett, G. (2011). Ethical issues in case study publication: "Making our case(s)" ethically. *Journal of Health Care Chaplaincy, 17*(1-2), 55-74.

Monod, S., Rochat, E., Büla, C., & Spencer, B (2010). The spiritual needs model: spirituality assessment in the geriatric hospital setting. *Journal of Religion, Spirituality and Aging, 22*, 271-282.

Morgan, M. (2015). Review of literature. Melbourne: Spiritual Health Victoria. Retrieved October, 16, 2016 from http://www.spiritualhealthvictoria.org.au/research

Mowat, H. (2008). The potential for efficacy of healthcare chaplaincy and spiritual care provision in the NHS (UK): A scoping review of recent research. Aberdeen, Scotland: Mowat Research Ltd. Retrieved September 13, 2009 from: www.nhs-chaplaincycollaboratives.com/efficacy0801.pdf

Myers, G. E., & Roberts, S. (Eds.) (2014). An Invitation to Chaplaincy Research: Entering the Process. Retrieved January 27, 2020 from: http://www.healthcarechaplaincy.org/docs/publications/templeton_research/hcc_research_handbook_final.pdf

Nash, P., Roberts, E., Nash, S., Darby, K., & Parwaz, A. A. (2019). Adapting the Advocate Health Care Taxonomy of chaplaincy for a pediatric hospital context: A pilot study. *Journal of Health Care Chaplaincy, 25*(2), 61-75.

Newitt, M. (2014). Chaplaincy Support to Bereaved Parents - Part 1: Liturgy, Ritual and Pastoral Presence. *Health and Social Care Chaplaincy, 2*(2), 179-194.

Nolan, S. (2016). "He needs to talk!": A chaplain's case study of nonreligious spiritual care. *Journal of Health Care Chaplaincy, 22*(1), 1-16.

Nolan, S. (2019). Lifting the Lid on Chaplaincy: A First Look at Findings from Chaplains' Case Study Research. *Journal of Health Care Chaplaincy, 2*, 1-23.

O'Connor, T. S., & Meakes, E. (1998). Hope in the midst of challenge: Evidence-based pastoral care. *Journal of Pastoral Care, 52*, 359-367.

Pargament, K. I. (1997). *The Psychology of Religion and Coping: Theory, Research, Practice.* New York: The Guilford Press.

Park, C. L. (2013). Religion and meaning. In R. F. Paloutzian & C. L. Park (Eds), *Handbook of the Psychology of Religion and Spirituality* (2nd ed.; pp. 357-379). New York: The Guilford Press.

Peery, B. (2012). Outcome Oriented Chaplaincy: Intentional Caring. In S. B. Roberts (Ed.), *Professional Spiritual and Pastoral Care: A Practical Clergy and Chaplain's Handbook* (pp. 342-361). Woodstock: SkyLight Paths Publishing.

Risk, J. L. (2013). Building a new life: A chaplain's theory based case study of chronic illness. *Journal of Health Care Chaplaincy, 19*(3), 81-98.

Schlauch, C. R. (2012). A Pastoral Theologian's Response to the Case Study. *Journal of Health Care Chaplaincy, 18*(1-2), 23-32.

Schultz, M. (2017). So that there will be one good and true thing to say about me in my eulogy [Hebrew]. In N. Bentur and M. Schultz (Eds.), *Meeting in the Midst: Spiritual Care in Israel* (pp. 183-206). Jerusalem: JDC Israel - Eshel.

Sherwood, H. (2017, September 4). *More than half UK population has no religion, finds survey.* The Guardian.

Snowden, A., & Telfer, I. (2017). Patient reported outcome measure of spiritual care as delivered by chaplains. *Journal of Health Care Chaplaincy, 23*(4), 131-155.

Torke, A. M., Maiko, S., Watson, B. N., Ivy, S. S., Burke, E. S., ... Cottingham, A. (2019). The Chaplain Family Project: Development, Feasibility, and Acceptability of an Intervention to Improve Spiritual Care of Family Surrogates. *Journal of Health Care Chaplaincy, 25*(4), 147-170.

Van Loenen, G., Körver, J, Walton, M., & De Vries, R. (2017). Case Study "Moral Injury." Format Dutch Case Studies Project. *Health and Social Care Chaplaincy, 5*(2), 281-96.

VandeCreek, L. (1999). Professional chaplaincy: An absent profession? *Journal of Pastoral Care, 53*(4), 417-32.

Walton, M., & Körver, J. (2017). Dutch Case Studies Project in Chaplaincy Care: A Description and Theoretical Explanation of the Format and Procedures. *Health and Social Care Chaplaincy, 5*(2), 257-280.

Wirpsa, J. M., Johnson, E. R., Bieler, J., Boyken, L., Pugliese, K., ... Murphy, P. (2019). Interprofessional Models for Shared Decision Making: The Role of the Health Care Chaplain. *Journal of Health Care Chaplaincy, 25*(1), 20-44.

Wirpsa, M. J., & Pugliese, K. (Eds.) (2020). *Chaplains as Partners in Medical Decision Making: Case Studies in Healthcare Chaplaincy.* London: Jessica Kingsley Publishers.

Chapter 3.

Putting Chaplaincy Research into the Picture
The Dutch Case Studies Project[2]

Jacques Körver

Introduction

For his project *Life Narratives*[3] the Greek photographer Nikos Markou made portraits of ordinary Greeks in the period 2012-2014. He also interviewed the people he portrayed. Part of the interview can be heard when looking at the portrait. However, the portrait is a still. The portrayed person comes more to life, while the spectator is listening to the story. The personal life stories merge into a greater story of the social and political developments affecting Greece during that period. The financial crisis, the stream of refugees, the growing poverty, but also personal ways of living (together), loving, and growing up, all come on the screen and become part of the portrait. The portraits become documents against oblivion showing how people seek coherence and lend to the larger portrait depth and perspective.

Something similar is occurring in the Dutch Case Studies Project (CSP). Although the viewfinder is focused on what chaplains actually do, the case studies also show how their interlocutors struggle with existential needs. With the help of (religious) rituals and stories, people try to find orientation for their lives and sources of strength. They testify of their courage and resilience, and often also of the desperation and tragedy. They find their way in sickness and health, guilt and penance, violence and reconciliation, autonomy and dependence, in good and bad times. The case studies are portraits of how people search for depth and perspective.

In this chapter we consider the development and context of the Case Studies Project in chaplaincy care in the Netherlands. One of the motives for the CSP is to provide chaplains themselves, but also others (managers, board members, care providers, citizens), with adequate language. All of them lack the words to describe properly what actually occurs in chaplaincy, what the goals are, and what the results. And which theories

2   This article is partly based on Körver, Bras, & Walton (2019/2020).
3   https://edgeofhumanity.com/2017/10/03/life-stories/ and https://nikosmarkou.com/life-narratives-2012-2014//. Retrieved January 24, 2020.

underlie those goals and interventions explicitly or implicitly. Usually chaplains emphasize the uniqueness of each contact, the importance of personal communication, and the conviction that chaplaincy is not about achieving anything (Körver, 2014). That is how they have been trained and socialized. The CSP emphasizes the opposite: not everything that happens in a contact is unique. It can therefore be described more generally. Explicitly and implicitly, chaplains are goal-oriented, they base themselves on theories and models, and they work towards a result. Chaplaincy represents a typical domain, specific interventions and observable results.

What do chaplains really do?

Since the end of the last century, there has been a trend in international research literature to carefully describe the actual practice of chaplaincy. There was a realization that we know little about this practice, that there are many models or theories about how chaplaincy should take place, the intentions, but that there is little or no insight into how and why chaplains act as they do in terms of interventions and underlying theories or models. Case studies research makes it clear that meaning and world view can indeed be identified in the practice of chaplains, but that they themselves do not refer to this as such (Körver, 2016). A few examples of this (quantitative) research are discussed below in an exemplary manner. It is impossible to give a complete picture, but the examples show how essential this type of research is.

In 2008, the *Journal of Health Care Chaplaincy* published three articles entitled "What Do Chaplains Really Do?" (Handzo, Flannelly, Kudler et al., 2008; Handzo, Flannelly, Murphy et al., 2008; Vanderwerker et al., 2008). The three publications analyze data on chaplaincy in thirteen New York care institutions in the years 1994-1996. The analyses in the first article showed that chaplains paid less frequent but longer visits in acute situations, that chaplains spent less time on patients who were alone in comparison with contacts in which family or friends also were present, and that the duration of the contact was longer if there was a referral. In the second study, the authors distinguished seventeen different interventions by chaplains, of which nine are religious or spiritual in nature and eight more general and not specifically religious. In most contacts, chaplains used the religious/spiritual interventions, alone or in combination with the more general interventions. Specific interventions varied somewhat according to the medical status of the people involved, with prayer and blessing being the most commonly used interventions in the accompaniment of dying and preoperative patients. No differences in interventions emerged with regard to the patient's religious background. In the third article, attention was paid to referral and referral patterns. Less than 20% of patient contacts were made by referral. The referrers turned out to be mainly nurses and relatives, few doctors. The reasons for referral were mainly patients' emotional problems, and less often religious or spiritual questions.

Although the figures are from more than twenty years ago, and the analysis was carried out ten years ago, some of the results are still recognisable, also for the Dutch situation. Chaplains have a special, often valued position in a care institution, but other professionals do not have a good (or only traditional) picture of what chaplaincy implies and can contribute to the care process. Hence perhaps the small percentage of referrals. In crisis situations and for patients with a more traditional religious background, chaplains make use of familiar religious or spiritual interventions. For people without this background, however, they have a smaller repertoire or feel insecure. What is most striking is that chaplains in most contacts use specific religious or spiritual interventions, while they themselves emphasise the meaning of the relationship and the more general interventions.

Another example of this research perspective is the report by Mowat and Swinton *What Do Chaplains Do?* (2007). In this Scottish study, chaplains, patients, relatives and staff members were interviewed. Conversations and contacts between chaplains and their interlocutors were observed. A first analysis was followed by another round of interviews. All this material together was condensed into a model that illustrates the core tasks and the process of chaplaincy. This in detail described process model identifies the core tasks as follows: a) tracking down people who are in need of chaplaincy by means of presence, referral or selection on the basis of certain criteria, b) determining the nature of the need on the basis of, among other things, experience, listening and spiritual and emotional sensitivity, and c) responding by means of theological and spiritual means or instruments to the need, without an agenda, on the basis of empathy and relational orientation. A few years later, this study was followed up, looking for new developments of chaplaincy in Scotland (Simpson, Collin, & Okekeke, 2014). The results were: the role of chaplaincy has broadened requiring priority setting; greater integration into the hospital organisation including increased work in this area; the need for continued professionalization; the need of coping with the limited or traditional imaging of staff and patients; and the search for a new professional identity. This study, too, shows that the results are comparable to the development of chaplaincy in the Netherlands (Schilderman, 2015).

A good overview of the empirical research that has taken place in the English-speaking world over the past ten years in the field of chaplaincy can be found in the collection of recently published articles *Evidence-Based Healthcare Chaplaincy* (Fitchett, White, & Lyndes, 2018). This publication has three parts: 1. Where do chaplains work and what do they do? 2. What are the spiritual needs of patients and their loved ones and how does chaplaincy fit in with those needs? And 3. What is the nature and effect of interventions by chaplains? The first part describes, among other things, the research on a taxonomy of chaplaincy, in which the various goals, methods and interventions have been mapped out, in order to arrive at a certain standardization of chaplaincy (Massey et al., 2015). The inventory (based on practice and theory) shows that the majority of interventions, goals and methods are not explicitly focused on meaning and world view, but are rather relational or more generally supportive in nature. In part two, specific target groups are discussed. The articles in this section show which spiritual/religious experiences and needs people in specific situations have and how religion and spirituality (and chaplaincy) can be helpful. In part three research about the effect of chaplaincy is included. The studies in this third part also have in common that they clarify the specific content of chaplaincy – meaning making and world viewing – in specific contexts or with respect to specific target groups.

What are chaplains in the Netherlands doing?

In the Netherlands, empirical research into chaplaincy has become more important in the last two decades. In 1996, Marijke Prins published a study in which she analysed conversations with patients and caregivers about the coping process of people with an incurable disease or a chronic disorder. An important result is that the world view in the process of illness or death is unmistakably present and indispensable (Prins, 1996). In 1997, the Trimbos Institute carried out a study based on questionnaires into the person, work and workplace of chaplains (De Roy, Oeneman, Neijmeijer, & Hutschemaekers, 1997). The aim of the research was to get a picture of how chaplains perform their tasks and what employers expect in this respect. An important result is that chaplains have great difficulty in describing their task. They describe their work mainly in opposition to other care providers who, according to the responding chaplains, are mainly guided by standards and protocols. Chaplains are oriented towards a holistic approach of patients and entitlement to sanctuary. They want to achieve this by "being there." The descriptions were not much more concrete than that (Oenema & Vandermeersch, 1999). A year later, Johan Bouwer published an overview of models of pastoral diagnostics

(Bouwer, 1998) as way of clarifying the content of the profession in a more methodical manner. Bouwer discusses ten models that originate mainly from the US. The following year, Jan-Hein Mooren published a study in which he describes the methodology of humanistic chaplaincy on the basis of case studies. The focus of the case studies is on the search for meaning (and the support for it). The methodology is mainly characterised by a socio-psychological and narrative approach to meaning making, in which the life stories of clients are central (Mooren, 1999).

In 2006, Wim Smeets obtained his PhD in a study into the attitudes of chaplains with regard to some relevant aspects of their profession. The starting point is that chaplaincy is a professional occupation in the health care sector and that it must meet the quality requirements like all other health care professions. The chaplaincy profession is placed in the context of developments in healthcare. A clear emphasis is placed on the importance of goal-orientation in the work. Smeets identifies a number of challenges for the profession: the plurality of religions and world views, the institutional embedding of chaplaincy and the implications for the training of chaplains to be(come) a real profession (Smeets, 2006). Smeets' dissertation heralds a new era with numerous (doctoral) studies on chaplaincy (Steggerda & Smeets, 2011).

It would go too far here to provide a complete overview. One of the findings in all these studies (see e.g. Kruizinga, 2017; Olsman, 2015; Körver, 2013) is that patients, clients and caregivers search for R/S questions, that can be expressed in clear and differentiated terms. This is in stark contrast to practice, where chaplains do not seem to notice these questions. Whereas others call on them, in want of suitable words, chaplains do not seem to recognise the questions.

Dutch Case Studies Project in chaplaincy care

A special line of research into what chaplains actually do was initiated by the American researcher George Fitchett (Fitchett, 2011). His starting point is that far too little is known about what actually happens in the interaction between chaplains and their clients, the client system and the (care) context, which themes are discussed, what type of interventions are used by chaplains, which goals they pursue and what the effects of their actions are. Fitchett also observes that, on average, chaplains are insufficiently able to properly describe and theoretically justify what they do. They quickly slip back into vague descriptions such as "working on the relationship," "recognising the uniqueness of each person" and "presence." Research using case studies is promising, especially since chaplains, as co-researchers, learn to express their explicit and implicit knowledge. This stimulates chaplains to participate in research that is in line with their daily practice. In all these case studies it is repeatedly apparent that chaplains do more than they say they do, and that this "more" relates to meaning making and world viewing. Other professionals observe that precisely the work's content is not addressed in the reflections by the chaplains themselves (Fitchett & Nolan, 2015, 2017, 2018). Moreover, it appears that case studies provide a very detailed picture, as if under a magnifying glass, of how meaning making and world viewing play a role in people's lives.

During a conference in Utrecht (2015) entitled "Making the Case on Chaplaincy & Spiritual Care," Fitchett repeated his plea. The conference was the stimulus for the CSP in which 56 chaplains from all fields and 10 researchers from four different universities are involved. The aim of the research is to trace good practices of chaplaincy, especially the active elements and criteria. It is necessary to pay attention to the relationship between practice and theory (on what chaplains base their actions or interventions), to the goals that chaplaincy pursues, and to the interventions that follow. The project uses an extensive and clearly described format to describe and reflect upon the case study. The relationship between practice and theory and the role of meaning making and world viewing are also discussed in detail. For this last aspect, the description of chaplaincy in the *Professional Standard of Chaplaincy Care* (2015) is used as a *sensitizing concept*: chaplaincy is focused on meaning making and world viewing. The reflection takes place in six research communities, five of which are composed on the basis of the field of work (hospital, elderly care, mental health care, prison and defence) and a sixth of mixed composition (youth care, care for people with a disability, rehabilitation, primary care) (Gärtner, Körver, & Walton, 2019; Walton & Körver, 2017). The design includes an opportunity for involved parties (clients, relatives, care providers) to respond to the description (*member check*) (Lub, 2014). In addition, reflection on the case study in the research community has the advantage that the study will be placed in a broader context and that consensus on what constitutes good practice can be strived for.

Context

It surprised the initiators of the CSP how much interest there was in participating in the project, in spite of the commitment to meet at least four times a year for four years and to provide at least two case studies. Three contextual developments created a *kairos* for the CSP: in the professional group, in health care, and in health care research.

The above overview has made it clear that over the past few decades a research tradition has slowly grown within the professional group of chaplains. The need for research and research literacy arose mainly in the health care sector, where (quantitative) research increases the status of the profession (Cadge, 2019). Recognition of chaplaincy requires accountability: what do you do, why and for what purpose? Can you as a chaplain substantiate that the intervention has a result or effect? The number of doctorates on chaplaincy or by chaplains has risen dramatically in recent years. In the CSP, chaplains themselves can contribute to the development of the profession. That appears to be one of the most important motivations for participating in the project. The project is based on the concrete activities of the chaplain, invites him or her to reflect on this practice together with fellow professionals, and it also directly benefits his or her own practice and professionalism. It appears also important that the project and the method fit in well with what chaplains have learned in their training, especially during their internship, in supervision and in Clinical Pastoral Education (CPE). Whereas in supervision and CPE the emphasis is on reflection on the person and biography (Körver, 2007), reflection in the CSP shifts to the content of the profession. It appears to be complicated for professionals to clarify on the basis of which theories or models they carry out an intervention. Many of the insights gained during their training and experience remain unconscious (Muthert, Van Hoof, Walton, & Körver, 2019). During the reflection in the research communities, these fundamentals come to the surface, so that chaplains can intervene more consciously in their practice and can substantiate their accountability for that practice more explicitly. This feeds professional self-awareness.

There is, certainly in the field of health care, a powerful development that stimulates the attention for meaning, world view and spirituality, also for chaplaincy. Health scientist Machteld Huber has developed a new concept of health and disease as a correction to the existing concept of the *World Health Organisation.* In the new concept, the emphasis is not on striving for a disease-free existence, but on being able to deal with the possibilities and limitations that are given by life itself. In this context, explicit attention is paid to meaning, world view and spirituality, because it is precisely the ability to deal with limitations and the finite nature of existence that raises questions about meaning and spiritual sources (Huber, 2014). This new health concept has been met with a great deal of resonance in the health care sector in the Netherlands and in some government organisations. This development enhances a clearer awareness of the importance of meaning, world view and spirituality and consequently of chaplaincy. This is also evident from the recent structural measures taken by the Dutch government to (financially) support chaplaincy in primary (palliative) care.

There is a slow paradigm shift with regard to the type of research that is necessary to support the evidence of interventions in healthcare. For a long time, large-scale quantitative research with the RCT has been regarded as the absolute gold standard for evidence in medical and social science research. In this respect, evidence-based was and still is interpreted very one-sidedly. Whereas in the original sense evidence-based should be the result of best scientific evidence, clinical experience and the client's values (Sackett, Rosenberg, Gray, Haynes, & Richardson, 1996), the last two elements are generally neglected. A discussion of dozens of researchers with the editors of the *British Medical Journal* made this painfully clear (Greenhalgh et al., 2016; Panter, Guell, & Ogilvie, 2016). In the Netherlands, the *Council for Health and Society* has pointed out that evidence-based care that does not take into account the context and the client's values cannot be good care. According to the Council good care is an illusion without accounting for the client's context and values. The Council even formulates quite provocatively: "No evidence without context" (Council for Health and Society, 2017). On the contrary, qualitative research, including case study research, is an excellent contribution to a profound understanding of a client's personal struggle with questions relating to sickness and health.

Against this background, it is the task of the chaplains who participate in the CSP to use their case studies to create portraits with depth and perspective of people who are looking for meaning and coherence. The motto of the American photographer Emmet Gowin comes to mind (2013, p. 64):

> And, finally, this is what I need to say to you.
> There are things in your life that only you will see,
> stories that only you will hear.
> If you don't tell them or write them down,
> if you don't make the picture,
> these things will not be seen,
> these things will not be heard.

References

Bouwer, J. (1998). *Pastorale diagnostiek. Modellen en mogelijkheden.* Zoetermeer: Boekencentrum.

Cadge, W. (2019). Healthcare Chaplaincy as a Companion Profession: Historical Developments. *Journal of Health Care Chaplaincy, 25*(2), 45-60.

Council for Health and Society (2017). *No evidence without context. About the illusion of evidence-based practice in healthcare.* Den Haag: RVS.

Gowin, E. (2013). New York: Fundación Mapfre – Aperture (exposition).

De Roy, A., Oeneman, D., Neijmeijer, L., & Hutschemaekers, G. (1997). *Beroep: geestelijk verzorger. Een verkennend onderzoek naar persoon, werk en werkplek van geestelijk verzorgers in de gezondheidszorg.* Utrecht: Trimbos-instituut.

Fitchett, G. (2011). Making our case(s). *Journal of Health Care Chaplaincy, 17*(1-2), 3-18.

Fitchett, G., & Nolan, S. (Eds.) (2015). *Spiritual Care in Practice. Case studies in healthcare chaplaincy.* London: Jessica Kingsley Publishers.

Fitchett, G., & Nolan, S. (Eds.) (2017). Special Issue: Chaplain Case Study Research. *Health and Social Care Chaplaincy, 5*(2).

Fitchett, G., & Nolan, S. (Eds.) (2018). *Case Studies in Spiritual Care. Healthcare chaplaincy assessments, interventions & outcomes.* London: Jessica Kingsley Publishers.

Fitchett, G., White, K. B., & Lyndes, K. A. (Eds.) (2018). *Evidence-based Healthcare Chaplaincy. A research reader.* London: Jessica Kingsley.

Gärtner, S., Körver, J., & Walton, M. (2019). Von Fall zu Fall. Kontext, Methode und Durchführung eines empirischen Forschungsprojekts mit Casestudies in der Seelsorge. *International Journal of Practical Theology, 23*(1), 98-114.

Greenhalgh, T., Annandale, E., Ashcroft, R., Barlow, J., Black, N., ... Ziebland, S. (2016). An open letter to The BMJ editors on qualitative research. *British Medical Journal, 352*, i563.

Handzo, G. F., Flannelly, K. J., Murphy, K. M., Bauman, J. P., Oettinger, M., ... Jacobs, M. R. (2008). What Do Chaplains Really Do? I. Visitation in the New York Chaplaincy Study. *Journal of Health Care Chaplaincy, 14*(1), 20-38.

Handzo, G. F., Flannelly, K. J., Kudler, T., Fogg, S. L., Harding, S. R., ... Taylor, B. E. (2008). What Do Chaplains Really Do? II. Interventions in the New York Chaplaincy Study. *Journal of Health Care Chaplaincy, 14*(1), 39-56.

Huber, M. (2014). *Towards a New, Dynamic Concept of Health. Its operationalisation and use in public health and healthcare, and in evaluating health effect of food.* Maastricht: Maastricht University.

Körver, J. (2007). Historisch bepaalde oriëntaties in pastorale supervisie. In J. Körver & W. Regouin (Eds.), *Professionele begeleiding en spiritualiteit. Pastorale supervisie nader verkend* (pp. 25-45). Houten: Bohn Stafleu van Loghum.

Körver, J. (2013). *Spirituele copingstrategieën bij longkankerpatiënten.* Eindhoven.

Körver, J. (2016). Wat doen geestelijk verzorgers? Met *case studies* op naar *practice-based evidence* van geestelijke verzorging. *Tijdschrift Geestelijke Verzorging, 19*(82), 10-19.

Körver, J. (Ed.) (2014). *In het oog in het hart. Geestelijke verzorging 2.1.* Nijmegen: Valkhof Pers.

Körver, J., Bras, E., & Walton, M. (2019/2020). Geestelijke verzorging onder de loep. Elementen van zingeving en levensbeschouwing als aanknopingspunt voor de christelijke traditie? In K. de Groot, J. Z. T. Pieper & S. Goyvaerts (Eds.), *Waar blijft het christendom?* (In press).

Kruizinga, R. (2017). *Out of the Blue. Experiences of contingency in advanced cancer patients.* Amsterdam: Universiteit van Amsterdam.

Lub, V. (2014). *Kwalitatief evalueren in het sociale domein. Mogelijkheden en beperkingen.* Den Haag: Boom Lemma uitgevers.

Massey, K., Barnes, M. J. D., Villines, D., Goldstein, J. D., Hisey Pierson, A., ... Summerfelt, T. (2015). What Do I Do? Developing a taxonomy of chaplaincy activities and interventions for spiritual care in intensive care unit palliative care. *BMC Palliative Care, 14*(1), 1-8.

Mooren, J. H. (Ed.) (1999). *Bakens in de stroom. Naar een methodiek van het humanistisch geestelijk werk.* Uitgeverij SWP: Utrecht.

Mowat, H., & Swinton, J. (2007). *What do chaplains do? The role of the chaplain in meeting the spiritual needs of patients.* Aberdeen: Mowat Research.

Muthert, H., Van Hoof, M., Walton, M., & Körver, J. (2019). Valuing One's Holding to a Suicide Appointment. Embodied moral counseling in a Dutch case study of chaplaincy in mental health care. *Tidsskrift for Praktisk Teologi, 36*(2), 81-89.

Oenema, D., & Vandermeersch, P. (Eds.) (1999). *Flarden. Geestelijke verzorging in het verpleeghuis.* Zoetermeer: Boekencentrum.

Olsman, E. (2015). *Hope in Palliative Care. A longitudinal qualitative study.* Amsterdam: Universiteit van Amsterdam.

Panter, J., Guell, C., & Ogilvie, D. (2016). Qualitative research can inform clinical practice. *British Medical Journal, 352*, i1482.

Prins, M. C. J. (1996). *Geestelijke zorgverlening in het ziekenhuis.* Dwingeloo: Kavanah.

Sackett, D. L., Rosenberg, W. M., Gray, J. A., Haynes, R. B., & Richardson, W. S. (1996). Evidence Based Medicine: what it is and what it isn't. *British Medical Journal, 312*(7023), 71-72.

Schilderman, H. (2015). Van ambt naar vrij beroep. *Tijdschrift voor Religie, Recht en Beleid, 6*(2), 5-23.

Simpson, J., Collin, M., & Okeke, C. (2014). What Do Chaplains Do Now? The continuous process of adaptation. *Health and Social Care Chaplaincy, 2*(2), 213-234.

Smeets, W. (2006). *Spiritual Care in a Hospital Setting. An empirical-theological exploration.* Leiden: Brill.

Steggerda, M., & Smeets, W. (2011). Onderzoek naar geestelijke verzorging in academische ziekenhuizen. *Tijdschrift Geestelijke Verzorging, 14*(62), 40-47.

Vanderwerker, L. C., Flannelly, K. J., Galek, K., Harding, S. R., Handzo, G. F., ... Bauman, J. P. (2008). What Do Chaplains Really Do? III. Referrals in the New York Chaplaincy Study. *Journal of Health Care Chaplaincy, 14*(1), 57-73.

VGVZ. (2015). *Beroepsstandaard geestelijke verzorging.* Amsterdam: VGVZ.

Walton, M., & Körver, J. (2017). Dutch Case Studies Project in Chaplaincy Care. A description and theoretical explanation of the format and procedures. *Health and Social Care Chaplaincy, 5*(2), 257-280.

Chapter 4.

Researching practices
Lessons from Dutch Youth Care

Jan Willem Veerman

Introduction

Recent publications in the field of spiritual care emphasize the need to make research practices more evidence based. Fitchett (2011), for instance, stressed the importance of research for the future of health care chaplaincy. He maintained that "evidence from research needs to inform our pastoral care" (p. 4), and "'the chaplain practices evidence-based care including ongoing evaluation of new practices" (p. 4). As an implication, chaplains should be involved in research. Walton and Körver (2017), taking the same stance, add that this research needs to take place "in the direct proximity to daily practice" (p. 259).

This situation in chaplaincy care shows striking similarities with developments in youth care[4] over the last 50 years (Barth et al., 2012; Kazdin, 2003; Van Yperen, Veerman, & Bijl, 2017; Weisz et al., 2017). Questions about the effectiveness of youth care were increasingly raised during that period, in the beginning mainly by researchers, later also by practitioners, administrators and policy makers. Answering questions about the effectiveness therefore not only gained scientific relevance, but also practical, political and financial. This development increased the pressure for delivering evidence-based treatment, which sounds logical and rather down to earth. Who would not want to deliver care that has been proven to be effective? What exactly was meant by "evidence-based," however, was not always made clear. Evidence-based became one of those container concepts that could take on almost every meaning, especially that of the speaker.

In the Netherlands these developments led us to further reflect on the meaning of evidence-based youth care (Veerman & Van Yperen, 2007; Van Yperen et al., 2017). Along the way we learned a number of lessons about how to use the concept evidence-based for (1) conducting research into the effectiveness of care, and (2) to connect this research to practice and policy (including financing). In this chapter seven of these lessons are discussed. They can also be applied to similar developments in chaplaincy care.

---

4   Youth care includes all forms of psycho-social treatment for young people and their families, in the fields of mental health care, social work and child welfare.

Lessons from Dutch youth care
1. Evidence-based is not the same as research-based
The "evidence" in evidence-based care is often equated with evidence from quantitative empirical studies. That is a misconception. From the first definition of Sackett, Rosenberg, Gray, Haynes, and Richardson (1996) to later definitions, wishes, values and preferences of practitioners and clients also fall under the "evidence." For instance: "Evidence-based practice in psychology is the integration of the best available research with clinical expertise in the context of patient characteristics, culture, and preferences" (APA, 2006). The lesson we learned here is that expertise, preferences and values of the two main actors in practice are just as important as results of empirical research. Sackett himself wrote that "... practice risks becoming tyrannized by external evidence, for even excellent external evidence may be inapplicable or inappropriate for an individual patient" (Sacket, 1997, p. 3).

2. Research-based is not the same as RCT-based
If we concentrate on the research part of the definition of evidence-based, we often see that evidence from research is equated with evidence from a randomized controlled trial (RCT). This is a research design in which one group receives the treatment one wants to investigate and another group, the control group, does not receive this treatment or gets a placebo treatment. Clients are randomly assigned to one of both groups. If the treatment group performs better than the control group, this can be interpreted as evidence of the effectiveness of the treatment being studied. The randomized controlled trial has become the gold standard for establishing evidence. Evidence from these trials, however, seems hardly useful for everyday youth care practice (Weisz, Krumholz, Santucci, Thomassin, & Ng, 2015). It was estimated that only 2% of the hundreds of youth psychotherapy RCT's that have been conducted in de the last 50 years focus on clinically referred clients, treated by practitioners in practice settings. In the Dutch database of effective youth care interventions only seven out of 235 interventions (3%) are supported by evidence from a RCT.[5] It is clear that the great majority of interventions carried out in everyday practice is not evidence-based according to the RCT yardstick (see also Kazdin, 2003). However, it is practically impossible and ethically unacceptable to withhold interventions and wait for that evidence. That need not be a problem for delivering evidence-based care. The lesson to be learned from this discussion is that the definition of evidence-based

5   See https://www.jeugdinterventies.nl (retrieved February 3, 2020).

does not automatically imply evidence from RCT's, but the "best available evidence."

3. The best available evidence lies in practice

In 2017 about 400.000 thousand children and adolescents received a youth care intervention in the Netherlands.[6] Inasmuch as there are very few interventions in youth care with evidence from RCT's, we came to realize that the "best available evidence" should be practice-based (see also Barkham & Mellor-Clarke, 2003). In this conviction we were strengthened by the findings of John Weisz, a leading investigator of childhood psychotherapy. From a meta-analysis of more than 50 RCT's comparing evidence-based youth psychotherapies with usual care, he and his co-workers only found a modest effect in favor of evidence-based youth psychotherapies. They concluded that these therapies may be less potent than some have assumed, that certain forms of usual care even outperformed evidence-based youth psychotherapies, and that those usual care interventions may deserve further study in their own right (Weisz, Kuppens, Eckshtain, Ugueto, Hawley, & Jensen-Doss, 2013). These conclusions make this lesson even more urgent. To ascertain evidence of effectiveness of youth care we must research practices.

4. Practice-based evidence has many shades of gray

Researching practices meant that existing views and classifications of evidence-based practice were not useful for studying practice-based evidence. A minimum requirement in this regard is that studies have included a control group, with or without randomization. (See for instance the growing number of internet databases that summarize effective treatments for youth, such as Blueprints for Healthy Youth Development, www.blueprintsprograms.com, and The California Evidence-based Clearinghouse, www.cebc4cw.org.) Given the virtually absence of evidence-based interventions in practice, we felt that more nuances were needed in order to give names to various indications of practice-based evidence and to communicate on them. For that purpose, we constructed an effect ladder, with steps that indicate increasing degrees of certainty on the evidence of effectiveness of an intervention, with sufficient degrees of freedom to choose a study design appropriate to the intervention under study (Veerman & Van Yperen, 2007). Figure 1 shows this ladder in its most recent version (Van Yperen et al., 2017).

6   https://www.cbs.nl/nl-nl/nieuws/2018/18/ruim-400-duizend-jongeren-krijgen-jeugd-zorg (retrieved February 3, 2020).

Figure 1. The effect ladder (slightly adapted from Van Yperen et al., 2017)

Level of evidence	Description	Types of research	Developmental level of the intervention
5. Strong empirical indications	As in 1 to 4, but there is now sound and substantial evidence that the outcome is caused by the intervention and/or clear evidence showing which elements of the intervention are responsible for the outcome.	Experimental studies (RCTs) or repeated quantitative case studies (N=1 studies) with convincing control conditions, both without follow-up	Efficacious
4. Good empirical indications	As in 1 to 3, but it has now been demonstrated that it is plausible that the outcome is caused by the intervention.	Quasi-experimental studies (without random assignment) Theory of Change studies Dose-respons studies Norm referenced studies Quality assurance studies Benchmark studies Quantitative case studies (N=1 studies) with some form of control	Plausible
3. First empirical indications	As in 1 and 2, but it has now been demonstrated that the intervention leads to the desired outcomes (e.g., goals are attained, target problems decrease, competencies increase, clients are satisfied).	Outcome monitoring Change studies (pre-post tests) Goal attainment studies Client satisfaction studies Quantitative case studies (N=1 studies) without control conditions	Functional
2. Theoretical indications	As in 1, but the intervention now has an acceptable rationale (a program theory) to explain why it should work with whom.	Meta-analyses Reviews Focus groups Delphi panels Intervention mapping Qualitative case studies	Promising
1. Descriptive indications	The essential elements of the intervention have been made explicit (e.g., goals, target group, methods and activities, requirements).	Descriptive studies Observational studies Conduct of interviews Analysis of documents Qualitative case studies	Explicit

The steps on the effect ladder can be conceived as levels of evidence of the effectiveness of an intervention (first column). At the same time, they provide an indication of the maturity of an intervention, i.e. the developmental phase the intervention is in (fourth column). From most interventions in practice we hardly have any evidence of their effectiveness, they reside in "the mud of practice" so to speak, hence they do not enter the effect ladder. A first glance of evidence will emerge if we know what practitioners are actually doing, for whom and to which ends. This yields descriptive evidence that something useful might be going on. This is not so much a piece of evidence as well as a condition for further development. From a developmental perspective the intervention is born and can be seen by everyone, the intervention is "explicit." A second step in the development of an intervention is that we know why it would lead to the desired outcomes. This provides a foundation of theoretical evidence. The intervention has become "promising." The next step is that first empirical indications are gathered which show that an intervention does what it is supposed to do, namely bringing about beneficial changes in the lives of clients. The intervention is "functional." However, we still do not know whether the intervention really caused these changes. Maybe there are alternative explanations, such as spontaneous remission or getting new friends or a new job. More certainty about evidence is acquired if these alternative explanations can be excluded and it therefore becomes clear that it is the intervention which has caused the changes. Ideally, this is the case when a successful RCT has been conducted, which would yield strong empirical indications of effectiveness and will put the intervention on the top of the effect ladder. It has reached the phase of "efficacious." Also, a number of quantitative controlled case studies (N=1 studies) may be sufficient for this level. The literature suggests that more than nine N=1 studies yield comparable evidence to that of a RCT (Chambless et al., 1998). Sometimes the designs of these RCTs or N=1 studies are not yet strong enough to rule out all the alternative explanations. This places the intervention just below the top, it is therefore "plausible" that the intervention has caused the changes.

Each step on the effect ladder describes types of research appropriate for that step. Within the framework of the ladder the search for evidence does not take place from a top-down method driven perspective (as with the RCT), but rather from a bottom-up practice driven perspective, which allows for more freedom to choose a research design. It is essential to choose a design which matches the level of development of the intervention under study. For instance, if there are no descriptions of what is actually done, for whom and to which ends, then the intervention is not yet on a descriptive level. This calls for a study on that level. It would be far too early to conduct a RCT. Jacobs (2003), a researcher in the social domain, coined in this regard the term "good enough study." She borrowed this term from the psychoanalytic writings of Winnicot about the "good enough mother." In order to foster the development of a child one does not need to be an "ideal mother," it is sufficient to be a "good enough mother." In the same vein we have argued that practitioners in collaboration with researchers should foster the development of their interventions by doing a good enough study instead of the ideal study (the RCT). In addition, the effect ladder stimulates further development of an intervention, but this is not obligatory. Sometimes an intervention is too complex to reach the highest level, sometimes practitioners (and their administrators) are satisfied with the evidence level they have already reached. The effect ladder has greatly enhanced the communication within the field of Dutch youth care. It facilitates collaboration among practitioners, administrators, policy makers, financers and researchers.

Summarizing this fourth lesson we can say that practice-based evidence is not black or white, but has many shades of grey dependent on the developmental level of an intervention. As a consequence, conducting evidence-based practice is not restricted to interventions that are empirically supported by RCTs, but includes all interventions that are supported by the best available evidence.

5. Outcome monitoring enhances the evidence

Without information about the outcome of an intervention it is as if one is shooting at a target while blindfolded (Sapyta, Riemer, & Bickman, 2005). In the ideal situation, data are collected at the start of an intervention, in the interim period and at the end of it. This has become known as routine outcome monitoring (ROM). With ROM practitioners receive feedback which helps them to track the progress of their clients and improve their treatment if the data suggest that it is necessary. There is strong evidence for the effect of this kind of feedback in adult care (Gondek, Edbrooke-Childs, Fink, Deighton, & Wolpert, 2016; Lambert, 2010). In youth care this effect has not yet been established as strongly as in adult care (Tam & Ronan, 2017).

The work of Michael Lambert and his colleagues is exemplary in this respect. In their studies a questionnaire containing questions about 45 psychiatric symptoms was used as the outcome monitor and filled out weekly by adult patients treated in outpatient settings. Feedback to therapists and/or patients consisted of a graph which plotted the total score over time along with color coded warning messages when improvement was not occurring or not of the expected magnitude (Lambert, 2010). Shimokawa, Lambert and Smart (2010) reported upon the combined results of six of their studies. Figure 2 shows the results for patients whose progress negatively deviated from the expected course of progress and hence were classified as not-on-track (NOT) cases, considered as being at risk for treatment failure. In these cases, in particular, feedback is assumed to have a positive effect on outcome. Figure 2 depicts the control condition (no feedback given) and three feedback conditions: feedback to the therapist only, feedback to both therapist and patient, and feedback to the therapist with additional clinical support tools (CST) for identifying the causes of deterioration and making suggestions for resolution of identified problems. These CST rely on assessment of therapeutic alliance, patient motivation, and social support with corresponding recommendations for effective actions. The bars in Figure 2 denote the percentages of patients that underwent a reliable positive change during treatment (i.e. a change in the score on the questionnaire that is statistically beyond chance).

Figure 2. Effects of routine outcome monitoring (taken from Shimokawa et al., 2010)

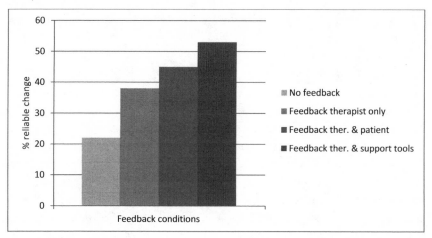

It appears from Figure 2 that feedback to the therapist is better than no feedback. More patients will demonstrate reliable change (38% versus 22% with no feedback). When both therapists and clients receive feedback, more patients show reliable change (45%). When therapists also receive suggestions how to adjust the treatment (the clinical support tools), this percentage increases further (53%). This pattern makes sense, because from left to right chances increase that relevant information is used to improve the treatment for clients who run the risk of deterioration. This is the core of receiving feedback: it must be used. It is important to note that although use is facilitated by researchers, it is in itself part of the work of practitioners. They are gathering practice-based evidence that might place their intervention on step 3 of the effect ladder.

Snowden and Telfer (2017) presented a short Patient Reported Outcome Measure (PROM) which might be used for ROM in chaplaincy care.[7] It contains five questions that aim to measure the impact of spiritual care, to be answered on a 5-point scale ranging from "none of the time" to "all of the time" in the last two weeks. Figure 3 shows these questions.

Figure 3. Patient reported outcome measure of spiritual care (Snowden & Telfer, 2017)

In the last two weeks I have felt:

- I could be honest with myself about how I was really feeling
- I had a positive outlook on my situation
- In control of my life
- A sense of peace
- Anxious

Answers: None of the time – Rarely – Some of the time – Often – All of the time

The lesson here is that monitoring the outcome of treatment increases the chance of a positive result, in particular for patients or clients who run the risk of treatment failure.

6. From protocols to personalized interventions

Over the years the emphasis in youth care (and also in adult care) was on the development of protocolized interventions for specific disorders, such as anxiety, depression, conduct disorder, attention deficit disorder. Mostly the interventions consist of a theoretically based "package" of core elements (therapeutic techniques) that are thought to ameliorate the disorder. Those elements must usually be presented in a prescribed order, in a number of sessions, within a certain period of time. All of which is laid down in a protocol. Nowadays this development is found troubling (Barth et al., 2012; Weisz, Bearman, Santucci, & Jensen-Doss, 2017):

- The number of interventions is no longer manageable;
- Interventions often look similar, they contain the same elements;
- Implementation is a huge problem;
- Practitioners usually take from interventions those elements that they need;
- The effects are not very impressive compared with usual care.

---

7   The PROM is currently being investigated in a research project of ERICH in Belgium, Estonia, The Netherlands, UK, Ireland and Germany, see https://www.pastorale-zorg.be/page/projects/#1 (retrieved February 3, 2020).

Recently the focus has shifted to the core elements that are responsible for change. Those elements are also known as active ingredients, practice elements, or kernels. The work of Bruce Chorpita and his staff provide a good example. They examined more than 600 youth treatment protocols from more than 300 RCTs and distilled 41 core elements that were part of most of the interventions (Chorpita & Daleiden, 2009), for instance exposure, goal setting, modeling, relaxation, time out. They called these core elements the "common elements" of youth psychotherapy, which can be the first options to choose from in treating individual clients. The lesson here is that practitioners can be liberated from the yoke of the protocol to create a personalized intervention for each client with the help of core elements that are common to a great number of evidence-based interventions.

7. Aggregating from cases facilitates further learning

In researching practices, it is a good choice to focus first and foremost on the case. That is in line with conducting practices, where the case also stands central. The collection of practice-based evidence that was advocated earlier in this chapter is in fact to a great extent the collection of case-based evidence. Practitioners can learn from studying cases. On the effect ladder in Figure 1 there are two kinds of case studies. Quantitative case studies or N=1 studies appear in steps 3 to 5. During treatment problems or competencies are repeatedly measured and some form of control is exerted to ensure changes are attributable to the treatment. The qualitative case study has no empirical measurements, therefore the interventions that are studied are not empirically supported. Hence, we place them on step 1 or 2, depending on the credibility of the theoretical underpinning.

To further promote learning, aggregation of case-based evidence is helpful. That can be done in different ways. One may think of qualitative methods to look for common themes in case studies in order to find general knowledge which might be used by individual practitioners. But quantitative methods can also be of use, particularly when measures were taken to monitor the outcome. To illustrate this for chaplaincy care a fictional example is given inspired by a study of Van Loenen, Körver, Walton and De Vries (2018). They describe how Van Loenen developed and conducted a ritual with a military veteran who killed several people in his active service in military war zone and as a result suffers from traumatization. At the time of his contact with the chaplain he is in a psychiatric hospital. He wants to set things right with God and asks if the chaplain has a ritual that can take care of that. Let us assume for the purpose of this chapter that it is possible that the steps of this ritual and the theoretical foundation could be described in such a way that it can be conceptualized as a core element in chaplaincy care, which could be used by other chaplains (of course adapted to the needs of their client). If the theoretical foundation is also clear it can be placed on step 2 of the effect ladder.

Assume further that we have data of 10 psychiatric hospitals about of the use of this ritual and that we want to aggregate these N=1 data to the group level. The fictional results of this aggregation are given in Figure 4. The bars in the graph denote the percentage of clients with whom the chaplains in the hospital performed a ritual with a client. The hospitals are denoted with a capital.

Figure 4. Frequency of the use of rituals in 10 psychiatric hospitals

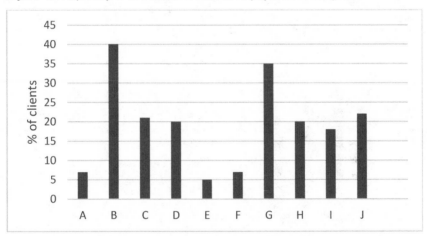

As one can see in most of the hospitals, rituals are used by chaplains with about 20% of their clients. However, there are some exceptions. In hospital A, E and F the frequency is much lower, and in two other hospitals (B, G) the frequency is much higher. This gives rise to interesting questions for learning purposes. For instance, why do chaplains in some hospitals use rituals more or less often? Are preferences or choices on the part of their clients responsible for this? Or has it to do with knowledge or values of the chaplain?

Let us further assume that the chaplains in the fictional hospitals are curious about the outcome of the ritual. They ask their clients to fill out the PROM for spiritual care that was previously mentioned, before and after the ritual. Remember that this questionnaire consists of five questions which are scored on a 5-point scale, with higher scores indicating favorable outcomes. The chaplains can calculate a sum score with values

from 5 to 25 for every client. They also can calculate the difference between the before and after measure and determine if this difference is
large enough to speak of a "reliable change." They used the formulae of
Jacobson and Truax (1991) for this purpose. With those formulae it can
be determined for each client whether the difference between the before
and after measure is statistically above chance level, which depends largely on the reliability of the questionnaire. That results in a decision of "yes"
or "no" reliable change. The outcome can be used in individual guidance
to learn if one is on the right track (see lesson 5). On the group level the
number of clients that underwent reliable change can be counted as an
indication of effectiveness of the intervention. Figure 5 presents the fictional results for the group in our example. The bars denote the percentage of clients in each hospital that showed reliable change.

Figure 5. Outcome of the use of rituals in 10 psychiatric hospitals

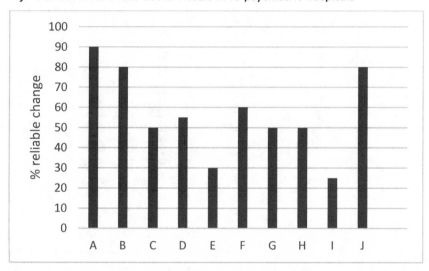

As can be seen, there is variability in the reliable change scores. Most
hospitals had 50 to 60 percent reliable change. However, some hospitals
have remarkably low percentages, indicating poorer outcome (see E, I).
And other hospitals score remarkably high (up to 90 percent, see A, B, J).
Again, this may lead to questions. Why are some hospitals scoring poorly
and others excellently? Characteristics of individual clients, individual
chaplains or the organization might offer a clue. Discussing answers on
these questions once again creates opportunities for learning.

In this fictional example it was assumed that the chaplains of the 10
hospitals had meetings in which they discussed their results. Maybe they

took part in a research project, or maybe they were in a research community. The lesson to be learned here is that results do not speak for themselves; they must be spoken about! Van Yperen et al. (2017), from whom we derive this lesson, envision an "outcome table" at which not only practitioners and researchers should have a place, but also managers, policy makers, financiers and clients. They all share a common goal: to learn from outcomes in order to reach joint decisions about evidence-based care.

Conclusion

The lessons we learned in researching practices of Dutch youth care in order to look for evidence of the effectiveness of interventions and that have been discussed in this chapter are also of relevance for studying the effectiveness of chaplaincy care. In this domain researchers and chaplains can also free themselves from the "tyranny" of the randomized controlled trial (lessons 1 and 2). Instead of meeting that gold standard they should strive to do a "good enough study" that is appropriate to the developmental level of the intervention under study (lesson 4). Our effect ladder suggests examples of such studies. Those studies can help to find an answer to the three important questions of Fitchett (2011) about chaplaincy care: "Who was the patient, what was the intervention, what changed" (p. 6); and those of Walton and Körver (2017) as well: "What do chaplains do, for what reasons and to what ends" (p. 258). (Level 1 to 3 on the ladder.) Moreover, with appropriate control conditions it can be demonstrated that the intervention has caused the changes (level 4 and 5). In addition, the focus lies on searching for practice-based evidence (lesson 3).

In answering these questions, it might also be fruitful to look for core elements that cut across many chaplaincy practices (lesson 6). That can help to construct a taxonomy of common elements that can be used to build "possible" effective interventions. Via routine outcome monitoring one can acquire empirical indications of the effectiveness of those interventions for individual clients (lesson 5). This is a first step in learning from outcomes. By aggregating data of individual clients (lesson 7) further learning can take place as to "what treatment, by whom, is most effective for this individual, with that specific problem, under which set of circumstances, and how does it come about?" Ironically, this is the "ultimate question" about the outcome of psychotherapy which Gordon Paul formulated more than 50 years ago (Paul, 1967), but that still has not received the ultimate answer. The theme of this chapter is that hitherto the answer has been looked for from a top-down method driven perspective, whereas a bottom-up practice driven perspective might be more fruitful.

References

APA Presidential Task Force on Evidence-Based Practice (2006). Evidence-based practice in psychology. *American Psychologist, 61,* 272-285.

Barkham, M., & Mellor-Clark, J. (2003). Bridging evidence-based practice and practice-based evidence. Developing a rigorous and relevant knowledge for the psychological therapies. *Clinical Psychology and Psychotherapy, 10,* 319-327.

Barth, R. P., Lee, B. R., Lindsey, M. A., Collins, K. S., Strieder, F., ... Sparks, J.A. (2012). Evidence-Based Practice at a Crossroads: The Timely Emergence of Common Elements and Common Factors. *Research on Social Work Practice, 22,* 108-119.

Chambless, D. L., Baker, M. J., Baucom, D. H., Beutler, L. E., Calhoun, K. S., ... Woody, S. R. (1998). Update on empirically validated therapies, II. *The Clinical Psychologist, 51,* 3-16.

Chorpita, B.F., & Daleiden, E.L. (2009). Mapping evidence-based treatments for children and adolescents. Application of the distillation and matching model to 615 treatments from 322 randomized trials. *Journal of Consulting and Clinical Psychology, 77,* 566-579.

Fitchett, G. (2011). Making our case(s). *Journal of Health Care Chaplaincy, 17,* 3-18.

Gondek, D., Edbrooke-Childs, J., Fink, E., Deighton, J., & Wolpert, M. (2016). Feedback from outcome measures and treatment effectiveness, treatment efficiency, and collaborative practice: A systematic review. *Administration and Policy in Mental Health and Mental Health Services Research, 43,* 325-343.

Jacobs, F. H. (2003). Child and family program evaluation. Learning to enjoy complexity. *Applied Developmental Science, 7,* 62-75.

Jacobson, N. S., & Truax, P. (1991). Clinical significance. A statistical approach to defining meaningful change in psychotherapy research. *Journal of Consulting and Clinical Psychology, 59,* 12-19.

Kazdin, A. E. (2003). Psychotherapy for children and adolescents. *Annual Review of Psychology, 54,* 253-276.

Lambert, M. J. (2010). *Prevention of treatment failure. The use of measuring, monitoring and feedback in clinical practice.* Washington, DC: American Psychological Association.

Paul, G. L. (1967). Outcome research in psychotherapy. *Journal of Consulting Psychology, 31,* 109-118.

Sackett, D. L. (1997). Evidence-based medicine. *Seminars in Perinatology, 21,* 3-5.

Sackett, D. L., Rosenberg, W. M. C., Gray, J. A. M., Haynes, R. B., & Richardson, W. S. (1996). Evidence based medicine. What it is and what it isn't. *British Medical Journal, 312,* 71-73.

Sapyta, J., Riemer, M., & Bickman, L. (2005). Feedback to clinicians: Theory, research, and practice. *Journal of Clinical Psychology, 61,* 145-153.

Shimokawa, K., Lambert, M. J., & Smart, D.W. (2010). Enhancing treatment outcome of patients at risk of treatment failure: Meta-analytic and mega-analytic review of a psychotherapy quality assurance system. *Journal of Consulting and Clinical Psychology, 78,* 298-311.

Snowden, A., & Telfer, I. (2017) Patient reported outcome measure of spiritual care as delivered by chaplains. *Journal of Health Care Chaplaincy, 23,* 131-155.

Tam, H. E., & Ronan, K. (2017). The application of a feedback-informed approach in psychological service with youth: Systematic review and meta-analysis. *Clinical Psychology Review, 55,* 41-55.

Van Loenen, G., Körver, J., Walton, M., & De Vries, R. (2017). Case study of "moral injury": Format Dutch Case Studies Project. *Health and Social Care Chaplaincy, 5,* 281-296

Van Yperen, T. A., Veerman, J. W., & Bijl, B. (Eds.) (2017). *Zicht op effectiviteit. Handboek voor resultaatgerichte ontwikkeling van interventies in de jeugdsector* (2nd rev. ed.). Rotterdam: Lemniscaat.

Veerman, J. W., & Van Yperen, T. A. (2007). Degrees of freedom and degrees of certainty. A developmental model for the establishment of evidence-based youth care. *Evaluation and Program Planning, 30,* 212-221.

Walton, M., & Körver, J. (2017). Dutch Case Studies Project in chaplaincy care: A description and theoretical explanation of the format and procedures. *Health and Social Care Chaplaincy, 5,* 257-280.

Weisz, J. R., Bearman, S. K., Santucci, L. C., & Jensen-Doss, A. (2017). Initial test of a principle-guided approach to transdiagnostic psychotherapy with children and adolescents. *Journal of Clinical Child & Adolescent Psychology, 46,* 44-58.

Weisz, J. R., Kuppens, S., Eckshtain, D, Ugueto, A. M., Hawley, K. M., & Jensen-Doss, A. (2013). Performance of evidence-based youth psychotherapies compared with usual clinical care. A multilevel meta-analysis. *JAMA Psychiatry, 70,* 750-761.

Weisz, J. R., Kuppens, S., Ng. M. Y., Eckshtain, D., Ugueto, A. M., ... Fordwood, S. R. (2017). What five decades of research tells us about the effects of youth psychological therapy: A multilevel meta-analysis and implications for science and practice. *American Psychologist, 72,* 79-117.

Weisz, J. R., Krumholz, L. S., Santucci, L., Thomassin, K., & Ng, M. Y. (2015). Shrinking the gap between research and practice: Tailoring and testing youth psychotherapies in clinical care contexts. *Annual Review of Clinical Psychology, 11,* 139-163.

Chapter 5.

Up and Down the Participation Ladder
The Use of Narratives in Collaborative Research

Gaby Jacobs

The Case Studies Project (CSP) uses a collaborative research methodology. In this contribution I will first outline a view on collaborative research. Since there are many different forms, I will discuss some differences and commonalities to find the form that is most akin to the Case Studies Project. Following this, the use of narratives in collaborative research is discussed. That discussion raises questions regarding the function of narratives in the CSP, the quality of the research and its outcomes.

Collaboration in research: what forms can it take?

Collaborative research can be defined as researchers working together to achieve the common goal of producing new scientific knowledge (Katz & Martin, 1995, p. 7). Research collaboration is often expressed by multiple authorship. Although this is not a perfect measure, it shows that different researchers have co-created knowledge in a specific area. Quite diverse causes can be indicated for the growing collaboration in research, including changing requirements for receiving funding;[8] the need for more complex instrumentation and methods; and increasing specialization and the need for innovation in science, a demand that often can only be met by pooling one's expertise with others (Katz & Martin, 1995). Another important factor that is not mentioned by Katz and Martin but that has influenced research collaboration is the demand to work in closer proximity to professional and institutional practices in order to build evidence-based practice.

Evidence-based practice is the use of current best evidence on providing good care or services (Sackett, 1997). It is based on a hierarchy of evidence with randomized controlled trials being the research method

---

8   Participatory research has received a boost in health care, with patients increasingly being actively involved as co-researchers and helping to determine research topics. Large funding programs in the Netherlands, such as the Netherlands Organisation for Health Research and Development (https://www.zonmw.nl/en; retrieved February 3, 2020), have made patient participation a requirement to be eligible for funds. Also, in the field of care for the elderly there is a focus on action research in which practitioners become researchers and change agents, learning and developing at the same time.

to produce the best evidence for a specific intervention and systematic reviews as the best way of collating and screening that evidence. In the last decades however, the notion of evidence-based practice has been criticized for its one-dimensional view on knowledge as scientific knowledge: "The prominence ascribed to research evidence has meant the relative neglect of other forms of evidence in the delivery of healthcare ..." (Rycroft-Malone et al., 2003, p. 83). Moreover, evidence-based practice is regarded as not taking the specific context into account, thereby not producing high ecological validity (The Council for Public Health and Society, 2017). Green (2008) argues that the research-practice gap is usually addressed by looking for ways to communicate evidence-based practice guidelines to practitioners more efficiently and by more effectively supporting them in implementing these guidelines within their practice. However, throughout the scientific pipeline in which evidence is produced, Green argues that:

> the research itself is rendered increasingly irrelevant to the circumstances of practice by the process of vetting the research before it can qualify for inclusion in systematic reviews and the practice guidelines derived from them. It suggests a "fallacy of the pipeline" implicit in one-way conceptualizations of translation, dissemination and delivery of research to practitioners. Secondly, it identifies a "fallacy of the empty vessel" implicit in the assumptions underlying common characterizations of the practitioner as a recipient of evidence-based guidelines. (Green, 2008, p. i20)

Consequently, a move is made to involve practitioners as researchers in building evidence from practice, the so-called practice-based evidence. Green argues that bringing the research closer to practice produces more actionable knowledge, that is tailored and relevant to the populations and their specific circumstances, and that delivers immediate feedback to the practitioners: "The promise of this 'pull' approach has led to the suggestion that if we want more evidence-based practice, we need more practice-based evidence" (Green, 2008, p. i23). Participatory research, action research and practice-based research taking place in cross-sector collaborations are all forms that help to deliver practice-based evidence. They are all forms of collaborative research, in which researchers work together with practitioners to create practice-based evidence.

In this contribution we are not so much interested in academic researchers working together, as has been increasingly the case in the last years. We will look at the collaboration between academic researchers and practitioners-as-researchers, more specifically chaplains-as-researchers. This already limits the number of different research forms but still shows some different traditions that are relevant for the CSP. I will discuss cross-sector collaboration, participatory research and participatory action research.

First of all, the CSP is a good example of cross-sector collaboration, i.e. the collaboration between several universities on the one hand and non-profit organizations on the other hand. Cross-sector collaboration can be defined as "the linking or sharing of information, resources, activities, and capabilities by organizations in two or more sectors to achieve jointly an outcome that could not be achieved by organizations in one sector separately" (Bryson, Crosby, & Stone, 2006, p. 44).

On an inter-institutional or macro level, an agreement of understanding has established the collaboration within the CSP. This is often an important precondition for collaborative research to take place. On the meso-level of the project in which groups work together, chaplains have a role as co-researchers, studying their own practice and writing it up as a case. They are supported by academic researchers and peers in this process. Would this be a kind of participatory research? The International Collaboration of Participatory Health Research (2013) defines participatory research as follows:

> The primary underlying assumption is that participation on the part of those whose lives or work is the subject of the study fundamentally affects all aspects of the research. The engagement of these people in the study is an end in itself ... recognizing the value of each person's contribution to the co-creation of knowledge in a process that is not only practical, but also collaborative and empowering. (ICPHR, 2013, p. 5)

This fundamental assumption is also found in participatory action research, because the persons who are affected by the research play an active role as co-researcher. However, action research explicitly aims at changing or improving the reality being investigated, which is not the case in participatory research as such. Participatory action research then is defined as:

> Social research carried out by a team that encompasses a professional action researcher and the members of an organization, community, or network ("stakeholders") who are seeking to improve the participants' situation. AR [Action Research] promotes broad participation in the research process and supports action leading to a more just, sustainable, or satisfying situation for the stakeholders. (Greenwood & Levin, 2007, p. 3)

In participatory research, the co-researchers can be anyone except for academic researchers, e.g. patients, citizens, practitioners or policymakers. They may be elderly people living in a deprived neighborhood where safety is at stake; or nurses who, due to understaffing, can no longer do their work with attention and dedication; or chaplains who join forces to reorient their practice within the healthcare organization. Together with a researcher as facilitator, they work step by step to implement changes and to monitor their significance and impact on a relevant situation. The active participation also means that the participants themselves are undergoing a development, also referred to as empowerment. They become aware of obstacles and develop new skills to overcome or avoid them as they work on the project. That is the educational component of action research. This form of research also explicitly uses a multi-stakeholder perspective because the stakeholders are involved in the research in one way or another. So, for example, when it comes to profiling chaplaincy in a care institution for the elderly, residents, family members, nurses, care-workers, doctors and management also have a stake. The different perspectives and knowledges are included in order to get a multi-perspective on the situation and to work with complexity in transforming practice.

Returning to the CSP, the aim is primarily to build evidence from practice and secondly to strengthen the professionalism of the chaplains, but not so much to transform chaplaincy practice. It is participatory research but without the action goal of participatory action research, and on a macro level collaboration between academy and professional practice is established. So far, it includes the practitioners' knowledge, but not so much a multi-perspective from other stakeholders on chaplaincy's practice. Besides this, calling the CSP a form of participatory research in itself does not tell us much about the nature of the participation. That is why we need to take a closer look at the chaplains' participation.

Participation can be viewed as a multilevel phenomenon with academic researchers and co-researchers achieving different levels and kinds of participation depending on the task at hand (Jacobs, 2006) (see Figure 1). Participation in research by practitioners then takes different forms and degrees in different phases or activities of a research project, ranging from information and consultation of practitioners at one end, to collaboration and assuming full responsibility by practitioners at the other. Well-known participation instruments are the Ladder of Arnstein (Arnstein, 1969) and the Ladder of Pretty (Pretty, 1995) which is a more "neutral" version of the former typology. The Ladder of Pretty has for the sake of this article been slightly modified to adapt it for research participation.

Figure 1. Ladder of participation (adapted from Pretty, 1995; in Jacobs, 2006, p. 572)

5. Self-mobilization	Practitioners set their own agenda and organize the project. Researchers have a role in the background, facilitating and supporting but only when asked.
4. Interactive participation	Practitioners and researchers work as equal partners in defining the topic and research strategies, sharing knowledge and valuing "local" knowledge, and taking decisions. Researchers facilitate and support the research process and outcomes.
3. Functional participation	Practitioners are involved in the development and conduct of project activities. Researchers are in control and have the responsibility for the process and outcomes.
2. Participation by consultation	Practitioners are asked to give their opinions and knowledge about the project plans or topics; researchers make the decisions.
1. Participation by information	Researchers are in control of the project; practitioners are informed about the project.
0. No participation	Practitioners are not informed about the project, i.e. only about the parts for which their information is sought.

Whether all levels in this figure should be defined as modes of participation and what levels of participation contribute to empowerment is open to discussion. In participatory action research which aims at empowerment and changing circumstances, participation should be empowering (i.e. levels 4 and 5) and not just a situation where practitioners work together with a researcher for the latter's convenience. In research collaboration with the aim of building practice-based evidence, level 3 participation may be sufficient. The research project is set and determined by academic researchers, but without the practitioners' knowledge of their practice it would not achieve valid outcomes. If participation does not exceed the level of informed consent (levels 0 and 1), it is questionable whether this can be called participatory research since it does not differ from traditional research approaches in which participants are the object of the research (Jacobs, 2006).

As a collaborator on the meso-level of a project, in which persons and groups work towards a common aim, one should be at least involved throughout the project's duration and make substantial and frequent contributions. Furthermore, one should be co-responsible for at least one of the main elements of the project, such as data collection or analysis. In the CSP chaplains work in small groups to contribute cases from their own practices. They are the primary actors for collecting data, whereas the researchers mostly take the lead in analyzing them and the process of writing up. However, in some cases, chaplains take the lead in the analysis and publication of a case study. Therefore, although the responsibility for the project lies with academic researchers, participation of chaplains shifts between levels 1 to 4, with level 1 and 2 when the project started to levels 4 where chaplains take an active lead in data collection or analysis and the writing up of cases. The higher levels of participation may contribute to the building of practice-based evidence as well as the professional development and empowerment of chaplains involved in the CSP. Both are narrative practices, in which professional and personal knowledge is built resulting in change, development or transformation. In the next section I will expound on this.

Research collaboration as a narrative practice

As human beings we are storytelling creatures. We use narratives to express our experiences, thoughts and feelings. We deliberate about our actions and whether we did the right thing. Stories do not only express the values of the teller, they also create values and meaning in the process of storytelling (McAdams, 1993). Chaplaincy care in large part is about storytelling: clients most of the times use stories to talk about their lives, their identities, their connections and their losses. Chaplains listen, ask questions, and tell stories (for example from literature, poetry, art, bible texts, their own lives and experiences) that convey certain meanings that they then can explore together. There are close links between chaplaincy as a narrative practice and the use of narratives in the collaborative CSP, which makes a case study methodology suitable for doing research on chaplaincy. In the remainder of this chapter I will explore three functions of narratives in collaborative research, i.e. building knowledge from practice; the learning and empowerment of the practitioners involved and the transformation of practice; and communicating about chaplaincy to the external world.

Knowledge building from experience: narrative-based evidence

Chaplains use stories about their own practice as part of a larger project that aims to obtain insight into the processes and outcomes of chaplaincy care. The narrative research tradition (see e.g. Bold, 2012) aims at building knowledge that expresses the meanings for the participants and local practices involved. It is situated in a constructivist or relational constructionist research tradition, in which knowledge is understood to be constructed within the interactions between persons. By telling stories, the tacit knowledge that practitioners have acquired comes to the fore, knowledge that they were possibly not able to articulate before.

Critics have posed some risks involved in narrative based research. According to them, narratives cannot be used to build evidence, as they are "subjective," incomplete and present a selective picture of "reality." Indeed, there is a problem of correspondence between stories that are told and practitioners' "actual" actions and relationships, a problem that is referred to as the discrepancy between theories-in-use versus espoused theories (Argyris & Schön, 1978). However, using narratives as data will not bring the "truth" of practice to the fore, but neither are they fictions. By analyzing these narratives, representative constructions (Bold, 2012, p. 145) can be made that highlight certain features and outcomes of practice which could not be accomplished in other ways. Especially when mixed data are used, such as video or audio recordings and patient reports alongside practitioner self-reports, the representativeness of the constructions gains validity. The CSP allows for the use of mixed methods, although the main data exist of practitioner's reports. Besides this, the subjectivity of case studies should not be seen as a limitation, but as a key characteristic of the method (Toledano & Anderson, 2017). Stories are already interpreted by the teller, and then re-interpreted by the researcher (*double hermeneutics*) and then even re-reinterpreted in the dialogue with other chaplains-researchers (see the next part). This again is a close resemblance with chaplaincy practice itself, in which client and chaplain co-construct the stories that are told. Instead of trying to reduce this subjectivity, reflexivity is needed as to what the role of the researcher is in selecting and interpreting stories. "A reflexive researcher is aware of the fact that the story has been created by him/her. He/she exposes his/her process of knowing to the readers" (Heikkinen, Huttunen, Syrjälä, & Pesonen, 2012, pp. 8-9).

Professional learning and empowerment through storytelling

Writing up a case study, telling it and sharing it with others can be seen as a way of collecting data in research but it is also a reflective practice (Bolton, 2005) in which chaplains develop new insights about their professional ways of being and acting. The simple act of telling and being listened to, leads to an interruption of normal practice for the chaplains in the CSP. By making explicit their own practice, trying to find the right words and language, learning takes place with regard to their professional and personal selves, their practice, and the collaborative research project they are involved in. A more critical consciousness emerges once the researchers start to question their stories in dialogue with others. Dialogue is a key to collaborative practice and the professional development that emerges from it (Ledwith & Springett, 2010). Story is the beginning of dialogue and is at the same time very much enhanced by dialogue that is characterized by connected knowing: empathetic, open, attempting to understand from deep inside (Belenky, Clinchy, Goldberger, & Tarule, 1997). In dialogue, chaplains become more aware of their habits of thought and acting by the mutual questioning of assumptions and actions, and the opening up of new perspectives offers new possibilities. Moreover, the insights are not kept individual but are shared within the group and in this way may influence chaplaincy practice in general: "The narrative method is a form in which people, cooperatively, co-create knowledge – i.e. an improved understanding of a phenomenon – and, consequently, a new social reality" (Toledano & Anderson, 2017, p. 13). Professional learning and empowerment through participatory practice may lead to transforming practice (Ledwith & Springett, 2010).

Communicating new stories and challenging dominant discourses

Until recently, narrative knowledge has not had a strong position in science because of the criticisms outlined before. It does however have a place in the original notion of evidence-based practice, in which not only knowledge from large randomized controlled trials (RCTs) counts as evidence, but also the practitioner's knowledge, experiential knowledge of clients or lay persons, and the local context knowledge (Rycroft-Malone et al., 2004). Currently, the collaborative – and narrative – research tradition is challenging the dominant discourse of science, truth and objectivity by demonstrating the power of small stories in building evidence from practice. The CSP thereby is part of a bigger movement that challenges traditional scientific rules.

> Personal stories challenge hegemonic narratives ... Such counternarratives are, as Lyotard explains, quintessentially "little stories" – the little stories of those individuals and groups whose knowledges and histories have been marginalized, excluded, subjugated or forgotten in the telling of official narratives. (Ledwith & Springett, 2010, pp. 108-109)

Moreover, narratives can be used to communicate these findings in the academic, policy and practice worlds. For the CSP, this bears the possibility of using stories to counter old or prejudiced views of chaplaincy or to enrich existing ones, which will strengthen the profession. The narratives may also be used in educational courses, for the professional development of future chaplains or other disciplines. They are powerful forms for communicating and learning, as they draw on the imagination, connecting experiences with meanings, past with present and future, and different locations, thereby enabling an understanding of what essentially matters in chaplaincy practice.

Conclusion

Chaplaincy is a narrative practice that acknowledges the storied nature of human beings (Bruner, 2004; McAdams, 1993). The CSP fits in with that practice by using a collaborative and narrative based methodology in which chaplains and academic researchers cooperatively co-create knowledge leading to an improved understanding of chaplaincy practice. The project is producing narrative based evidence: chaplains tell their stories, interpret them, share and validate them. Questions remain regarding the process of the CSP and its goals and outcomes on a professional and practice level, as will be discussed next.

The process of co-creation requires dialogical competencies: the ability to empathetically engage with the others in the project and questioning each other's stories in order to construct knowledge from them. Without narrative, it would be almost impossible to work collaboratively. Chaplains tell stories and build common stories (as knowledge) in working together. However, this is not per se a harmonious process: everyone looking and "travelling" in the same direction (Jacobs, 2016). It is important to keep asking what stories may not be voiced or heard; who determines the structure for narrating the stories; what language or words are chosen? The CSP might also be broadened by inviting the stories of other disciplines about chaplaincy, the stories of clients and their family members, the stories of policy makers; as well as other sources of data and analysis, such as observations or conversation analysis. The cases then may not be a single coherent story about a chaplaincy practice, but a multi-layered, polyphonic one in which different voices can be heard, recognized and valued.

In participatory action research transforming practice and empowerment of stakeholders is the main aim. In the CSP the primary goal is building evidence. However, collaborative research has an enormous potential for change in other areas. Alongside the CSP, a PhD study (see chapter 20 by Niels den Toom), is conducted to learn about the knowledge and skills chaplains develop in participating in the CSP. Other relevant questions we need to ask are: What new stories are being told about chaplaincy, e.g. to students, other disciplines, policy makers? How does the CSP spread to new domains? Is the CSP methodology used in other chaplaincy projects? How does it lead to new ways of practicing, such as a more critical-reflective and dialogic practice? How does it lead to the empowerment of clients by "making their voices heard"? These and other questions may bring new insights and innovations in conducting case study research. The use of narratives will remain a key in this:

When our concern is with particular occurrences, human interactions, or personal life experiences, logical principles and laws cannot be used to organize them; they cannot explain their richness ... It is in such cases that narratives demonstrate their greatest potential. (Toledano & Anderson, 2017, p. 10)

References

Argyris, C., & Schön, D. (1978). *Organisational learning: a theory of action perspective*. San Francisco: Jossey-Bass.

Arnstein, R. S. (1969). A ladder of citizen participation. *Journal of the American Planning Association, 16*(2), 187-195.

Belenky, M. F., Clinchy, B. M., Goldberger, N. R., & Tarule, J. M. (1986). *Women's ways of knowing: The development of self, voice, and mind*. New York: Basic Books.

Bold, C. (2012). *Using narrative in research*. London: Sage.

Bolton, G. (2005). *Reflective practice: writing and professional development*. London: Sage.

Bruner, J. (2004). Life as narrative. *Social Research, 71*(3), 691-710.

Bryson, J. M., Crosby, B. C., & Middleton Stone, M. (2015). Designing and Implementing Cross-Sector Collaborations: Needed and Challenging. *Public Administration Review, 75*(5), 647-663.

Jacobs, G. (2006). Imagining the flowers, but working the rich and heavy clay: participation and empowerment in action research for health. *Educational Action Research, 14* (4), 569-581.

Jacobs, G. (2016). "A guided walk in the woods": boundary crossing in a collaborative action research project. *Educational Action Research, 25*(4), 575-593.

Green L. W. (2008). Making research relevant: if it is an evidence-based practice, where's the practice based evidence? *Family Practice, 25,* i20-i24.

Greenwood, D. J., & Levin, M. (2007). *Introduction to action research. Social research for social change*. Thousand Oaks: Sage.

Heikkinen, H. L. T., Huttunen, R., Syrjälä, L., & Pesonen, J. (2012). Action research and narrative inquiry: five principles for validation revisited. *Educational Action Research, 20*(1), 5-21.

International Collaboration for Participatory Health Research (ICPHR) (2013). *Position Paper 1: What is Participatory Health Research?* Version: May 2013. Berlin: International Collaboration for Participatory Health Research. Retrieved May 5, 2019, from http://www.icphr.org/uploads/2/0/3/9/20399575/ichpr_position_paper_1_defintion_-_version_may_2013.pdf

Katz, J. S., & Martin, B. R. (1995). What is research collaboration? *Research Policy, 26,* 1-18.

Ledwith, M. & Springett, J. (2010). *Participatory practice. Community-based action for transformative change*. Bristol: Policy Press.

McAdams, D. (1993). *The stories we live by: personal myths and the making of the self*. New York: Guilford Press.

Pretty, J. N. (1995). *Regenerating agriculture: policies and practice for sustainability and selfreliance.* London: Earthscan Publication Ltd.

Rycroft-Malone, J., Seers, K., Titchen, A., Harvey, G., Kitson, A., & McCormack, B. (2004). What counts as evidence in evidence-based practice? *Journal of Advanced Nursing, 47*(1), 81-90.

The Council for Public Health and Society (2017). *No context without evidence. About the illusion of evidence-based practice in healthcare.* The Hague: RVS.

Sackett, D. L. (1997). Evidence-based medicine. *Seminars in Perinatology, 21*(1), 3-5.

Toledano, N. & Anderson, A. R. (2017). Theoretical reflections on narrative in action research. *Action Research, 0*(0), 1-17.

Chapter 6.

The Science of the Particular[9]

Jacques Körver

Introduction

The impressive ten-part documentary *The Vietnam War* (Burns & Novick, 2017) shows the developments in that war step by step. In the course of 1966/1967, the American army command and government doubted their approach and wondered what they were actually doing. More and more troops and equipment were being deployed, but it was completely unclear whether this had any effect, and whether the war was moving in a desired direction. A former general later formulated this comment: "If you can't count what's important, you make important what you can count."[10] In fact, this meant that it was decided to choose the number of killed Vietcong soldiers as a measure of success: the more people killed, the better the war would go on. However, there was absolutely no correlation whatsoever with the course of the war. Moreover, the statistics proved to be extremely unreliable; they were often exaggerated in order to prove success at all costs. The real impact of the American strategy could only be seen through stories from those directly involved and on the basis of observations on the spot, as the documentary does 40 years later. Precisely those stories, however, were excluded from the official reports.

In chapter 3, the occasion and context of the Dutch Case Studies Project in chaplaincy care (CSP) were discussed. In this chapter I consider a number of theoretical and methodological starting points that have led to the specific approach in the project. A number of these principles have been extensively discussed in several articles published elsewhere, including the format for the description and reflection of the case studies (Gärtner, Körver, & Walton, 2019; Walton & Körver, 2017). Thereupon I describe the characteristics of a naturalistic case study, an approach that fits in seamlessly with the principles of the CSP. Finally, I list some of the characteristics of the CSP.

9   The title is borrowed from the article by Abma & Stake (2014). The chapter is a partial adaptation of Körver & Walton (2019).

10   The statement makes a striking reference to a remark by Robert McNamara, the Secretary of Defense in that period, saying just the opposite: "Measure what is important, don't make important what you can measure."

Basic principles

One of the basic principles of the CSP's design is the observation that the case studies published at that time made it clear that chaplaincy often involves more than chaplains themselves articulate. That holds for the interventions, the goals, the accountability and the results (see e.g. Baird, 2018). Another observation was that for the descriptions in the case studies very different formats were used making it difficult to compare them. In addition, the use of theoretical models and concepts was not or hardly noticeable in the material and the relationship between theory and practice was barely visible in the case studies described. These observations have led to a research design that makes use of an extensive and clearly described format to describe and reflect upon the case study. In the format extensive attention is paid to the relationship between practice and theory. Discussion takes place in six research communities[11], in numbers varying between 8 and 12 participants. Five research communities have been compiled on the basis of the field of work (hospital, care for the elderly, mental health care, prison and military) and a sixth is of mixed composition (youth care, care for people with a disability, rehabilitation, primary care, students) (Gärtner et al., 2019; Walton & Körver, 2017).

The aim of the research is to trace good practices of chaplaincy, especially criteria for good practices. It is necessary to pay attention to the relationship between practice and theory ("On what do chaplains base their actions or interventions?"), to the goals that chaplaincy pursues and to the interventions that are employed together with their effect. That requires an accurate and detailed description of the chaplain's behavior. Moreover, involved clients are invited to read and respond to the description, along with other parties involved in the case study (relatives and caregivers). In addition, the reflection on the case study in the research community has the advantage that the case study will be placed in a broader context and a consensus on (the criteria for) the good practices will be worked on.

In the context of the CSP, a case study is conceived as an informative story, based on a methodical description and reflection, in which the counseling process and the contribution of chaplaincy are presented and argued. The CSP concentrates on individual contacts and contacts with a small group (without neglecting the context). Case studies can then be examined from different perspectives, e.g. from the perspective of the faith or world view of the client and/or the chaplain, of the field of work, of the relationship between relationship and goal-orientation, of rituality, of the importance of metaphors, of a specific target group, of contingency

---

11   A contraction of "research group" and "learning community."

or finiteness, or many other perspectives. The practice described in a case study consists of a coherent pattern or network of observations, interactions, interventions, reflections, emotions, motivations, intentions, effects, etc. (Reckwitz, 2002). The choice of a specific case study is made by the chaplain himself or herself on the basis of his or her assessment that it is an example of good practice. During the reflection in the research community, this initial assessment is further investigated, and it may turn out that the case study (1) is representative of the target group; (2) paradigmatic with regard to the method of chaplaincy; (3) unusual because its erratic character makes something visible; and/or (4) critical because the presuppositions or the existing method of chaplaincy are being tested (this classification is based on a combination of Flyvbjerg, 2006; Thomas, 2011; Yin, 2014).

An underlying issue is the nature of the evidence provided by case studies. It is true that a case study is often considered to be research with low evidence, but it appears to be a valuable research approach suitable for research into chaplaincy and is also increasingly (re)appreciated in other areas of science (Flyvbjerg, 2006; Greenhalgh et al., 2016; Panter, Guell, & Ogilvie, 2016). The focus is primarily on the development of practice-based evidence as a first step towards evidence-based practice. Although the outcome of a single case study is somewhat ambiguous, research based on several case studies can lead to a degree of plausibility and reliability much greater than often assumed, especially in the context of practice-based research in which researchers and chaplains work together. This type of research is in line with the current level of development of the interventions, is embedded in professional practice, can be used immediately at all levels of practice (primary process, team, institution, and policy), and is focused on and based on cooperation between the researchers and all levels of the practical organization (Van Yperen, Veerman, & Bijl, 2017).[12] It is a form of responsive research in which interaction with the subjects studied is sought (Abma, Nierse, & Widdershoven, 2009; Visse, Abma, & Widdershoven, 2012). In fact, there are three levels of interaction: between the chaplains and their clients, between the chaplains and other professionals involved, and between the chaplains (as co-researchers) and the researchers.

12   See further chapter 4 by Jan Willem Veerman that discusses this theme in more detail.

Naturalistic case study

As argued above, case studies are particularly suitable for studying the multicolored and multi-layered nature of reality. Case studies serve to capture the complexity of and interactions in a specific situation and to approach the meanings that people give to situations and events. Case studies explicitly contribute to evidence-based practice (EBP), especially by clarifying clinical practice and experience and by paying attention to clients' values and contexts. After all, according to the original views on EBP, it is precisely these two elements – clinical experience and values of the client – that should be explicitly combined with the best scientific insights and research results (Council for Health and Society, 2017; Sackett, Rosenberg, Gray, Haynes, & Richardson, 1996).

Case studies constitute "the science of the particular," in terms of Abma and Stake (2014). In their perspective on the naturalistic case study, they formulate five distinguishing features of the case study. These characteristics fit in particularly well with the CSP's aims and methods. Moreover, it will become clear that these characteristics fit in particularly well with the professional ethics and skills of chaplains. This is also, by the way, characteristic of other professions, such as a psychologist taking part in a narrative study who suddenly realizes: "I have been doing narrative research for 30 years" (Josselson, Lieblich, & McAdams, 2003). Below is a brief description of each characteristic. For each characteristic a short description of a case study from the CSP is included, which accurately typifies the characteristic in question.

(1) A case study concerns so-called emic issues, i.e. issues that arise from the case and are not imposed from the outside. The purpose of a case study is to better understand a specific situation or case, especially the embedded values and meanings. Although in the beginning a case study is always approached from a certain focus and research question (which is also the case in the CSP and is mainly expressed in the format for the description and reflection), the design is not fully defined in advance. Issues, questions and points of attention arise from the case (emic versus etic) and can be further developed and investigated.

> In a case study the chaplain very accurately describes an anointing of the sick. During the reflection the research community observes that the chaplain paid an exceptional amount of attention to establishing contacts and connections between the various parties involved: family (the patient's wife and their children), nurses and doctors in the intensive care, and the other therapists. He explains that he always does

this, that he considers it important to make clear to everyone what is happening and what the importance of the ritual is. He sees himself as a kind of liaison officer, who especially – as the research community concludes – is able to make a connection between the lifeworld of the patient and his family and the system world of treatments, protocols and procedures (Abma, 2010; Habermas, 1987). The chaplain also makes a connection with the time after death (what should be done in a practical sense?, the first steps in the mourning process, thoughts about the afterlife) - partly in response to a question from the wife after the ritual: "What is going to happen now?" Perhaps Ronald Grimes' statement also resonates here: "To be cured is to be fixed, to be healed is to be reconnected" (Grimes, 2000, p. 342).

(2) In a case study, the influence of the context is constantly taken into account. The meaning of an experience is always situationally determined. There are constant interactions with the context, a case is never an isolated fact. Within each case, parts, dimensions and domains can be distinguished, each of which has its own influence on the whole and on other parts. Studying these parts contributes to the comprehensibility and meaning of the case as a whole.

In another case study, a wax coat suddenly turns out to have a great meaning. The patient, who has been staying in a medium care department for months, on a respirator, has had the coat explicitly hung up, close to the door, always in her field of vision. Sometimes the woman can get off the respirator for a while, but more often the conversation takes place by means of written notes. Earlier in the process, the chaplain discussed a number of images and metaphors with this woman. The exploration of the meaning of a mechanical singing bird (in a cage, on the bedside table, received from a friend) gives back a voice to the patient, as it were, and expresses her desire to be no longer caged. She has been breathing with a respirator for months and it is unclear if she will ever be able to get off of it. The wax coat adds to the imagery with regard to the ambivalence between remaining dependent on respiration and being able to walk around freely, the desire to be no longer caged, which is in sharp contrast to her current situation and anxiety.

(3) A case study pays explicit attention to meaning and interpretation. A case study is more about understanding (*Verstehen*) than about explanation (*Erklären*). The presupposition is that precisely in the dialogue between person and environment meaning arises. Meaning is not given in

advance, but arises in dialogue, in interaction. And precisely this meaning making in interaction and experience are central to a case study. At the same time, this means that the researcher does not occupy an objective, distant position, but is involved in the interaction, and therefore also in the process of interpretation and the construction of meaning. It is also necessary to obtain the necessary distance, so that the broader context and different perspectives remain visible. Multiple partiality is required.

> In yet another case study, the chaplain explains during the reflection in the research community that the case study also includes recognition of the client. It concerns a client with a bipolar disorder who is regularly admitted to the hospital, and who over and over again has to manage to give the disorder a place in her life, has to tell her story to other care providers, and has to rediscover her place in her family. The chaplain wants to pay tribute to the woman through the case study, "recognition for the fact that she lets herself be known" and trusts others, including her as a chaplain. The chaplain becomes involved in the interaction, senses in herself the great influence that it has on the client to tell her story over and over again, and in this way discovers the courage and perseverance of this client. The case study is therefore also a tribute to this client.

(4) A case study focuses on holistic understanding, i.e. it concerns the organic relationship of events, interactions, contexts, perspectives and influences, and does not focus on single causal relationships. Understanding reality is served by investigating and taking into account the multiple perspectives of those involved and stakeholders. The researcher observes, listens, asks questions, gauges and interprets, and is therefore himself the instrument to arrive at such a holistic understanding.

> The reflection of a case study shows that the interaction with the patient, admitted with metastases after a major oncological intervention a year before, is not unequivocal. She tells a lot, laughs a lot, and seems to want to stay away from the seriousness of the situation. She is appreciated by doctors and nurses as "a nice woman." The chaplain gauges, sometimes very directive, her feelings about her illness and situation. Sometimes she dwells upon it for a brief moment, but then she quickly switches to another subject. Focusing on a single behavior or expression does not take into account the changing ways in which the patient tries to cope with what is happening to her. The chaplain wants to consider the contact and the interaction in their connectedness. Typing

her attitude as resistance or denial does not do justice to the situation, in the belief of the chaplain, who has the very idea that in the back and forth between seriousness and humor awareness of the reality is indeed present. The contact feels like that with an old acquaintance, an approach that helps the chaplain to get a picture of the breadth of the patient's story. The research community characterized this way of working as "diluted seriousness."

(5) The purpose of a case study is to provide detailed information. It is not so much about representativeness as about what we can learn from a particular case. It is all about the learning potential. At the beginning of a case study, it is often not yet clear whether it will provide relevant information. In the mutual comparison, it becomes clear which cases do have this potential, lead to challenging and promising insights, and can clarify the complexity and dynamics of specific situations. Case studies provide local knowledge that is specific to time and context, and often leads to a so-called vicarious experience for those who are able to translate the described experiences into their own context. The latter is more successful if the study makes use of thick description (Geertz, 1973), and the case is presented in a narrative form. A story is accessible through the development of characters as the story progresses, the problems that present themselves, the dialogue and struggles that will arise in the course of time. A story clarifies the complexity and context, offers room for ambivalence and thus shows the general human character of a situation.

The patient is a 46-year-old man who is suddenly admitted after an intestinal examination. He has to undergo an urgent operation in which a stoma will be placed. He is completely unprepared for this and doubts whether he wants to undergo the operation. The chaplain was asked for a consultation but did not have the opportunity to speak with the man before the operation. With regard to the operation the doctor made it very clear that the man had no choice. Two days after the operation, the chaplain manages to talk to the patient. They reflect on what has happened. The chaplain introduces himself as a "spiritual caregiver," but during the conversation the man asks, *what* exactly he *is*. When the chaplain then names himself as "chaplain," the conversation takes a turn. A new conversation arises; the man asks for prayer. Surprisingly in this case, which was chosen more or less by chance with the intention to present "the first patient on Monday morning" as a case, is that the presentation as a spiritual caregiver does indeed give rise to an open discussion about the situation, and the impact that all this has on the patient, but that after becoming known as a "chaplain," a new, different type of openness arises, visible in facial expressions and the openness of speaking. The faith of the man is discussed, and he expresses the wish to pray with the chaplain. The reason for selecting this case is, as indicated, to take a "normal contact" as a starting point, but now it has also become a critical case for the chaplain (and the research community) that raises the question: how do you present yourself, and what influence does this presentation have on the accompaniment?

A few characteristics of the CSP

From the start of the project, a fixed format was chosen for the description and reflection of the case study (Gärtner et al., 2019; Walton & Körver, 2017). The format encourages the contributing chaplain to express the different layers, aspects and perspectives of a situation. As a result, participating chaplains find that they are doing much more than they initially thought they were doing. The complexity and far-reaching nature of cases are highlighted more sharply. A regular observation during the discussion is that chaplains do have a goal to which they attune their interventions, even though they often first say: "I did not have a clear goal when I started the accompaniment." What was done intuitively reflects a greater degree of professionalism than was initially assumed. Tacit knowledge (Polanyi, 1967) becomes conscious and can be better differentiated. The different features of the format form sensitizing concepts (Bowen, 2006) that guide the initial description and analysis. These sensitizing concepts include the Professional Standard's definition of what constitutes chaplaincy, which distinguishes four dimensions of a world view: existential, spiritual, ethical and aesthetic (VGVZ, 2015). The use of sensitizing concepts in the format and of the fixed structure for reflection increases the comparability of specific parts of the case studies. Although each case is unique and describes in great detail a situation of chaplaincy, comparisons can make clear which case represents a good practice paradigmatic for the profession and which criteria for and active elements of promising interventions can be identified (Van Yperen et al., 2017).

In the research communities, the chaplain who introduces his/her case study speaks of himself/herself in the third person: "this chaplain." This appears to contradict how Abma and Stake (2014) talk about the close involvement of the researcher. Nevertheless, we have chosen this option, especially since the case study is a description of the chaplain's own practice. The degree of involvement could be too great to perceive more perspectives in and the broader context of the case. The contributor must be both involved and able to obtain distance at the same time. It is an example of what in another context Scheff called aesthetic distance: not too close so that it is not a re-experience, not too far away to prevent it from becoming a list of facts (Scheff, 2001). Moreover, speaking in the third person accentuates the fact that the research community is not a supervision group, in which the emphasis would be on the personal learning process of the chaplain. The emphasis is on the description and analysis of the case from the perspective of the profession.

An important element in the working method is the member check (Lub, 2014; Madill & Sullivan, 2018). Those involved in the case study can read the report and, if necessary, comment on it. If possible, the report will be presented to the client and, if necessary, to the next of kin, but also to other care providers involved. This way of working, which is customary in qualitative research, regularly leads to nuances, additions and corrections to the original report. Sometimes clients react with great restraint and do not want to read the report. "Too confronting" is the most common motivation, although, until now, clients always give their consent for the use of the case study in the context of the research. The reactions of care providers can be very different: "I recognize it altogether," "Never before have I had such an insight into the work of chaplains, I will be more attentive to it in the future," or "There are no errors in the report from a medical point of view." Gradually it became clear that the format for the case study and the reflection on the report in the research community functions as a member check for participating chaplains. The check is given form in the focus on concrete behavior and on the question of working with goals or not, the attention for the results or effects and for the theoretical basis of the interventions. The member check can work as a mirror or be seen as a portrait, it can evoke ambivalent reactions or, on the contrary, be challenging. In any case, there is an exchange of knowledge that invites transformation and validation (Madill & Sullivan, 2018).

In conclusion

The project is complex in terms of design and infrastructure and required a long development time. As results become available step by step, it appears that we have found a very suitable way to lay the foundations for the wonderful and indispensable profession of chaplaincy in cooperation with the professionals themselves.

References

Abma, T. A. (2010). *Herinneringen en dromen van zeggenschap. Cliëntenparticipatie in de ouderenzorg.* Den Haag: Boom Lemma.

Abma, T. A., Nierse, C. J., & Widdershoven, G. A. M. (2009). Patients as Partners in Responsive Research. Methodological notions for collaborations in mixed research teams. *Qualitative Health Research, 19*(3), 401-415.

Abma, T. A., & Stake, R. E. (2014). Science of the Particular. An advocacy of naturalistic case study in health research. *Qualitative Health Research, 24*(8), 1150-1161.

Baird, J. (2018). Critical Response to Paediatric Case Studies. A paediatric nurse's perspective. In G. Fitchett & S. Nolan (Eds.), *Case studies in spiritual care* (pp. 78-84). London: Jessica Kingsley.

Bowen, G. A. (2006). Grounded Theory and Sensitizing Concepts. *International Journal of Qualitative Methods, 5*(3), 12-23.

Burns, K., & Novick, L. (Writers) (2017). *The Vietnam War* [movie]. Washington: Florentine Films - WETA.

Council for Health and Society (2017). *No evidence without context. About the illusion of evidence-based practice in healthcare.* Den Haag: RVS.

Flyvbjerg, B. (2006). Five Misunderstandings about Case-study Research. *Qualitative Inquiry, 12*(2), 219-245.

Gärtner, S., Körver, J., & Walton, M. (2019). Von Fall zu Fall. Kontext, Methode und Durchführung eines empirischen Forschungsprojekts mit Casestudies in der Seelsorge. *International Journal of Practical Theology, 23*(1), 98-114.

Geertz, C. (1973). Thick Description. Toward an interpretive theory of culture. In C. Geertz (Ed.), *The interpretation of cultures* (pp. 3-30). New York: Basic Books.

Greenhalgh, T., Annandale, E., Ashcroft, R., Barlow, J., Black, N., ... Ziebland, S. (2016). An open letter to the BMJ editors on qualitative research. *British Medical Journal, 352,* i563.

Grimes, R. L. (2000). *Deeply into the Bone. Re-inventing rites of passage.* Berkeley: University of California Press.

Habermas, J. (1987). *Lifeworld and System: a critique of functionalist reason. The theory of communicative action - vol. 2.* Cambridge: Polity Press.

Josselson, R., Lieblich, A., & McAdams, D. P. (2003). *Up Close and Personal. The teaching and learning of narrative research.* Washington: American Psychological Association.

Körver, J., & Walton, M. (2019). Geestelijke verzorging in beeld. Onder het vergrootglas van de case study. *Handelingen, 46*(2), 17-25.

Lub, V. (2014). *Kwalitatief evalueren in het sociale domein. Mogelijkheden en beperkingen.* Den Haag: Boom Lemma.

Madill, A., & Sullivan, P. (2018). Mirrors, Portraits, and Member Checking: Managing difficult moments of knowledge exchange in the social sciences. *Qualitative Psychology, 5*(3), 321-339.

Panter, J., Guell, C., & Ogilvie, D. (2016). Qualitative research can inform clinical practice. *British Medical Journal, 352,* i1482.

Polanyi, M. (1967). *The Tacit Dimension.* New York: Doubleday.

Reckwitz, A. (2002). Toward a Theory of Social Practices. A development in culturalist theorizing. *European Journal of Social Theory, 5*(2), 243-263.

Sackett, D. L., Rosenberg, W. M., Gray, J. A., Haynes, R. B., & Richardson, W. S. (1996). Evidence Based Medicine: what it is and what it isn't. *British Medical Journal, 312*(7023), 71-72.

Scheff, T. J. (2001). *Catharsis in Healing, Ritual, and Drama.* Lincoln: Authors Guild Backinprint.com Edition.

Thomas, G. (2011). *How to Do Your Case Study? A guide for students & researchers*. London: Sage.

Van Yperen, T. A., Veerman, J. W., & Bijl, B. (Eds.) (2017). *Zicht op effectiviteit. Handboek voor resultaatgerichte ontwikkeling van interventies in de jeugdsector* (2nd rev. ed.). Rotterdam: Lemniscaat.

VGVZ (2015). *Beroepsstandaard geestelijke verzorger*. Amsterdam: VGVZ.

Visse, M., Abma, T. A., & Widdershoven, G. A. (2012). Relational Responsibilities in Responsive Evaluation. *Evaluation and Program Planning, 35*(1), 97-104.

Walton, M., & Körver, J. (2017). Dutch Case Studies Project in Chaplaincy Care. A description and theoretical explanation of the format and procedures. *Health and Social Care Chaplaincy, 5*(2), 257-280.

Yin, R. K. (2014). *Case Study Research. Design and methods* (5th ed.). Los Angeles: Sage.

II.   From Methodology to Initial Findings

Chapter 7.

Chaplains' Case Study Research
Building Towards a Theory of Chaplaincy Care?

Steve Nolan

Introduction

When George Fitchett initiated a project aimed at encouraging healthcare chaplains to publish case studies of their work, he was very clear about the purpose (Fitchett, 2011). Fitchett saw case studies as foundational to healthcare chaplaincy research and argued that a body of robust case studies would provide the much-needed depth of understanding about spiritual care interventions that could enable more advanced stages of research (Fitchett, 2011, p. 4). Although research was the primary reason for Fitchett initiating the case studies project, he also acknowledged that case studies would add value in educating chaplains and the wider healthcare community about spiritual care (Fitchett, 2011, p. 6). I want to suggest another way in which chaplains' case studies have value, namely, in the area of building towards a theory of chaplaincy.

At present, chaplaincy care lacks a coherent theory regarding what it is and how it fits within contemporary healthcare practice. In this review of case studies published to date, I will argue, first, that chaplains' case study research is in continuity with the recent and sustained questioning of what it is that chaplains do. In this context, I will suggest that chaplains' case study research uniquely addresses this question from the perspective of practice-based research and can be used to build theory from the ground up. To date, the theoretical assumptions made about chaplaincy have been that it is essentially a religious practice. However, reviewing the cases, I will show that the case studies so far published are ambiguous about this. On the one hand, the cases can be read as confirming this widely held theory; but equally, they can be read as confounding that theory. Using a select but representative sample of cases, I will argue that the common and constant factor that is apparent across the cases is *relationship*, which elsewhere I have argued should be an important focus for chaplaincy and spiritual care research (Nolan, 2015). I will claim that the care reported in the cases parallels the care offered in psychotherapies, which similarly offer interventions in and through relationship (the therapeutic alliance). Noting the longstanding debate within psychotherapy about whether the efficacy of a treatment should be located in the specifics of a particular psychotherapeutic technique or in elements that are common across all the psychotherapies, I will show how chaplaincy care shares elements in common with the psychotherapies but has its own unique specificities. I will show how the case studies reveal the way chaplaincy care, like psychotherapy, works first of all in and through relationship, and in many cases uses the same relational techniques employed by psychotherapists (of which I will discuss five), yet also how it has its own unique features that distinguish it from any other form of psychotherapeutic intervention (again, I will discuss five). I will conclude by asking the question: if we were not already predisposed to think that (by and large) chaplaincy care is care delivered by religious professionals – and perceived, therefore, to be a religious intervention – what categories would we draw from in order to speak about chaplaincy care?

What do chaplains do?

For some years now, and in different forms, chaplaincy researchers have been considering the question of what it is that chaplains do.

In 2007, Mowat and Swinton completed a two-year qualitative study that explored the question with 44 Scottish chaplains (Mowat & Swinton, 2005, 2007). They identified that chaplains work to what they called an active "process model" of chaplaincy, a model that focuses on three core tasks. First, chaplains *seek out* people who require their services; next, they *identify* (or assess) the nature of the person's particular need; then, finally, they *respond* to that need through forms of spiritual practice, "some of which are informed by the chaplains' theological and spiritual tradition, but others that call for chaplains to expand on and move beyond this core knowledge base" (Mowat & Swinton, 2007, p. 33).

In 2008, George Handzo and a group of US researchers addressed much the same question when they analyzed data from 30,995 chaplain visits, collected at 13 healthcare institutions in the Greater New York City area during 1994-1996. These researchers identified 17 different types of chaplain intervention: eight general or not specifically religious activities (crisis intervention; emotional enabling; ethical consultation/deliberation; life review; patient advocacy; counseling; bereavement; and empathic listening); and nine activities they regarded as religious or spiritual in nature (hearing confession or amends; faith affirmation; theological development; performing a religious rite or ritual; providing a religious item; offering a blessing; praying; meditation; and other spiritual support) (Handzo, Flannelly, Kudler, Fogg, Harding, Hasan, Ross, & Taylor, 2008, pp. 43-44). Of all the interventions identified in this study, *prayer* was the most common, although the performance of religious rites or rituals was rare, and of those interventions that were not specifically religious, *emotional enabling* – inviting "the patient or family member to share feelings" (Handzo et al., 2008, p. 53) – and *life review* were the most frequently used. However, it is interesting to note, as Handzo and colleagues highlight, that many of the chaplains who took part in the study disagreed with the authors' classification of interventions. These chaplains felt that interventions the researchers classified as non-religious should actually have been classified as spiritual (Handzo et al., 2008, p. 50).

The question of what it is that chaplains do has most recently been explored in research by Massey and colleagues (Massey, Barnes, Villines, Goldstein, Lee, Pierson, Scherer, Vander Laan, and Summerfelt, 2015). Their study aimed at developing a standardized vocabulary or taxonomy that chaplains might use to communicate what they do more consistently and therefore more effectively to their healthcare colleagues. These researchers identified a 100-item list of chaplains' activities, which they sub-divided under three headings: intended effects, methods, and interventions. Of these 100 items, 33 could be said to be identifiable as broadly religious/spiritual care, with only 18 items requiring a religiously authorized figure. Fully two-thirds of the items could be said to be non-religious in nature, that is, deliverable by a person with no faith affiliation. Significantly, none of the items rated in the top ten by importance were specifically religious:

> Active listening (5); Demonstrate caring and concern (4.9); Provide a pastoral presence (4.8); Preserve dignity and respect (4.8); Collaborate with care team member (4.8); Build rapport and connectedness (4.8); Establish a relationship of care and support (4.8); Demonstrate acceptance (4.7); Provide emotional support (4.7); Provide support (4.7). (Massey et al., 2015)

My reason for highlighting these studies is to locate the chaplains' case studies project as research that is in continuity with a wider set of projects that are independently aiming to understand, explain and justify what it is that chaplains do. What is distinctive about chaplains' case studies, and what marks their peculiar and vital contribution, is that, while the other studies attempt to answer, at a high-level of generalization, the question of what it is that chaplains do, chaplains' case studies are addressing the question from the perspective of the bedside. These case studies seat us right alongside the chaplain, in a place where we can look over her shoulder and listen in to the intimacy of her conversations with the person in the bed. To put it otherwise, chaplains' case studies are providing practice-based evidence of what chaplains do when they do what they do.

Practice-based, case study research: building towards theory

It is important to recognize that practice-based evidence is not an alternative to research-based or evidence-based practice. Practice-based evidence supports and is complementary to research-based practice. But there is a sense among some researchers that practice-based evidence has less validity than evidence-based practice. So, the immediate challenge posed to chaplains' case studies is that the knowledge generated by case studies is of limited scientific value. Flyvbjerg (2006), a Danish social scientist, articulates the reasons for this challenge in the following way:

> (1) The knowledge generated by case studies is, and can only ever be, context dependent. As such, (2) it is not possible to generalize from case study knowledge and, while (3) case study knowledge may have value in the early stages of research, for example in generating hypotheses, scientific development depends on other research methods to test the hypotheses and to build theory. Consequently, case study knowledge cannot contribute to scientific development in the way that context-independent or theoretical knowledge can and does. In addition, case studies (4) tend to build in bias towards verifying the researcher's preconceptions and also, they (5) tend to be difficult to summarize.

Against this, Flyvbjerg argues, forcefully, that what are considered to be "reasons" to doubt the scientific value of case studies are in fact "misunderstandings" about case studies. As himself a case studies researcher and a frequently cited scholar in social science methodology, Flyvbjerg approaches these misunderstandings informed by the phenomenology of human learning and from the perspective that "research is simply a form of learning" (Flyvbjerg, 2006, p. 236). He highlights how research on human learning has pointed to the way expertise is built on the foundation of context-dependent knowledge, of the kind produced by case studies, and he underscores the fact that human learners develop from being rule-dependent beginners to functioning as independent experts (or, borrowing an expression from Pierre Bourdieu, as "virtuosos") because of their experience with thousands of individual cases.

To counter these misunderstandings, Flyvbjerg argues that, in the study of human affairs – the area with which chaplains' case studies are concerned – predictive theories and universals are just not available:

(1) Concrete, context-dependent knowledge is all we have. Nonetheless, (2) it is possible to generalize on the basis of a single case (Flyvbjerg cites the case example of Galileo's fabled experiment at the leaning tower of Pisa, by which he falsified Aristotle's view of gravity, which had dominated scientific understanding for nearly two thousand years). The point is that, as a source of scientific development, formal generalization is frequently overvalued at the expense of "the force of example," which is generally underestimated. So, while case studies are accepted as having value in generating and testing hypotheses, (3) they also provide research strategies when, for example, we wish to investigate *extreme* or *critical cases*, cases of *maximum variation* or *paradigmatic cases*.[13] With regard to bias, (4) case studies are actually more likely to be biased toward falsifying rather than verifying a researcher's preconceived notions, and while it is true that summarizing case studies can be difficult, (5) these difficulties are more often due to the properties of the reality studied than to the case study as a research method. Human life is difficult to summarize. (Paraphrased from Flyvbjerg, 2006)

Stiles extends this thinking about the concrete, context-dependent knowledge that case studies provide and argues that, as practice-based evidence, single cases can contribute to theory-building in what he calls "theory-building case study research" (Stiles, 2010, p. 91).

Theories are essentially ideas about the way that the world – or aspects of it – works. The kinds of theories we are concerned with are constructed from observation of, or reflection on, practitioner experience. As a construct, it is important to keep in mind that "a theory is not a fixed formula but a growing and changing way of understanding" (Stiles, 2010, p. 94); it is a "living document," open to change, development and refutation. When practitioners buy in to a particular theory, they are buying in to a set of assumptions and principles that supply the intellectual tools they need to inform their practice. No theory can supply full step-by-step instructions for every situation and practitioners must interpret and apply the theory to their own practice. In the process of applying theory, practitioners typically find that they have to modify or perhaps elaborate

13 *Extreme* or deviant cases are those that are considered especially problematic or especially good; *critical cases* are those that might permit logical deductions of the type, "if it is (not) valid for this case, then it applies to all (no) cases"; cases of *maximum variation* are cases that are different on a given dimension: size, form of organization, location, etc.; *paradigmatic cases* establish an exemplar for the domain that the case concerns (Flyvbjerg, 2006, p. 230).

or even critique the theory. It is this process of modification, elaboration and/or critique that Stiles terms "theory-building" (Stiles, 2010, p. 92).

As practice-based research, case studies capture data that can be used to interrogate theory. As such, case study research may aim at either *enriching* theory, by extending or illuminating understanding, in which case it seeks *transferability*; if the aim is to find *generality*, the research can aim at *theory-building* (Stiles, 2010, p. 94). Stiles goes on to argue that, while it is difficult to build theory based on a single case, a single case may be enough to modify, elaborate or critique a given theory. Multiple cases further strengthen such theory-building.

On its specific contribution to theory-building, Stiles contrasts case study research with hypothesis testing. Whereas the research strategy of statistical hypothesis testing is to test one statement against many observations, in case study research, the strategy is "to compare each of many theoretically-based statements with one or a few observations. It does this by describing the case in theoretical terms ... At issue is the correspondence of theory and observation" (Stiles, 2010, p. 93).

The point of this is to underline the fact that case study research has the potential to contribute to and shape a theory of chaplaincy. Heretofore, the theoretical assumptions made about chaplaincy have been that it is essentially a religious practice or the practice of religious professionals. Anecdotally at least, we know this is the assumption of many healthcare practitioners. It is certainly the assumption that underwrites the little that exists in the way of chaplaincy theory (Jacobs, 2012; Plummer, 2012; Caperon, Todd, & Walters 2018; Williams, 2018), which is largely constructed in terms of Christian theology.

Findings from the chaplains' case studies

In part, the chaplains' case studies confirm this widely held theory of chaplaincy as a religious practice. However, in part they also confound that theory. I want to explore that ambiguity.

To date (so far as we are aware), 28 cases have been published. Figure 1 breaks down the published cases by nationality, gender, faith and medical specialty.

Figure 1. Cases published to date

Cases published to date					
Case nationality	15 USA		7 UK		1 (each) Australia, Canada, Germany, Iceland, Israel, The Netherlands
Chaplain's gender	15 Female		12 Male		1 Mixed team
Recipient's gender	14 Female		13 Male		1 Transgender
Chaplain's faith	25 Christian		2 Jewish		1 Mixed team
Recipient's faith	18 Christian	5 Humanist/ no religious faith	2 Jewish	2 Culturally/ religiously mixed	1 Spiritual but not religious
Medical specialty	11 Hospice/ palliative care	5 Pediatrics	4 Psychiatry	2 (each) Oncology, psychosexual, rehabilitation	1 (each) Chronic care and geriatrics
Note: Categorization is not straightforward as some cases would fit multiple categories. At the time of writing, a further collection of 9 cases is in press (Wirpsa & Pugliese, forthcoming, 2020).					

These cases represent significant amounts of rich, compelling data. Perhaps most significantly, and in a way that other research has not previously shown, they provide data on the diversity of spiritual need that chaplains address. Among the cases, I would highlight:

- Two people – a gay man and a transsexual-woman – have spiritual needs that concern their emergent identity, as they try to express sexual identity in relation to identities constructed for them by their religion and culture;
- Two people have their spiritual needs addressed in rituals that perform and speak to their multiple identities: their indigenous cultural identities (Native American and Australian Aboriginal) layered with their Roman Catholic religious identity;
- One man's spiritual needs emerge in the conflict between his rationalism that had allowed him to live his adult life at ease with an atheist worldview and his underdeveloped emotional life that, as he lives toward his death, unexpectedly craves comfort in beliefs he knew in his childhood but rejected in his youth;

- A family, for whom the religion of their parents has little meaning or relevance, has unacknowledged spiritual needs, that include the existential transitions of welcoming new life while navigating the death of an elder (their father), addressed in the religious rituals and pastoral care of the Lutheran Church.

Sociologically, these and other cases speak to the emerging awareness that, within postmodernity, people frequently realize the potential they have to perform multiple identities. But these cases confirm what the more generalized research into what chaplains do is showing, namely that spiritual need is no longer cast in traditionally religious terms.

Where the data become more interesting, and arguably more useable, is where they illuminate the interventions that chaplains and spiritual carers provide. And what is immediately apparent is that, despite the specificity of these otherwise disparate cases, there is a common and constant factor that runs through them all, which is *relationship*. This observation touches upon a debate that has circulated within psychotherapy almost from its inception. In the 1930s Rosenzweig (1936) argued that, although there were significant differences between the emerging models of psychotherapy, the efficacy of any treatment was to be found in certain elements that were common across the therapies. Since then, psychotherapists have argued about where the therapeutic effect of their work should be located: is it in the factors that therapies have in common, which are fundamentally relational; or is it in the specific factors of a particular therapy's techniques?

This debate between *common* or relational factors and *specific* or technical factors remains unresolved. But the distinction, I suggest, offers a framework within which to think about the data emerging from the case studies. I suggest that chaplaincy care, as it is reported in the cases, consists of factors that are both common to and distinct from the psychotherapies, and here I will highlight five common factors and five specific factors of chaplaincy care. I will identify the common factors with reference to one particular case and use examples from several cases to discuss the specific factors. In brief, the common factors are: making assessments, building rapport, using active listening, intentionally using self and challenging, and demonstrating core therapeutic attitudes. The specific factors I identify are: affirming the divine or supporting transcendence, working with belief or life philosophy, creating and conducting ritual (religious or otherwise), being-with (presence), and supporting the institution. It is important to keep in mind *both* that the examples are paradigmatic and equally evident in many of the cases, *and* that the categories are heuristic and overlapping rather than definitive.

Common factors in chaplaincy care: Angela

Angela was an average 17-year-old when Katherine Piderman (2015) met her. Angela had few friends and her home setting was troubled: in fact, she had argued with her mother on the morning of her car accident. When the emergency personnel arrived, they found Angela's car turned over and down an embankment. She was conscious but unable to move. Scans later determined that her spinal cord had been severed at a high cervical level and she was paralyzed from the neck down.

1. Chaplains make assessments

Chaplain Piderman's role in the Rehabilitation Unit includes conducting spiritual assessments and facilitating or providing spiritual care. She frames her assessment approach with the FICA Spiritual Assessment Tool (Puchalski & Romer, 2000). She also uses a self-devised tool, called the 4C Spiritual Assessment Tool, which looks at how the person feels *centered* or anchored, *called* or motivated, *connected* to relationships beyond themselves and *contributes* to the good of others. Using these tools, Piderman assesses that Angela is anguished on several levels:
- Physically, she is facing challenges that go with paralysis;
- Emotionally, she is enraged at her helplessness and feels profound despair as she looks to the future;
- Spiritually, she feels devastated by God's silence and apparent absence, compounded by her sense that God is responsible.

Piderman's assessment is ongoing and, as their relationship develops, she regularly reassesses Angela's state of being.

2. Chaplains build rapport

Piderman goes on to report that her initial goals are to build rapport, to get to know Angela and to understand the role that spirituality and religion play in her life. She reports that Angela is in membership at a small evangelical Protestant church; that she considers herself a Christian despite no longer actively attending church; and that, since her accident, she is trying to get closer to God. Piderman tells us that, although Angela feels unconnected to her church pastor, she enjoys talking with the chaplain about how God is working in her life and that she has requested daily visits.

3. Chaplains use active listening

During their first meeting, Angela tells Piderman that her mother believes "God never gives you more than you can take" and "If you pray hard enough, God will give you a miracle." Piderman tells us she is congruent to her own negative reaction to this belief but decides not to challenge it since, at that point, it is fueling Angela's optimism. However, she holds Angela's words in her mind.

As Angela comes to realize that the prayed-for miracle is not happening, her mood becomes extremely low. On one visit, Piderman finds Angela angry and feeling trapped, unable even to wipe her own tears. When Angela brings up her belief that God is responsible for her accident and injuries, Piderman wants to offer an alternative perspective. However, she recognizes it will be unhelpful to try to impose her belief that God does not orchestrate every event in our lives but is with us to guide us through them. She wants to be present with Angela and remain faithful in her darkness and senses that Angela is using their conversations to look at huge questions that are haunting her as she struggles to make sense of what she believes.

4. Chaplains make intentional use of self and challenge
When Angela askes where in the Bible it says, "God doesn't give you more than you can handle?" Piderman sees this as the opportunity gently to challenge Angela's theology. She records that she reaches inside to center herself in her belief that God is with us always and especially in our deepest darkness, then points Angela to 1 Corinthians 10:13:

> None of the trials which have come upon you is more than a human being can stand. You can trust that God will not let you be put to the test beyond your strength, but with any trial will also provide a way out by enabling you to put up with it. (NJB)

As a result of this conversation, Angela begins to see that perhaps God will give her a way out or help her deal with her situation and she begins to pray for patience and strength.

5. Chaplains demonstrate core therapeutic attitudes: particularly unconditional positive regard and empathy
Through these visits and conversations, Piderman describes (almost incidentally) how she offers Angela unconditional positive regard. For example,
- When she finds Angela in the darkest of moods, she expresses no judgement but simply accepts that is where Angela is on that day;
- And when Angela optimistically shares her belief about prayer and miracles, Piderman recognizes but withholds her negative reaction to it.

Piderman's skill in imaginatively entering Angela's inner world and describing it so that Angela feels herself understood, demonstrates her real ability to communicate empathetic understanding of Angela's experience. For example,

- When she tells Angela, "It's so dark for you, Angela. You thought you could count on God to get you through and even change things, but now it seems as if that isn't going to happen and worse, that God is the cause," Angela's reply is emphatic, "That's it exactly";
- And when Piderman says, "I don't know if this is true for you, but sometimes we ask questions when we're too mad to really seek an answer," Angela responds, "Yeah, you're right. I don't really care what the answer is. I still hate it. I guess I just want to be mad."

What is evident from these five factors is that a good deal of what chaplains do is common to the work of the psychotherapies. As with the psychotherapies, so too with chaplains: both make assessments, build rapport, use active listening, make intentional use of self and demonstrate core therapeutic attitudes: particularly unconditional positive regard and empathy.

Specific factors in chaplaincy care: paradigmatic examples
This takes us to the question of what is distinctive about chaplaincy care.

1. Affirming the divine or supporting transcendence
For chaplains, religion is the most obvious specific factor. Amy Goodman and Joel Baron (2018) take us into an intimate space in which Mrs. Pearlman, an 82-year-old woman with advanced Alzheimer's disease, is supported to keep the Jewish High Holy Days. In this case, the chaplain acts as the *shaliach tzibbur* or prayer leader to Mrs. Pearlman, skillfully tailoring the liturgy to her capacity to engage and tenderly singing familiar prayers and hymns to her.

Yet this chaplain's action is about more than leading prayer; it is about mediating a series of connections: the chaplain connects Mrs. Pearlman with her culture and history; he also connects her with her community; and significantly, the chaplain helps Mrs. Pearlman to connect with the Divine. Goodman and Baron highlight their perspective that an important outcome for Mrs. Pearlman is the affirmation of the presence of the Divine and also that she is encouraged in her value as a person.

In this case, we see a journeying towards transcendence that moves in two different but related and mutually reinforcing directions. Mrs. Pearlman is enabled to experience connection with the Transcendent and, in so doing, she is helped to transcend the mundanity of her condition and experience connection with herself. Both experiences, I would argue, are profoundly spiritual.

2. Working with belief or life philosophy

In presenting her case, Rosie Ratcliffe (2015) very skillfully demonstrates how a chaplain can work with a person's belief or life philosophy. Yesuto is an African man tormented by his belief in witchcraft. He believes his young son to be in danger of being cursed by an African witch and that the boy will die prematurely. Yesuto's anxieties have led to psychiatric hospitalization and his beliefs are a source of tension between him and his medical team.

Ratcliffe reports that the team members are dismissive of Yesuto's fears and beliefs. They tell him that he is ill and that, if only he will take his medication, his fears about witchcraft will disappear. Ratcliffe admits that she knows little to nothing about witches. Crucially, however, because she does understand how belief operates to construct reality – of whatever kind – and how it enables us to live in those constructions *as if* they are really real, Ratcliffe is able to accept that, for Yesuto, his beliefs articulate the reality he is living. Knowing this, Ratcliffe empathically enters into his world in order to work with his beliefs and gently but effectively challenge his thinking from the inside.

3. Creating and conducting ritual (which may or may not be religious)

We see this same kind of empathic working with beliefs in the case presented by Guus Van Loenen and his colleagues (Van Loenen, Körver, Walton, & De Vries, 2017), this time being acted out in ritual that effects an inner, spiritual healing. Over a period of a few weeks, Van Loenen works with Hans, a former military marksman, who on a tour with the United Nations killed 37 people. Now a civilian, these people are stalking Hans down the dark corridors of his dreams.

Van Loenen records how, collaborating with a psychiatrist, he is able sensitively to establish a relationship with Hans and then help him to reframe his experience, first by showing him a way to understand what he has done in a way that could be redemptive, and then by crafting a ritual that symbolizes Hans' need for redemption and allows him to act out receiving that redemption. In this case, ritual seems to operate as a form of spiritual psychodrama.

4. Being-with (presence)

I suggested above that we should understand the chaplain's offer of presence as a common factor. But there is a sense in which presence can also be regarded as a factor specific to chaplaincy. This is because so many chaplains see their work in terms of offering a "ministry of presence." Nina Redl's (2015) presentation of her work with "David," a Jewish man in his 60s, exemplifies the power of being-*with* (Nolan, 2012).

Brought up an Orthodox Jew in the old city of Jerusalem, David's mother was killed in a street bombing when he was 16. This precipitated his father's suicide, leaving David prematurely the head of his family. Dutifully, he assumed responsibility for keeping his younger siblings fed and housed but when eventually they left home, David found he was unable to move on and realize his ambitions. When Redl met him, David had been diagnosed with stage IV pancreatic cancer and had opted for palliative and end of life care. Fiercely independent, Redl's attempts to support David are met with distrust and total rejection of anything religious – which includes the person of Redl herself. Undeterred, through the cumulative effect of many small acts of loving kindness, she makes herself available to David, if he wants to accept her unconditional offer. Eventually, Redl overcomes David's suspicion, winning his confidence and ultimately his friendship. In this way, she facilitates an otherwise lonely and isolated man to receive love and to die surrounded by people he finally allowed to care for him.

5. Supporting the institution

Chaplains support their institutions in a variety of ways: formally, by providing expert advice or by their membership of ethics or policy committees; informally, through supportive relationships with staff at all levels. In the UK, longevity is a feature of many chaplains' service and as such they act as carriers of institutional memory.

Patricia Roberts (2018) reports on work that supported her institution by caring not only for Daisy, a former colleague, but for an extended network of staff, who had been Daisy's colleagues and friends. A long-serving and well-liked member of the nursing staff, Daisy was in her mid-60s. Her diagnosis of aggressive cancer shocked her colleagues and, newly in post, Roberts finds herself needing to support not only Daisy but many of those who knew her and cared about her. Roberts' case deals with helping Daisy plan a bespoke funeral. Following the funeral, Roberts acknowledges the need Daisy's colleagues have to grieve and decides she must go against Daisy's expressed wish not to have a memorial service. In this way, Roberts responds to the bereavement needs of the nursing staff.

Conclusion: The case for a new theory of chaplaincy care?

As I read the data emerging from these case studies, and especially when set in the context of the research that is addressing the question of what it is that chaplains do, it seems to me that these ten factors articulate a model of chaplaincy that at least questions, if not challenges the current theory of chaplaincy as a religious practice and suggests chaplaincy needs to be theoretically relocated.[14]

For me at least, the common and specific factors pose an interesting question, which is this: if we were not already predisposed to think that (by and large) chaplaincy care is care delivered by religious professionals – and perceived, therefore, to be a religious intervention – what categories would we draw from in order to speak about chaplaincy care? Might we, I wonder, be inclined to describe chaplains' work as some class of psychological therapy, a *psychospiritual therapy*? It certainly appears to me that much of what is essential chaplaincy care makes direct and effective use of factors that are common to the psychotherapies – assessing a person's psychospiritual state, building rapport, listening actively, intentionally using the self and demonstrating core therapeutic conditions. And what specifies chaplaincy – affirming transcendence, working with life philosophy, creating ritual, being-*with* and supporting the institution – is broadly spiritual rather than narrowly religious. On this point, it is particularly instructive to note how small a percentage of the chaplaincy care reported in the cases is explicitly religious – despite the fact that the majority of the data from the case studies comes from care given by religiously affiliated professionals to religiously affiliated recipients. This fact indicates how great the need is to have cases written by religiously unaffiliated chaplains and about chaplaincy care that is non-religious.

Despite the fact that a number of the cases have a religious theme, I would argue that in many of these, religion is actually a sub-theme and not the main focus of the work.[15] With this in mind, I would argue that *chaplaincy care has the form of psychological therapy*, which is not the same thing as saying that chaplaincy care *is psychotherapy*, but it might be a way of saying that chaplaincy could be theorized as a specialized and dynamic form of pastoral therapy.

14 I lack the space here to explicate this claim, except to say that it is based on an understanding of spirituality and spiritual need/asset in humanistic-phenomenological terms. For such a definition, see Elkins et al. (1988). For further elaboration of my own thinking, see Nolan (2011, 2017).
15 A particularly clear example of this is the case reported by Alice Hildebrand (2015). On the face of it, Hildebrand's case may appear to be about religion, but religion serves to provide common ground on which she and Erica meet.

Nor is claiming *chaplaincy care has the form of psychotherapy* the same thing as saying that chaplains should position themselves as psychotherapists. This is the proposition advanced by Raymond Lawrence, of the College of Pastoral Supervision and Psychotherapy. Lawrence claims, in my view with some degree of self-contradiction, that chaplains or "pastoral clinicians" should be psychoanalytically trained to attend to patients' "transferential data," by which he means the "evidence of unconscious as well as conscious material at play, in the patient, in the chaplain him/herself, and between the two of them" (Lawrence, 2018). He proposes that "competent pastoral counseling and psychotherapy" demands an "agnostic posture" and argues that if a "clinical chaplain" should offer prayer s/he will blur the boundary between pastoral and religious care, which for Lawrence cannot be combined in the work of one person. I do not believe he is right, and I do not believe the evidence supports his view. For specific examples, I would point to the work I have already cited by Katherine Piderman (2015), Karen Murphy (2017) and Guus Van Loenen (2017), among others.

Putting it positively, to claim that *chaplaincy care has the form of psychotherapy* is to claim that chaplaincy care is a highly specialist form of psychological or (better) psychospiritual therapy that can be understood in terms of what it has in common with the psychological therapies but that also makes its own specific and distinctive contribution to psychospiritual wellbeing.

The practice-based evidence emerging from the chaplains' case studies published to date is resonant with the findings of other recent research into what chaplains do (Mowat & Swinton, 2005, 2007; Handzo et al., 2008; Massey et al., 2015). Cumulatively, the evidence is beginning to challenge the widely assumed understanding that chaplaincy is (and perhaps should be) a religious practice and is offering interesting data in support of the case that chaplaincy and spiritual care needs to be re-theorized. The publication of more cases, written by both religiously affiliated and unaffiliated chaplains that report on care that is both religiously and non-religiously oriented, will further enrich our understanding of what it is that chaplains do and provide the additional data needed for theory-building.

References

Caperon, J., Todd, A., & Walters, J. (2018). *A Christian Theology of Chaplaincy*. London: Jessica Kingsley Publishers.

Elkins, D. N., Hedstrom, L. J., Hughes, L. L., Leaf, J. A., & Saunders, C. (1988). Toward a humanistic-phenomenological spirituality: Definition, description and measurement. *Journal of Humanistic Psychology, 28*(4), 5-18.

Fitchett, G. (2011). Making our case(s). *Journal of Health Care Chaplaincy, 17*(1), 3-18.

Flyvbjerg, B. (2006). Five misunderstandings about case-study research. *Qualitative Inquiry, 12*(2), 219-245.

Goodman, A., & Baron, J. (2018). "For myself and for Your people with whom I pray" – Mrs. Pearlman, an 82-year-old woman with a terminal diagnosis of advanced Alzheimer's disease. In G. Fitchett and S. Nolan (Eds.), *Case Studies in Spiritual Care: Healthcare Chaplaincy Assessments, Interventions and Outcomes* (pp. 187-204). London: Jessica Kingsley Publishers.

Handzo, G. F., Flannelly, K. J., Kudler, T., Fogg, S. L., Harding, S. R., ... Taylor, B. E., (2008). What do chaplains really do? II. Interventions in the New York Chaplaincy Study. *Journal of Health Care Chaplaincy, 14*(1), 39-56.

Hildebrand, A. A. (2015). "I can tell *you* this, but not everyone understands" – Erica, mother of a 2-year-old girl with cancer. In G. Fitchett and S. Nolan (Eds.), *Spiritual Care in Practice: Case Studies in Healthcare Chaplaincy* (pp. 51-68). London: Jessica Kingsley Publishers.

Jacobs, M. (2012). Creating a personal theology to do spiritual/pastoral care. In S. B. Roberts (Ed.), *Professional Spiritual and Pastoral Care: A Practical Clergy and Chaplain's Handbook* (pp. 3-11). Woodstock, VT: SkyLight Paths.

Lawrence, R. J. (2018, February 21). A new construct. *Pastoral Report*, College of Pastoral Supervision and Psychotherapy. Retrieved September 9, 2019, from http://www.cpsp.org/pastoralreportarticles

Massey, K., Barnes, M. J. D., Villines, D., Goldstein, J. D., Lee, A., ... Summerfelt, W.T. (2015). What do I do? Developing a taxonomy of chaplaincy activities and interventions for spiritual care in intensive care unit palliative care. In G. Fitchett, K. B. White & K. Lyndes (Eds.) (2018). *Evidence-Based Healthcare Chaplaincy: A Research Reader* (Reprint; pp. 66-81). London: Jessica Kingsley Publishers.

Mowat, H., & Swinton, J. (2005). *What do chaplains do? A report on a two year investigation into the nature of chaplaincy in the NHS in Scotland*. Edinburgh: Scottish Executive.

Mowat, H., & Swinton, J. (2007). *What do chaplains do? The role of the chaplain in meeting the spiritual needs of patients* (2nd ed.). Aberdeen: Mowat Research Limited.

Murphy, K. (2017). "I'm Being Swallowed Up by this Illness, So Much Pain Deep Inside": Claire a 40 Year old Woman with Cancer. *Health and Social Care Chaplaincy, 5*(2), 210-223.

Nolan, S. (2011). Psychospiritual care: New content for old concepts – Towards a new paradigm for non-religious spiritual care. *Journal for the Study of Spirituality, 1*(1), 50-64.

Nolan, S. (2012). *Spiritual Care at the End of Life: The Chaplain as a "Hopeful Presence."* London: Jessica Kingsley Publishers.

Nolan, S. (2015). Healthcare chaplains responding to change: Embracing outcomes or reaffirming relationships? *Health and Social Care Chaplaincy, 3*(2), 93-109.

Nolan, S. (2017). Searching for identity in uncertain professional territory: Psychospirituality as discourse for non-religious spiritual care. In G. Harrison (Ed.), *Psycho-spiritual Care in Health Care Practices* (pp. 175-187). London, UK: Jessica Kingsley Publishers.

Piderman, K. M. (2015). "Why did God do this to me?" – Angela, a 17 year old girl with spinal injury. In G. Fitchett & S. Nolan (Eds.), *Spiritual Care in Practice: Case Studies in Healthcare Chaplaincy* (pp. 69-89). London: Jessica Kingsley Publishers.

Plummer, D. B. (2012). Creating a personal theology to do spiritual/pastoral care. In S. Roberts (Ed.), *Professional Spiritual and Pastoral Care: A Practical Clergy and Chaplain's Handbook* (pp. 12-18). Woodstock, VT: SkyLight Paths.

Puchalski, C. M., & Romer, A. L. (2000). Taking a spiritual history allows clinicians to understand patients more fully. *Journal of the American Medical Association, 3*, 129-137.

Ratcliffe, R. (2015). "I am frightened to close my eyes at night in case the witch comes to me in my sleep." Yesuto, an African man in his early thirties troubled by his belief in witchcraft. In G. Fitchett & S. Nolan (Eds.), *Spiritual Care in Practice: Case Studies in Healthcare Chaplaincy* (pp. 113-132). London: Jessica Kingsley Publishers.

Redl, N. (2015). "What can you do for me?" – David, a mid-60s Jewish man with stage IV pancreatic cancer. In G. Fitchett & S. Nolan (Eds.), *Spiritual Care in Practice: Case Studies in Healthcare Chaplaincy* (pp. 223-241). London: Jessica Kingsley Publishers.

Roberts. P. (2018). "I do want to get this funeral planned" – Daisy, a former colleague in hospice care. G. Fitchett & S. Nolan (Eds.), *Case Studies in Spiritual Care: Healthcare Chaplaincy Assessments, Interventions and Outcomes* (pp. 170-186). London: Jessica Kingsley Publishers.

Rosenzweig, S. (1936). Some implicit common factors in diverse methods of psychotherapy. *American Journal of Orthopsychiatry, 6*(3), 412-415.

Stiles, W. B. (2010). Theory-building case studies as practice-based evidence. In M. Barkham, G. E. Hardy & J. Mellor-Clark (Eds.), *Developing and Delivering Practice-Based Evidence: A Guide for the Psychological Therapies* (pp. 91-108). Chichester: John Wiley & Sons Ltd.

Van Loenen, G., Körver, J., Walton, M., & De Vries, R. (2017). Case study of "moral injury": Format Dutch Case Studies Project. *Health and Social Care Chaplaincy, 5*(2), 281-296.

Williams, R. (2018). *A Theology for Chaplaincy: Singing Songs in a Strange Land*. Cambridge: Grove Books.

Wirpsa, J., & Pugliese, K. (2020, forthcoming). *Chaplains as Partners in Medical Decision-Making: Case Studies in Healthcare Chaplaincy*. London: Jessica Kingsley Publishers.

Chapter 8.

Comparing Multiple Case Studies of (Military) Chaplaincy Care

Methodological issues

Theo Pleizier, Carmen Schuhmann

Introduction: Case data, case analysis, and case comparison

The Dutch Case Studies Project (CSP) aims to answer the question of what chaplains do, for what reasons and to what ends (Walton & Körver, 2017). The answer to this research question is sought in a series of single case studies of chaplaincy care. In this project we coordinate a research community of military chaplains in which case studies of chaplaincy care within the Dutch Armed Forces are collected. Speaking about "collecting" cases, however, is methodologically not precise enough. The cases have a rather high level of construction (Mason, 2018). They are constructed or generated in two phases. In the first phase, one chaplain describes and interprets one case of pastoral care from her or his own chaplaincy practice according to a detailed list of observational, interpretative, reflective and evaluative questions. This phase one case description is then presented to the research community of fellow chaplains and (a) researcher(s). In the second phase, the case is further interpreted and evaluated in the research community.

This procedure is unique and does not fit into the existing models of case study research described by authors like Yin (2014) or Thomas (2016). For instance, there is no obvious answer to the question of what counts as the data that are to be analyzed. Nor is there a clear distinction between data and analysis. Do the data consist of the "raw" data – the recordings or verbatim reports of conversations – or do the data consist of the phase one description by the chaplain? It is also possible to understand the data as the entire generated case, the "raw" material, the case description by the chaplain and the reflections of the research community generated in phase two. Hence, the understanding of "data" remains rather vague in the format that is used in the CSP. The format suggests that the phase one case descriptions by the chaplain are the data which are then analyzed in the research community. In that case the entire case report – description (phase one) plus analysis (phase two) – is an unusual "hybrid case report" consisting of data followed by analysis. Literature on case study research points to a distinction between cases as "data" or as "outcome" (Thomas & Myers, 2015; Ridder, 2017). For the CSP the question remains whether the entire case study (phase one and two) counts as data or as outcome of research?

In the project, the eventual case studies are in the first place seen as provisional outcomes of research. The methodological picture becomes even more complex when the question of case comparison comes in. Walton and Körver (2017) write that "the approved text (of the case study) then can be kept for later comparison or offered for publication" (p. 268). They mention the need for comparing multiple case studies and argue for a "cumulative effect" of building up evidence by adding single cases that in themselves may be rather idiosyncratic (Walton & Körver, 2017, p. 269). This suggests that the final case reports as a whole can also be considered as data that are in need of further analysis. Hence, the idea of "data" in the CSP is multilayered. First, we have the "data" generated by the chaplain, the phase one case description. Second, there are the phase two "data" generated in the discussions in the research community in search for interpretative perspectives of the case. Thirdly, there are "data" on the level of the entire case: each complete case study becomes data in a comparative analysis with other case studies. This raises the question of what properly counts as data in relation to the CSP's central research question. In this article we propose an approach of multiple case analysis in which single case descriptions are seen as pieces of data that require further analysis instead of as outcomes.

In the military chaplaincy research community that we are both involved in as researchers, the issue of case comparison emerged while discussing single cases. This research community consists of six military chaplains, working in multiple contexts of the Dutch Armed Forces: the army, the navy, the air force, the military police, and the institution for veteran care. In our meetings we started, unplanned, to compare new cases with cases we had discussed earlier. We also questioned the selection of cases: do they adequately capture the variety of practices within the field of military chaplaincy? Against the background of our conversations in the military chaplaincy research community, this article positions the analysis of cases within the wider field of case study research and addresses issues that are involved in setting out a route for analysis across cases.

Chaplaincy in the Dutch Armed Forces

In the Netherlands, military chaplaincy has a dual structure of legitimacy. On the one hand, the Ministry of Defense appoints chaplains within the Dutch military, where they "contribute to the (existential) wellbeing of

soldiers, civilian personnel, veterans and the home front, and to the mo-
rality of the Armed Forces as a whole."[16] Military chaplains always work
within a particular military unit like the navy or the air force. Depending
upon the scope of the unit, the chaplain works within small multi-deno-
minational chaplaincy teams. On the other hand, the sending agencies (for
instance the churches or the Dutch Humanist Association) are responsible for the personal, professional and spiritual competencies that are
required in chaplaincy. Given this structure, chaplains do not exclusively
work within their own denomination but serve the military of an entire
base, platoon, or unit in a mission abroad. Military chaplains must therefore be able to work across denominations. The chaplains in the military
chaplaincy research community represent three different religious/world-
view backgrounds: Protestantism, Roman Catholicism and humanism.

In collecting cases of military chaplaincy, we therefore need to be
aware of the following aspects. First, the cases presented by the chaplains
usually involve situations where the worldview background of the soldier
does not match that of the chaplain. Only in a few cases do the soldier
and the chaplain share a similar religion or worldview. Second, cases usually concern a particular military unit, for instance the navy or veteran
care. Third, some cases concern so called "base care": chaplains interact
with the military personnel at the base that they are assigned to. Other
situations concern deployment care: the chaplain serves a unit that is part
of a (peacekeeping) mission. For the Case Studies Project, this entails the
methodological question of what kind of chaplaincy care is studied. It is
reasonable to state that, in the military chaplaincy research community,
individual cases are cases of *military chaplaincy care*, but we have to bear in
mind the diversity of the military context, according to denomination, to
military unit, and to care situation (base care or care during deployment).

Methodological challenges of single case analysis

According to Thomas (2016), a case study offers "a rich picture with many
kinds of insights coming from different angles, from different kinds of
information" (p. 21). The format that is used in the CSP collects descriptions, verbatim reports of conversations, and interpretations by the chaplain (phase one) and interpretations of this particular, unique instance
of chaplaincy care by the research community (phase two). The description by the chaplain counts as one source of information and the analytical perspective of the research community, including its consensus and

---

16   Translated from https://www.defensie.nl/onderwerpen/personeelszorg/geestelijke-
     verzorging (retrieved February 3, 2020).

discussions, as additional sources. In the research format, there is also room for feedback on the case by the client or by other professionals. Still, the perspective of (the) chaplain(s) is dominant. The eventual case studies are, in the first place, narratives of care provided by chaplains. The data collected in single cases in the CSP do not seem to meet the criteria for offering a "rich picture" according to the methodologies of scholars who call for using multiple sources, such as documents, interviews, field notes, etc. (Yin, 2014; Thomas, 2016).

Even when we understand a case as "one unique story," its uniqueness only makes sense in relation to broader analytical categories. Hence, we have to ask: what is this a case *of*? In the case of single narratives on military chaplaincy, the question "what is this a case of" can be answered on two levels of abstraction. First, the single cases that are collected in the Case Studies Project can be understood as single incidents of interactions between a chaplain and a soldier. Each single case tells a part of the story of the larger case of "military chaplaincy in the Dutch army at the beginning of the 21st century." The larger case is defined by time (beginning of the 21st century) and place (in the Dutch Army). Time and place function as boundaries of the case "military chaplaincy." Multiple cases actually count as multiple pieces of information of the single case "military chaplaincy in the Dutch Army." Next, on a more abstract level we can take military chaplaincy itself as "an instance of a class of phenomena ... which the case illuminates and explicates" (Thomas & Myers, 2015, pp. 7, 56–58). Comparing military chaplaincy with chaplaincy in other domains, larger cases are compared to the largest case, namely "chaplaincy" (the object, that of which it is a case *of*).

The denominational, contextual, and situational differences sketched above, emphasize the importance of comparing different cases when answering the research question - what do chaplains do, for what reasons and to what ends? In the discussions of our research community, chaplains regularly commented in relation to a particular case that certain aspects of the case were characteristic for chaplaincy care in the context of the Dutch Army or even in the context of a specific unit within the army. These comments are partly captured in the research format under the heading of the case selection: does it concern a "representative" case, a "paradigmatic" case, an "outsider" case, or a "critical" case? Still, the question remains how a single case contributes to answering the broader research question. By comparing multiple cases we obtain theoretical ideas for analytic patterns across cases.[17] A single case then functions as incident for a pattern that transcends the single incident.

Examples of analytic patterns across cases

In order to demonstrate what the outcome could be of an approach of cross-case comparison, we present three patterns that started to emerge when discussing single cases in the military chaplaincy research community. These patterns are tentative as they have been generated by comparing the first four cases of military chaplaincy, but, given this limitation, they illustrate sufficiently the need for (reflection on) multiple case analysis: comparing more cases will provide a more nuanced and theoretically richer picture. In the project we aim to collect around 15 cases in total.

Positioning within Ministry of Defense

The first pattern concerns the behavior of the chaplain in relation to the larger institution of the Ministry of Defense (MoD). In one of the cases, an officer visits the chaplain for advice concerning a letter he got, indicating that he could no longer serve within the army because of financial cuts within the organization. In the conversation with the soldier, the chaplain did not side with the soldier against the MoD. In another case, a chaplain pays a home visit to a soldier who, due to physical, psychological, and social problems, is allowed time off from work during the last two years before his official retirement. In the conversation with the soldier the chaplain empathizes fully with the soldier and takes a critical stance towards the MoD. In a third case, the chaplain provides a completely different view of the mental health of a soldier than the military psychologist. The chaplain is open for a religious interpretation of experiences of the soldier, while the military psychologist interprets these experiences as pathological. In each of these three cases we see how the soldier is an actor in a large organizational system. While supporting the soldier, the chaplain constantly has to choose his or her position in the system.

Distinguishing between soldier and human being

In the case of the soldier who received the letter from the MoD resulting in his resignation, the chaplain challenges the soldier's self-understanding. He feels how the soldier identifies himself with the work in the military. In his response, the chaplain challenges the soldier to move beyond this self-understanding to envision a future outside the military. In another

---

17   This raises the question of how to take into account the type of case (representative, paradigmatic, outsider, or critical) when comparing single cases.

case, the chaplain talks about the price that the soldier and his family have to pay for his work in the air force. The chaplain is able to connect the difficulties that the soldier experiences at work with his larger biographical story. In doing so, the chaplain invites the soldier to look beyond his military functioning and to relate to himself as a human being. This pattern re-occurs in other cases. Military chaplains refuse to see the soldier only from the military perspective. They help the soldier to look at himself as a human being instead.

"Being known" as a chaplain

In several cases, soldiers emphasize the importance of having met and spoken with the chaplain before. In one case, a soldier contacts a chaplain who is not associated with his unit but whom he has met during a mission. The trustworthiness of the chaplain seems to reside in "knowing" this individual chaplain and having established a connection with her or him. There is, however, also a case where the soldier contacts a chaplain that he had never spoken before, in order to discuss religious struggles. In this case, the soldier does not know the individual chaplain from earlier meetings but recognizes the chaplain as a representative of religion. "Being known" as chaplain – either as an individual chaplain or as a representative – seems to be an important precondition for providing chaplaincy care in the military. Further cases are needed in order to gain more insight into the role of different kinds of "knowing the chaplain" in chaplaincy care.

Comparing cases: Sampling issues

The eventual aim of the CSP is "to make the case for what chaplains do, for what reasons and to which ends" (Walton & Körver, 2017, p. 271). The focus in the project is on the single case: the idea is to gather multiple single cases from multiple contexts (military chaplaincy, prison chaplaincy, elderly care, hospital chaplaincy, etcetera) in order to provide practice-based evidence for chaplaincy care. According to Yin (2014), cross-case synthesis is helpful for "making a case": "The analysis is likely to be easier and the findings likely to be more robust than having only a single case" (p. 164). Even when we question the notion that multiple case analysis provides more "robust" findings than single case analysis, in view of the aim of the project – using single case studies for building an argument that transcends specific situations, contexts and denominations – the cases need to be analyzed in relation to each other. With a view to cross-case analysis, questions concerning sampling explicitly come to the fore. "How one compares and contrasts cases will depend on the purpose of the study and how cases were sampled" (Patton, 2002, p. 452). At the start of the project, one sampling criterion was formulated: the chaplain who describes the case must understand the case as an example of "good chaplaincy practice."

Sampling strategies will inevitably influence what aspects or sub-questions of the CSP's rich and broad research question will be emphasized and which ones will tend to disappear from view. When we asked the chaplains in the military chaplaincy research community halfway the project about their views on the picture of military chaplaincy that was emerging from the case studies so far, they were skeptical. They felt that cases that fit the research format are not representative of military chaplaincy. Practices of "being present" and of "making small talk" are missing. They also felt that typical themes that soldiers discuss with chaplains had not come up in the cases: boredom, drug use, loss of a beloved one and mourning, getting into a fight when going out, and loss over time of the ideals with which soldiers enter the military. We as researchers noticed that there were only few cases in which experiences of war and violence played a central role, and that religion and worldview were generally not explicit themes in the cases. These observations might lead to different sampling strategies: we might want to add as a sampling criterion that one of the missing themes plays a role, or that religion/worldview is an explicit theme in the case. Looking at the three emerging patterns described earlier, we might also adapt sampling to "make the case" for one of the three patterns. Cases that help us gain insight in how the military system resonates in chaplaincy care (first pattern) do not necessarily also help us gain insight in how chaplains address soldiers as complex human beings (second pattern) or into the significance of "being known" in chaplaincy care (third pattern). Moreover, when we look at the three patterns from a perspective of the Case Studies Project as a whole, the question arises which issues emerging in the military chaplaincy research community also play a role in other domains than the Military, and which ones are relevant for "making the case" for chaplaincy as such. From the perspective of cross-case comparison in the project as a whole, different sampling strategies might be decided upon. Currently, sampling is done by the individual chaplains somewhat haphazardly: they decide which case they present. In the military chaplaincy research community, we discussed the sampling of cases in order to create a more balanced and diverse sample of cases. We think that the project as a whole may be served with intentional strategies for data selection. Cross-case analysis could provide the necessary methodology. For instance, if the entire case of military chaplaincy is the object of research, single cases should be purposefully selected to account for the rich data that are necessary for describing the broader case of military chaplaincy.

Reflecting on the aim of the project and on sampling strategies seems especially important given the inevitable political aspect of research. Whether intentionally or not, the CSP has an impact on how chaplaincy is perceived and understood by chaplains and other stakeholders such as the sending agencies (churches) or managers in care facilities or in governmental institutions like the ministry of Justice and Security or the ministry of Defense. A crucial question in "making the case for chaplaincy" is which audiences we are addressing in our research: what kind of audiences do we think or hope to find the evidence from the project convincing (Damen, Schuhmann, Leget, & Fitchett, 2019)? In the case of military chaplaincy, this question is especially relevant. Findings from the project might, for instance, suggest that the denomination of the chaplain is not a decisive factor in chaplaincy care, which might question the denominational structure of chaplaincy care provisions. Or, findings might suggest that military chaplains play a role in reducing health-related absence, which could have as a result that the value of military chaplaincy is henceforth evaluated in terms of reduction of absenteeism. All in all, it seems worthwhile to reflect with various stakeholders on purposes and strategies of case comparison from a viewpoint of the project as a whole before the project ends.

Conclusion

Case studies have been around in practical theology for a long time as a means for educating students for pastoral practice (Schipani, 2014). In case study projects, including the CSP, case studies are collected in order to sustain and improve the chaplaincy profession (Fitchett, 2011). Our reflections on comparing single cases of military chaplaincy care suggest that, with a view to the original research question, we need a two-sided focus on both single and multiple case analysis. A single case describes and explains a phenomenon sufficiently and adequately according to its uniqueness and completeness. Apart from being a case in itself, the single case narrative is also "just" another piece of data that adds to the "many and varied angles" from which the subject – namely (military) chaplaincy – can be looked at (Thomas & Myers, 2015, p. 8). These incidents, though, need to be compared, because "each individual case is less important in itself than the comparison that each offers with the others" (Thomas & Myers, 2015, p. 62).

With its emphasis on the research value of the single case, the project is in need of a methodology to compare cases. Given the amount of cases generated in the project, the research possibilities for cross-case comparison are endless. There are multiple ways to proceed: we might, for instance, focus on comparison of case studies collected within a specific setting of chaplaincy care, or use other selection criteria like the denomination of the chaplain, specific spiritual needs of clients, or a specific intervention. We might even take the analysis one step further and compare results of cross-case comparison of different strata – settings, denominations, interventions – in the total collection of case studies.

In order to unlock the project's potential for cross-case comparison, we need to reflect on the question of what methods to use for multiple case analysis. Walton and Körver (2017) state that "the comparison will take different forms" (p. 269). Methods for case comparison need to be chosen in relation to (the aim of) the specific aspect or sub question of the overarching research question that the comparison aims to address.[18] For instance, when the aim of the comparison is descriptive, thematic analysis (Braun & Clarke, 2006) offers a versatile approach. According to Fitchett (2011), description is the main aim of case studies: "Before we can do good clinical trials about our spiritual care, we need good case studies describing our work" (p. 4). In the CSP, case studies are located higher up in the research hierarchy. Cases are not "just" evidence to base practice upon but, instead, constitute "practice-based evidence." For cross-case development of theory, we need methods that aim "to move qualitative inquiry beyond descriptive studies into the realm of explanatory theoretical frameworks" (Charmaz, 2006, p. 6). Methods that include constant comparison, such as Grounded Theory (Charmaz, 2006; Glaser & Strauss, 1967; Holton & Walsh, 2016), are promising candidates to move beyond the single case studies towards a more integrated conceptual understanding of chaplaincy care. Including "constant multiple case comparison" in the research while the project is still running enhances flexibility – in particular the cyclical flow between data collection and data analysis – and reflexivity in the research process, which does justice to the qualitative character of the project.

---

18 Reflection is also needed on the question of what are the data that are used for cross-case comparison, "original data" used for writing the phase one case descriptions, or one/both of two different parts of the final phase two case reports.

References

Braun, V., & Clarke, V. (2006). Using thematic analysis in psychology. *Qualitative research in psychology, 3*(2), 77-101.

Charmaz, K. (2006). *Constructing grounded theory: A practical guide through qualitative analysis.* London: Sage.

Damen, A., Schuhmann, C., Leget, C., & Fitchett, G. (2019). Can outcome research respect the integrity of chaplaincy? A review of outcome studies. *Journal of Health Care Chaplaincy.*

Fitchett, G. (2011). Making our case(s). *Journal of Health Care Chaplaincy, 17*(1-2), 3-18.

Glaser, B. G., & Strauss, A. L. (1967). *The Discovery of Grounded Theory. Strategies for Qualitative Research.* Chicago: Aldine.

Holton, J. A., & Walsh, I. (2016). *Classic grounded theory: Applications with qualitative and quantitative data.* Los Angeles: Sage.

Mason, J. (2018). *Qualitative Researching* (3rd ed.). Thousand Oaks: Sage.

Patton, M. Q. (2002). *Qualitative research & evaluation methods* (3rd ed.). Thousand Oaks: Sage.

Ridder, H.-G. (2017). The theory contribution of case study research designs. *Business Research 10*(2), 281-305.

Schipani, D. S. (2014). Case Study Method. In B. J. Miller-McLemore (Ed.), *The Wiley Blackwell Companion to Practical Theology* (pp. 91-101). Oxford: Wiley-Blackwell.

Thomas, G. (2016). *How to do your case study* (2nd ed.). Los Angeles: Sage.

Thomas, G., & Myers, K. (2015). *The anatomy of the case study.* Los Angeles: Sage.

Walton, M., & Körver, J. (2017). Dutch Case Studies Project in chaplaincy care: A description and theoretical explanation of the format and procedures. *Health and Social Care Chaplaincy, 5*(2), 257-80.

Yin, R. K. (2014). *Case study research: Design and methods* (5th ed.). Los Angeles: Sage.

Chapter 9.

Professional Proximity

*Seeking a Balance between Relation and
Content in Spiritual Counseling*

Myriam Braakhuis

What do chaplains do, for what reasons and what is the effect of their work? That is the central question of the Case Studies Project (Körver, 2016; Walton & Körver, 2017). There are many descriptions of the work of chaplains (De Roy, Oeneman, Neijmeijer,, & Hutschemaekers, 1997; Mowat & Swinton, 2007; Cadge, Calle, & Dillinger, 2011; Mooren, 2013; Simpson, Collin, & Okeke, 2014; Walton, 2014; Cadge, 2017), but it is not always clear what chaplains are exactly focused on or what the effect of their work is (Mackor, 2007; Körver, 2014). It is remarkable that what the work of chaplains yields remains vague. What might be the reason? During my research, I began to notice that chaplains often describe their work in terms of their attitude, like: "being there" or "presence," "empathy," "attention" (De Roy e.a., 1997; Mackor, 2007; Cadge, 2017), rather than in terms of what they actually do and what they focus on.

A likely explanation is that chaplains are strongly focused on building a relationship of trust with their client. However, I think that chaplains run the risk of placing too much emphasis on this relationship of trust. Such a strong focus on a trusting relationship exposes chaplains to certain risks. Within this article, I will elaborate on these risks. Through literature research on these risks, I found that both a trusting relationship and a clear goal-orientation are important for the success of an accompaniment process. I will introduce the concept of professional proximity as helpful for finding a balance between relationship and content within spiritual counseling.

Let us first look at the relational attitude of chaplains. Within their field of expertise – spirituality and meaning of life – the necessity of building a relationship of trust with a client follows naturally. Without a basis of trust, it is hard to talk about personal life issues and existential questions (Ganzevoort & Visser, 2007). Therefore, it is not surprising that chaplains place so much emphasis on an empathic, attentive attitude. That indeed many chaplains prioritize a relational attitude appears clearly within a survey held among participating chaplains in the Case

Studies Project. The questionnaire was held in 2017 among chaplains in the Netherlands and was completed by 395 chaplains from diverse fields of work. The Presence approach, elaborated in the Dutch *Een theorie van de presentie* (Baart, 2001/2011) is a guiding theory and model for 34% of the respondents. In addition, 120 respondents (30%) did not answer the question about guiding theories and models.

Another factor is that chaplains usually have certain values and ideals, embedded in their own philosophy of life. Human dignity and love seem to be important values to chaplains (Campbell, 1985; Baart, 2001/2011; Leget, 2017). They regard a relational attitude as valuable in itself: the client feels taken seriously, experiences acknowledgement and understanding. This in itself has a beneficial effect (Walton, 2014). The value of this relational attitude is important and should not be underestimated. However, too much emphasis on a trusting relationship and "being there" for the other can have adverse effects on the guidance process. There is a chance that the chaplain loses sight of specific goals. Within each counseling situation, it is important that the chaplain has in mind what goals are being pursued (Smit, 2015), goals that are, of course, to be established in accordance with the client. In the following section, I will explain what risks are involved when a chaplain places too much emphasis on a trusting relationship. Through this, it will be also made clear why a clear goal-orientation is important in facing these risks.

Risks of too much emphasis on a relational attitude
Based on literature study, I can distinguish three major risks of too much emphasis on a trusting relationship with the client:
1. The chaplain does not dare to confront;
2. The chaplain loses track of existential and spiritual themes;
3. The chaplain crosses boundaries, either hers or the clients.

1. The chaplain does not dare to confront the client
In most cases, clients come to a chaplain with a life story that is impeded or broken. Confrontation can be needed at some point, in order to offer the client a different perspective (Ganzevoort & Visser, 2007). Confrontation should always be done in a non-judging and non-explaining way: reflecting on the contradictions in what a client is saying or doing (Mooren, 2013, p. 151). However, it is possible that the chaplain is afraid to confront the client, because doing so might influence the relationship (Smit, 1997; Nauta, 1998). In those cases, it feels safer for the chaplain to simply follow the client in her story. This will protect the trusting relationship, but the client will not be afforded sufficient opportunity to grow. Furthermore,

Smit (1997) explains that many chaplains did not learn to make goals explicit in counseling. If they could be clearer about the goals of their counseling, both towards their clients and themselves, they would be more secure and focused in the accompaniment process. That would prevent superficial talks or conversations running around in the same circles.

2. The chaplain loses track of existential and spiritual themes

From literature and from the questionnaire of the Case Studies Project, it appears that chaplains focus strongly on "presence": being fully attentive to the other person (Baart, 2001/2011; Cadge et al., 2011; Cadge, 2017). However, if being there is an end in itself, the focus on existential and spiritual themes can shift to the background. In the previously mentioned descriptions of the work of chaplains, it is not clear how they focus on existential and spiritual themes. They often encounter people in severe situations and have an eye for the existential questions that are at stake, but it remains unclear how the chaplains deal with these questions, how they guide their clients in profound reflection on those questions. In *Spiritual Care in Practice* (Fitchett & Nolan, 2015) this point is emphasized by Cotton, a psychologist who responds to the case studies of chaplains within pediatrics. He observes that the relationship of trust with the client plays a major role in several case studies and wonders whether this relationship should be a goal in itself or a means to something else. He points out various existential issues that are not being addressed by the chaplains. Too much emphasis on "being there" and listening can result in life questions expressed but not explored (Cotton, 2015).

3. The chaplain crosses boundaries, either hers or the client's

Too much emphasis on a relationship of trust can also lead to an unhealthy relationship. It may result in the client relying so much on the chaplain that she finds herself in a dependent position and hindered from assuming her own responsibility. According to Jongerius (2009), people with an intellectual disability are often accustomed to being in a dependent position. That can be reinforced by the attitude of a caregiver. If a caregiver maintains a relationship with the client that is too close, there is no room for the client's individuality and personal growth. That applies equally to a much wider group of clients. Ganzevoort and Visser write that the goal of spiritual guidance must be "as concrete and achievable as possible, because that helps to get moving" (Ganzevoort & Visser, 2007, p. 152). By formulating goals, the chaplain stimulates her conversation partner to find her own way forward and thus prevents undesirable dependence.

On the other hand, it is possible that the chaplain feels so closely connected to the client that she projects her own thoughts or feelings on the client. It is extremely important that the counselor is aware of her own moral and spiritual views, because of the risk that she otherwise projects or transfers them to the client. Both Dubbeldam and Mooren (2012) and Zwaan (2017) therefore emphasize the importance of self-care and self-reflection for chaplains.

Summarizing: within all three risks, the importance of being goal-oriented can be seen. A chaplain needs to know what goal she has in mind during counseling and to be able to confront a client in a helpful way. A clear goal-orientation also helps to focus on existential and spiritual questions. Furthermore, focusing on a concrete goal ensures that one will not lose herself in countertransference. The art of successful counseling is therefore to combine a relational attitude with a clear goal-orientation.

Professional proximity

To combine a trusting relationship with a clear focus on goals, the concept of "professional proximity" might be helpful. In the Netherlands, this concept is used within the Salvation Army. This concept is being mentioned more frequently in health care (Soldevilla, Pepegrino, Oriol, & Filella, 2012; Timmerman, Schreuder, & Kievitsbosch, 2017; Brown, Winter, & Carr, 2018). Inspired by the research of Jongerius (2009), I define professional proximity as: "A relationship in which the counselor is concerned with the client with attentiveness and empathy. In this relationship the autonomy of the client is acknowledged, and the client can manifest herself. Together, the counselor and the client determine key questions and objectives."

The concept of professional proximity is mostly used to counter the concept of "professional distance," in which the latter refers to a purely professional attitude with little space for personal involvement (Cummins, 2015; Netten, 2016; Van der Wedden, 2018). That indicates a development towards more attention for the whole person within health care. We consider that to be a positive development, because there is an "often heard complaint of patients that they are not seen as a person" (Van der Wedden, 2018). Fortunately, the balance is tipping over towards more attention for the client as a whole and unique person. Chaplains can, of course, contribute to that. However, for chaplains the challenge is on the other side of the spectrum: they could lose themselves in personal involvement and attention, with the three risks mentioned above as a result. In that case, the concept of professional proximity can also prove helpful. Within spiritual counseling, the relationship with a client is always professional, i.e. a human and loving relationship, but at the same time that relationship is restricted and based on an agreement. The chaplain must care for the boundaries of a relationship. It is the job of the chaplain to always be aware that the relationship is about guidance and that certain goals are being pursued. In that way, chaplains can contribute as much as possible to the wellbeing of a client: discovering new perspectives, finding motivation and being inspired.

Needed are examples of a successful combination of a relational attitude with a focus on concrete goals in the case studies. Those good practices can be analyzed: what makes these chaplains successful, and what are important success factors for professional proximity in practice? This can help us to give a more elaborated interpretation of the concept of professional proximity.

References

Baart, A. (2001/2011). *Een theorie van de presentie.* Utrecht: Boom Lemma.

Brown, T., Winter, K., & Carr, N. (2018). Residential child care workers. Relationship based practice in a culture of fear. *Child & Family Social Work, 23*(4), 657-665.

Cadge, W., Calle, K. & Dillinger, J. (2011). What Do Chaplains Contribute to Large Academic Hospitals? The Perspectives of Pediatric Physicians and Chaplains. *Journal of Religion and Health, 50,* 300-312.

Cadge, W. (2017). God on the Fly? The Professional Mandates of Airport Chaplains. *Sociology of Religion: A Quarterly Review, 78*(4), 437-455.

Campbell, A. V., & Browning, D. S. (1985). *Professionalism and Pastoral Care.* Philadelphia: Fortress Press.

Cotton, S. (2015). Critical Response to Pediatric Case Studies. A Psychologist's Perspective. In G. Fitchett & S. Nolan (Eds.), *Spiritual care in practice. Case studies in healthcare chaplaincy* (pp. 98-106). London: Jessica Kingsley Publishers.

Cummins, R. (2015). *Waarom professionele nabijheid zo belangrijk is in de zorg.* Online blog, retrieved August 8, 2018, from https://www.psychosenet.nl/professionele-nabijheid/

De Roy, A., Oeneman, D., Neijmeijer, L., & Hutschemaekers, G. (1997). *Beroep: geestelijk verzorger. Een verkennend onderzoek naar persoon, werk en werkplek van geestelijk verzorgers in de gezondheidszorg.* Utrecht: Trimbos-instituut.

Dubbeldam, A., & Mooren, J. H. (2012). Afstand en nabijheid. Een oneindige dans van verwijdering en toenadering. *Tijdschrift Geestelijke Verzorging, 15*(67), 12-20.

Fitchett, G., & Nolan, S. (Eds.) (2015). *Spiritual care in practice. Case studies in healthcare chaplaincy.* London: Jessica Kingsley Publishers.

Ganzevoort, R., & Visser, J. (2007). *Zorg voor het verhaal. Achtergrond, methode en inhoud van pastorale begeleiding.* Zoetermeer: Meinema.

Jongerius, L. F. (2009). *"Dag Schat!" Een onderzoek naar de professionele nabijheid in de hulpverlening.* Nijmegen: Hogeschool Arnhem en Nijmegen, Opleiding Creatieve Therapie.

Körver, J. (Ed.) (2014). *In het oog in het hart. Geestelijke verzorging 2.1.* Nijmegen: Valkhof Pers.

Körver, J. (2016). Wat doen geestelijk verzorgers? Met *case studies* op naar *practice-based evidence* van geestelijke verzorging. *Tijdschrift Geestelijke Verzorging, 19*(82), 10-19.

Lang, G., & Molen, H. T. van der (2012). *Psychologische gespreksvoering. Een basis voor hulpverlening* (16th ed.). Amsterdam: Boom/Nelissen.

Leget, C. (2017). *Art of Living, Art of Dying. Spiritual Care for a Good Death.* London: Jessica Kingsley Publishers.

Mackor, A. R. (2007). Standaardisering en ambtelijke binding. Lopen de idealen van geestelijk verzorgers gevaar? In J. Kole & D. de Ruyter (Eds.), *Werkzame idealen. Ethische reflecties op professionaliteit* (pp. 89-103). Assen: Van Gorcum.

Mooren, J. H. (Ed.) (2013). *Bakens in de stroom. Naar een methodiek van het humanistisch geestelijk werk* (2nd ed.). De Graaff: Utrecht.

Mowat, H., & Swinton, J. (2007). *What do chaplains do? The role of the chaplain in meeting the spiritual needs of patients* (2nd ed.). Aberdeen: Mowat Research.

Nauta, R. (1998). Theologie als handicap. *Praktische Theologie, 25*(3), 93-102.

Netten, C. (2016). *"Professionele nabijheid" in plaats van professionele afstand.* Online blog, retrieved August 8, 2018, from, https://www.humanconcern.nl/blog/blog-carmen-netten-professionele-nabijheid-in-plaats-van-professionele-afstand

Peters, R. (2016). *Professionele nabijheid in plaats van distantie.* Online blog, retrieved August 8, 2018, from https://nivoz.nl/nl/professionele-nabijheid-in-plaats-van-distantie

Simpson, J., Collin, M., & Okeke, C. (2014). What do chaplains do now? The continuous process of adaptation. *Health and Social Care Chaplaincy, 2*(2), 213-234.

Smit, J. H. (1997). Pastoraat als tegenspraak. *Praktische Theologie, 24*(3), 297-314.

Smit, J. D. (2015). *Antwoord geven op het leven zelf. Een onderzoek naar de basismethodiek van geestelijke verzorging.* Delft: Eburon.

Soldevila, A., Peregrino, A., Oriol, X., & Filella, G. (2012). Evaluation of residential care from the perspective of older adolescents in care. the need for a new construct: Optimum professional proximity. *Child & Family Social Work, 18*(3), 285-293.

Timmerman, M. C., Schreuder, P. R., & Kievitsbosch, A. F. (2017). Professional proximity in perceiving child sexual abuse in residential care. The closer the better? *Children and Youth Services Review, 76,* 192-195.

Van der Wedden, H. (2018). Professionele nabijheid. *Nursing, 24*(1), 12.

Walton, M. N. (2014). *Hoe waait de wind? Interpretatie van geestelijke verzorging door cliënten in de ggz.* Tilburg: KSGV.

Walton, M. & Körver, J. (2017). Dutch case studies project in chaplaincy care: A description and theoretical explanation of the format en procedures. *Health and Social Care Chaplaincy, 5*(2), 257-280.

Zwaan, B. (2017). *Een prachtige dans: De therapeutische afstemming van afstand en nabijheid in het werk van Carl Rogers, Martin Buber en Henri Nouwen.* Tilburg: KSGV.

Chapter 10.

Effects of Health Care Chaplaincy
A Qualitative Study with Case Reports

Nika Höfler, Traugott Roser

Background

How do health care chaplains working in German hospitals perceive and describe their contribution to health care? How do they measure effectiveness? While German academic literature on health care chaplaincy has seen a rise in contributions to the controversial debate on the concept of spiritual care versus traditional models of pastoral care, only a small number of empirical studies has been published. In particular, in the German-speaking area no one has ever examined the question of what determines effectiveness and how all participants perceive it in a pastoral encounter. As a result, the University of Münster has launched a new project in Germany with the aim to investigate the effectiveness of health care chaplaincy in a visible way. We have done this from the point of view of all participants in combination with statistical methods. While the Department of Practical Theology at the University of Münster (Prof. Dr. Traugott Roser) leads the research project within an academic setting, the project is a rare cooperation of active health care chaplains and academic theology.

In this article, we discuss in detail questions of methodology used in our research with case studies. The first stage of the project aims to collect and evaluate chaplains' narratives describing effects of their work and presence from their personal experience. Starting from the chaplains' perspective, we hope to find practice-based categories to describe effectiveness of health care chaplaincy. In passing, we note that in order to understand and interpret the data and results of this study, one needs to know that health care chaplaincy in Germany is (almost) exclusively provided by the established churches (Protestant denominations and Roman Catholic). All chaplains recorded in the study described below work on behalf of a Protestant church. Most chaplains are ordained pastors and are perceived as such by all parties. That also determines their self-image.

Research goals

As already mentioned, this study is part of a research project on questions of effectiveness of health care chaplaincy for all parties involved: patients, relatives, hospital staff, chaplains, and institutions. The main research question is: How effective is health care chaplaincy for *anyone involved* and *how and where* does it work? The aim is, first, to scientifically describe, evaluate and demonstrate forms of action and effectiveness of health care chaplaincy *based on (self-reported) practical experience and interventions*. Those parameters have not hitherto been available and have not been adapted from non-pastoral professions like physicians or psychiatrists. Our research field consists of clinics and institutions offering health care chaplaincy services. The project is a joint venture by the associations of health care chaplains of the Protestant churches of Rhineland (Evangelische Kirche im Rheinland – EKiR) and Westphalia (Evangelische Kirche von Westfalen – EKvW) and the Department of Practical Theology at the University of Münster, Germany. Essentially, we follow the approach of projects of the European Research Institute for Chaplaincy in Healthcare (ERICH) at the Catholic Faculty of the University of Leuven in Belgium to gain insight into the reality of today's clinical chaplaincy in different European countries through *case reports and case studies*.

The entire project spans a period of three years ending in early 2021. It consists of three phases. First, we want to gain access to the field through *case reports written by chaplains* from the two regional churches in Rhineland and Westphalia. We focus on their self-reported practical experience in order to understand in what way the participants describe and conceptualize effectiveness in their own terms. In December 2017, we issued a call for case reports to all members of the chaplains' associations. We will publish the results of the first phase in 2020. The phases two and three will complete our work with case reports. Starting in the fall of 2019, we will work with narrative interviews with patients, relatives and hospital staff in order to understand caretakers' perspectives on effects of health care chaplaincy. In the third and final phase, we will take a quantitative approach, statistically recording time quotas and contacts of a representative cross-section of hospital chaplains within a defined period. We will therefore work qualitatively in the first two phases and quantitatively in the last phase. Altogether, we follow a multiple methods approach – both in the survey (case studies, narrative interviews and statistics) and in the evaluation of the material (qualitative and quantitative methods). We have therefore chosen a combination of qualitative and quantitative methods, because it allows a comprehensive picture to emerge. We begin by letting the persons involved in a chaplaincy action speak directly (in the

first phase the chaplains, in the second phase patients, relatives and staff).
Only qualitative methods can capture all the phenomena of their subjective views and personal experiences. Only in the last step will statistical
analysis follow, in which we record contact numbers and time quotas. In
the end, we hope to gain a comprehensive view of the effectiveness of
health care chaplaincy among all participants.

Methods of the first phase

Based on the work of George Fitchett and Steve Nolan (Fitchett & Nolan,
2015), an expert discussion took place to generate a letter of invitation
mailed to the health care chaplains indicated above. We asked them to
write a case report about an experience that describes their work and its
effects. We leave it to the participants to focus either on patient- and fami-
ly-related care or chaplaincy care to members of other professions, with
regard to ethical consultations, institutions, etcetera. The case reports are
essentially based on the form of the Fitchett and Nolan reports, although
in a shortened form. The reports are two to five pages long and focus on a
significant encounter between a chaplain and a counterpart in which the
chaplains had noticed some sort of change. It is up to the interpretation of
the participants how they perceive that "change," whether it is perceived
by only one of the persons or by all those involved, and whether it is
perceived in similar ways. A definition of "change" is therefore not given.
In addition, the chaplains outline briefly the context of the persons and
the situation of the encounter. At the end of the description, the authors
provide a reflection in which they describe where and how change was
perceived and observed. Here he or she describes where and how one
perceives and observes change and who or what led to it in his or her
opinion, the counterpart, the institution as a whole and/or the chaplains
themselves. The change can be of physical, psychological, spiritual and/
or of social nature.

    We were able to collect 47 reports for evaluation. Data collection was
done at the University of Münster. We anonymized the cases for analysis,
following ethical standards for research. The analysis was done within a
research group. Methods and results were discussed both within the research setting and among health care chaplains. For this reason, our evaluation in the first two phases is based on qualitative methods. Qualitative
research is particularly suited for learning something about another person's point of view by recording subjective views, interpretations of the
situation and narrative identity. In that way, one can make the subject's
experience accessible to theory. We only use the case study method as a
survey method, not as an *evaluation* method. Our letter of invitation did

not ask for "best practice" narratives but for cases regarding effectiveness of an intervention/accompaniment process. Searching for a method to identify objectively the matters of interest, we decided to *evaluate* by using a Grounded Theory approach (Glaser & Strauss, 2010; Strauss & Corbin, 1996). While we make use of the case reports for pure data collection, we *evaluate* the existing texts by working with Grounded Theory. This approach allows the development of a theory "grounded" in the words of the participants. It is primarily used when there is not yet an existing theory. Grounded Theory allows us to develop inductive parameters from case reports (and from interviews in phase II of the project) that can capture and objectively represent the effectiveness of a measure. Grounded Theory is used where numbers alone cannot grasp the complexity of reality, but where contexts of action and meaning are conveyed linguistically. Thus, the method largely corresponds to the basic qualitative paradigm.

The researcher does not use a fixed working method but a systematic series of procedures, from which then emerges a theory about a phenomenon, anchored in the object. The aim is therefore to develop and generate a theory (Strauss & Corbin, 1996). By creating classifications and typologies based on several cases, data is literally "broken up like a surface" (Strübing, 2009) and broken down into individual components. Later, they are assigned to more general concepts. Through the process of coding, the original text is transformed, text quantities are reduced, and the constructed types form the basis for theory formation (Krumm, 2009). The category scheme directs the attention of the researcher to the research question. Based on this, the researcher groups the characteristics recognized as relevant into categories. This results in main- and subcategories, which are later classified into a scheme. A coding guideline is then developed, and the coding of the material starts. By comparing and correlating the text passages, one seeks to find structures and patterns in the material that can serve to further differentiate and categorize the material. The result should be empirically based typologies. The peculiarity consists first of all, as already mentioned, in the fact that the theory is anchored in the data itself, that the participants themselves are there in the discussion, and that categories are developed from this without material from outside being brought to the criteria (Hermisson & Rothgangel, 2018). This approach characterizes its mode of operation above all by the method of constant comparison. The data are repeatedly compared with each other in relation to an examined phenomenon. Similarities as well as different characteristics and variations are recognized. In this way, the researcher can also adopt unfamiliar perspectives and gain new insights. Permanent analysis questions are asked in the form of simple standard questions ("Who?," "When?," "Where?," "What?," "Why?," "How many?" etc.) and specify the research question.

In our understanding, to "ground" theory on participants' experience and reports, it is imperative that the caregiver's, i.e. the chaplain's subjective view should relate to the perspective of the counterpart. Therefore, in the second phase we will extend the work with case reports to narrative interviews with patients, staff and relatives in hospitals and conclude with a quantitative survey. At the end of the study it will be interesting to see whether and how the different perceptions of chaplaincy and the associated changes, and generally the "effectiveness," will differ among all persons involved. It is possible that a chaplain identifies these aspects at completely different points than staff members, or that a patient feels completely different about an encounter than a relative who was present experiences it. It is of utmost importance for us to let all participants have a voice and let them speak directly through qualitative working methods. Only in a latter step will quantitative data be added to the analysis. Thus, we are able to obtain a comprehensive picture of the effectiveness of health care chaplaincy.

Sample

As we will publish the results of the first phase of the project in the beginning of 2020, we provide here a look at the material and some preliminary findings. Until the present day, hospital chaplains in German speaking countries are not familiar with empirical studies in their field. We often encountered skepticism during the study. From the beginning, participation was very hesitant. When we only received very few reports at the beginning, we continued to advertize the project for more than a year and had to extend the deadline repeatedly. After initially hoping for 80 reports, we were, in the end, more than satisfied with the number of 47 reports. For the future, we hope for greater familiarity with research. Acceptance of research methods that respect chaplains' own experience will improve this.

The overall nature of the reports is as follows:

Figure 1

Valid reports[19]:	39			
	Male	**Female**		
Gender of chaplains	18	21		
	30-49 years	**50-60 years**	**> 60 years**	
Age	5	31	3	
	< 1 year	**1-10 years**	**10-20 years**	**> 20 years**
Years of experience[20]	4	12	16	7

Due to reasons of anonymity, we did not relate reports to one of the two church bodies (Rhineland and Westphalia).

Preliminary results

Since we did not specify the type of health care chaplaincy provided in the call for case reports, we have a variety of available reports, ranging from the accompaniment of patients and relatives to institutional tasks. The latter mainly concern ethical issues and events within the framework of ethical consultations. Not surprisingly, overlaps between these areas within one report occur quite often. It is understandable that accompanying a patient sometimes includes contact with relatives and can involve institutional and ethical questions. Most of the case reports concern an accompaniment with multiple contact moments. This, too, is not surprising, since an intimate relationship can often only arise through repeated and closer contact. Sometimes it is necessary to build trust. However, there is a number of one-time contacts without pre- or post-history. Some reports include more or less intensive "post-history" results connected with subsequent expressions of gratitude or the possibility for the chaplains to observe longer-term effects and effects with the patients and relatives afterwards. "Explicit" gratitude on the part of the patient or the institution (in the form of conversations, cards, e-mails or even presents) seems to be a rarity, nevertheless deserving of emphasis. This is particularly interesting when the renewed contact occurs after a very long time, and both – the counterpart as well as the chaplain – still remember it as salutary. This was the case five times in the relatively small number of cases, i.e. comparatively often. However, it is obvious that the chaplains

19   Eight reports were written in a format that we could not include in the evaluation.
20   In the institution in which the described encounter took place.

submitted such "special cases" (some of which are explicitly referred to as such) which stand out in their everyday work as having been particularly effective.

Working with case reports in order to evaluate them with the use of Grounded Theory after the first phase of the project has proven to be a rewarding enterprise. Our material covers a wide variety of chaplains' experience and practice, offering a broad understanding of effects and effectiveness of chaplaincy in health care settings. Case studies, in our project, serve as a survey tool for further research. They are the most useful way to investigate the chaplain's perspective directly and more inductively.

References

Fitchett, G., & Nolan, S. (2017). Guest Editors Special Issue: Chaplain Case Study Research. *Health and Social Care Chaplaincy, 5*(2), 167-173.

Fitchett, G. (2015). Introduction. In G. Fitchett & S. Nolan (Eds.), *Spiritual Care in Practice: Case Studies in Healthcare Chaplaincy* (pp. 11-24). London: Jessica Kingsley Publishers.

Fitchett, G., & Nolan, S. (Eds.) (2015). *Spiritual Care in Practice: Case Studies in Healthcare Chaplaincy.* London: Jessica Kingsley Publishers.

Glaser, B. G., & Strauss, A. L. (2010). *Grounded Theory. Strategien qualitativer Forschung.* Bern: Verlag Hans Huber.

Hermisson, S., & Rothgangel, M. (2018). Grounded Theory. In M. Pirner & M. Rothgangel (Eds.), *Empirisch Forschen in der Religionspädagogik. Ein Studienbuch für Studierende und Lehrkräfte* (pp. 111-126). Stuttgart: W. Kohlhammer.

Krumm, T. (2009). Grundlagen der qualitativen Datenanalyse. In B. Westle (Ed.), *Methoden der Politikwissenschaft* (pp. 297-323). Baden-Baden: Nomos Verlagsgesellschaft.

Strauss, A. L., & Corbin, J. (1996). *Grounded Theory: Grundlagen qualitativer Sozialforschung.* Weinheim: Beltz.

Strübing, J. (2009). *Grounded Theory: Zur sozialtheoretischen und epistemologischen Fundierung des Verfahrens der empirisch begründeten Theoriebildung.* Wiesbaden: VS Verlag für Sozialwissenschaften.

Walton, M., & Körver S. (2017). Dutch Case Studies Project in Chaplaincy Care: A Description and Theoretical Explanation of the Format and Procedures. *Health and Social Care Chaplaincy, 5*(2), 257-280.

III. Case Studies and Critical Issues

Chapter 11.

Personal Experiences in Writing a Case Study

Paul Galchutt

This essay bears my reflections on combining health care chaplaincy and case study research.[21] The first half of the essay is structured by philosophical and theoretical tenets of phenomenology, narrative hermeneutics, and dialogue. It is Fitchett's article (2011) that will structure the latter half of this chapter. In his article, Fitchett describes six, ideally seven, components to comprise "good" (p. 12) case studies. Among the seven components, the first four are: 1) it makes a point or tells an important story; 2) it makes our case among cases; 3) it begins with background; and 4) it describes the chaplain-patient relationship. The remaining three components (spiritual assessment, summary, and theory/measurement) are important, but will not be addressed here as these three are a little less focused on the personal experience in writing a case study.

As a chaplain and a researcher, I am a part of two communities. In the spirit of reflexivity and because these are reflections on the personal experience of writing a case study, I state that I am from the United States in the upper Midwest region from the State of Minnesota. I am a cisgender man, middle aged, and white. I am married and have two children.

Professionally, I served a Lutheran congregation as a pastor. The role of bereavement coordinator is also among my former positions. Most of my vocational life, however, has been dedicated to health care chaplaincy. I have either worked in the outpatient cancer chemotherapy infusion clinic, inpatient acute care, or inpatient palliative care. I, cumulatively, write from these perspectives. I left full-time chaplaincy in the fall of 2017 to pursue a Master of Public Health (MPH) degree.

Completing my Transforming Chaplaincy Research Fellowship and MPH (June 2019) has enabled me to learn research methods and skills.

---

21 I feel privileged to write this chapter for two reasons. First, because I am having a case published that I presented at the international conference on chaplaincy case study research hosted in Amsterdam, February 2019. Inspiration to host this gathering came from George Fitchett's article (2011), "Making Our Case(s)." Second, with the editors' generous invitation, I am honored to submit this essay on the personal experience of writing a case study.

As a result, I now work as a research chaplain[22] at University of Minnesota Health. While pursuing the MPH, I worked part-time in an outpatient cancer infusion clinic. That is where I met Keith Simons. Keith is the person discussed in a case study being published among a collection regarding chaplains being involved in shared medical decision making (Galchutt, in press). Keith is his real name. Reflections about Keith, our relationship and our experiences with one another are shared in the second half of this chapter.

The first half of this chapter reasons that the work and action of chaplaincy happens in dialogue with patients and loved ones. It also contends that chaplains interpretively and unavoidably conduct their work through the lens of their own experiences and story. Chaplains bring their storied selves into these dialogues with patients and loved ones to understand and participate in the patient's experience of illness. The personal experience of a chaplain conducting research through a case study then is intertwined with a patient's illness experience. Essentially, it is not possible to write a chaplaincy case study as research without including the chaplain in it. The illusion that any research or knowledge producing exploration can be conducted without noting how the care provider influenced it is just that, an illusion (Lincoln & Guba, 1985). The first half of this essay continues with the significance of seeking to understand a patient's experience (phenomenology) through the interpretive lens (narrative hermeneutic) of a chaplaincy researcher in caregiving dialogue with patients.

Phenomenology

I savored the moment when the lecturer in my qualitative methods class explained that phenomenology examines the lived experience of how someone understands their world amid their specific circumstances. I remember my excitement about this explanation of phenomenology for research because it also connected with my personal comprehension of a health care chaplain seeking to understand a patient's personal experience of illness. My enthusiasm grew as I realized that my chaplaincy care skills such as active listening (Nolan, 2019) to invite dialogue for revealing patients' experiences could also be used in my work as a researcher with case studies. The difference is that the phenomenological motivation for

---

22 As a healthcare research chaplain, I oversee original research development, which includes such components as the literature review, study design, methodology, analysis, and dissemination. This role also includes the provision of research literacy among chaplain colleagues as well as chaplain students.

chaplaincy is to contribute toward healing, whereas the goal as a researcher is to generate knowledge through evidence.

"Phenomenology is a philosophical approach to the study of experience" (Smith, Flowers, & Larkin et al., 2009, p. 11). German philosopher, Hans Georg Gadamer, contributed to phenomenology with his assertion that as people engage experience, they are perpetual interpreters. In Gadamer's seminal work, *Truth and Method*, he writes, "understanding is always interpretation, and hence interpretation is the explicit form of understanding" (p. 306). In seeking to understand the experience (phenomenology) of others, as both a chaplain and/or a researcher, there is an endless process of (hermeneutical) interpretation toward that goal.

Narrative hermeneutics

Hermeneutics is the philosophical and research term for the art and science of interpretation. Finnish philosopher, Hanna Meretoja, defines narrative in the context of narrative hermeneutics, "Narratives are second-order interpretations that weave together experiences by showing how they are related and by creating meaningful connections between them" (2018, p. 62). Meretoja is not alone in her contention that narrative is the primary means by which a person communicates a meaningful interconnection of experiences (Becker, 1997; MacIntyre, 2007; Meretoja, 2018; Polkinghorne, 1988).

Health care chaplains hear narrative when there has been a breach in the expected state of someone's life. The philosopher, Paul Ricoeur (2008), also describes this expected state of our future as our sense of emplotment. My experience in working with people with advanced cancer or as part of a palliative care team has been that a breach of the patient's emplotted future often requires reconfiguration work. As people reconfigure their emplotted narrative based upon their circumstances, reconstruction takes place (Mattingly & Garro, 2000). This narrative re-construction occurs when those with serious illness, for example, seek to "restore to reality its lost coherence and to discover, or create, a meaning that can bind it together again" (Hawkins, 1999, pp. 2-3). These reconstructed narratives are not worked out alone. They involve dialogue with various professional health care workers, including chaplains. In hearing the narratives as chaplains, healing can occur. In hearing the narrative as case study researchers, evidence emerges through the researcher's narrative interpretation.

Dialogue

Chaplains become a part of a patient's unfolding drama (Riesman, 2008) and a character within his/her story. This is where chaplaincy formation and the cultivation of self-awareness becomes important. Self-awareness amid caregiving helps a chaplain discern what belongs to his/her story and what belongs to that of the patient. The act of chaplain caregiving typically creates dialogue and with it a shared moment in time. An event occurs and with it, the unavoidable role as interpreters as chaplains seek "not to stand over the story, speaking about it," but as interpreters to be in "an ongoing dialogue with the story" (Frank, 2012, p. 104). In this dialogue chaplains seek to understand the patient's illness experience and interpretation of it while also seeking to understand their own experience of this shared event. Chaplains become case study researchers when they perceive there is an outcome worth sharing and contributing to the field of practice and knowledge.

Arthur W. Frank, sociologist and bioethicist, offers in *The Wounded Storyteller*, "Storytelling is less a work of reporting and more a process of discovery" (2013, p. xvi). Chaplains as case study researchers integrate a narrative interpretation to understand and communicate a patient's experience through their perception. This communication gives chaplain researchers the opportunity to contribute to the creation of knowledge through reflection and discussion of practice. To help refine the personal experience of writing a case, the first four components presented by Fitchett (2011) serve as an important framework for guidance.

1. The point

The point is that there is "something" worth telling a colleague about concerning a difference made through his/her work. These "somethings" are the substance of stories chaplains tell colleagues back in the office or the non-chaplain co-workers on the medical ward. When chaplains pause to recollect on moments that created positive outcomes, the makings of a case study are present. Amid all the details, there is usually a point concerning what was most effective about a chaplain's intervention within a specific context or moment, or with regard to the person with whom it was shared.

In the case study involving Keith, two interventions are worth highlighting. Upon meeting Keith, it was evident that he cultivated a vibrant sense of openness and curiosity about his life, despite his adverse circumstances and resultant distress with having advanced bladder cancer. Among the nine encounters we shared, it was not uncommon for him to repeat, "I need to always keep asking myself what I can learn from this situation."

Based on his sense of wonder, I discerned Keith would be an ideal partner for an intervention based on a group expressive writing practice, the Amherst Writers and Artists (AWA) Method (Schneider, 2003). I adapted the AWA method for mutual expressive writing. Core to this writing practice are the beliefs that every person is a writer and has a unique voice. The mutual expressive writing process involves picking a short poem or prose passage in advance and then reading it as a prompt twice. Participants then write for five minutes, and if comfortable, read aloud from what was written. The only feedback permitted is what was heard as meaningful or powerful. There is no critique or editing. Importantly, I mutually write alongside patients. Keith and I wrote together three times. He chose to read what he wrote each time, and each time he wept in response. I have experienced joy and a sense of the sublime when sharing this practice with patients. Meaning is created together through memories evoked, the words selected, and the emotions often aroused through writing expressively and sharing it with another as an act of connection. I included mutual expressive writing in this case as, to my knowledge, no other chaplain has published on this practice as an intervention to enhance a sense of meaning, purpose, transcendence, and connection (Puchalski, Vitillo, Hull, & Reller, 2014).

I also invited Keith into a ritual of treatment completion as he was finishing his chemotherapy. The ritual recognizes the extended process a patient has encountered through diagnosis, treatment, and its completion. It seeks to mark that completion moment in time as a significant event in someone's illness narrative and life. "In our rituals, like our stories, we narrate our existence" (Anderson & Foley, 1998, p. 26). When sharing the ritual with patients, it is adapted and customized, to the meaning systems to which a patient is oriented (Pargament, 2001).

2. A case among cases

The second component Fitchett highlights concerns chaplains making cases among the cases of other professional health care workers. By writing a case study chaplains function as narrative analysts (Riessman, 2008). Like any research, there is intent that it will provide benefit to a perceived audience. Each case is written with the recipient in mind (Riessman, 2008).

When writing a case, chaplains write for two audiences. First, chaplains write for one another. Cases are an ideal way for chaplains to learn from one another. While chaplains communicate interventions and outcomes, it is also true that "people find their stories easier to live through when they hear other people's stories" (Strauss, 2010, p. 151). There is comfort in knowing chaplains located elsewhere encounter similar outcomes and challenges. Additionally, cases are accessible as no knowledge of statistical method or analysis is required. It is evidence through a narrative.

Second, chaplains write for other professional partners to help them understand chaplaincy contributions. As Steve Nolan (2019) descriptively identifies, chaplains often come out of care encounters with improved patient outcomes, but professional colleagues sometimes do not understand how. Chaplains must describe it in a language that is not a chaplaincy code requiring a translation (Lee, Curlin, & Choi, 2017), but is easily understood.

3. Background

Case studies require a background component, which Fitchett describes as "detailed information about the patient, the chaplain, and the institutional context in which they meet" (2011, p. 13). Amplifying the importance of reflexivity in this section of a case study is Fitchett's admonition that the background includes "information about the chaplain(s) who provided the care and who wrote the case study" (2011, p. 13). A case then involves at least two characters, a chaplain and a patient, in a context. A chaplain often cares for a patient by sitting with him/her. Bioethicist scholar and physician, Eric Cassell, reflected, "Whenever two people sit opposite each other they tell stories" (2009, p. 157). This background section primarily develops narrative ingredients of the two main characters of the case.

Because cases are narratively mediated (Meretoja, 2018) with this background section, it is important to grasp what stories do. Through his work, *Letting Stories Breathe*, Arthur W. Frank (2012) helps explain how stories function. Some of these functions demonstrate distinctive chaplaincy specialization. Stories, for example, "provide people with a guidance system" (p. 46), are "the source of all values" (p. 69), and "belief systems are the performative effects of stories" (p. 108). So, hearing a story is so much more than just hearing a story.

The stories chaplains tell instruct one another and professional partners about that to which chaplains pay attention and how chaplains represent those within their care. As highlighted by clinical practice guidelines for palliative care within the United States, the core of chaplaincy work is this specialization of caring for the existential, spiritual, and religious aspects of a person (Ferrell, Twaddle, Melnick, & Meier, 2018). Also essential to the telling of any story in the context of serious illness is that it will necessarily involve emotion. Medical anthropologist, Gay Becker, wrote,

"Narrative is a conduit for emotion and a means through which embodied distress is expressed" (1997, p. 14). When patients tell chaplains their stories, emotions are revealed as they are "perceptions of significance" (Furtak, 2005, p. 6).

This background section is where the role of a chaplain researcher being a privileged storyteller of the case comes into sharp relief. Chaplains select the details and order the narrative. Writing a case is a discovery about that to which a chaplain pays attention. A case study is written in a way that seeks to tell a coherent story about lives that are disrupted by illness as Keith's was. His story could not be shared without naming some of his background such as being a loving husband, father of two adult children, a Christian with a Baptist background, an African American, and a former professional athlete. He also fiercely loved the life he was living and was forced to reimagine how it would end. His treatments did not reverse the course of his advanced cancer. This is some of what I highlighted when I chose to represent Keith. And yet, it must be named that I did not, nor could I ever finalize Keith's story. So much of a person's life can never be known from a case.

4. Relationship

The fourth component: "The heart of the case study is the story of the chaplain-patient relationship" (Fitchett, 2011, p. 13). Arthur W. Frank also reflects on relationships in narrative research, "In a dialogical framing, no one can ever take him- or herself out of relationships with others" (2012, p. 99). While chaplains are different from those written about, chaplains are never distant, nor separate. Case study chaplaincy research is a proximal endeavor. To say that people are separate denies our humanity and the I-Thou (Buber, 1970) nature of our relationships.

Chaplaincy care is bigger and wider than the intervention of active listening. It is only a part, albeit a crucial part, of our doing and being. This is an important action, but it only works best when this listening supports a patient being able to share a broader narrative. As explored above, the sharing of a narrative is so much more than the stringing together of events and details. It is a configuration of values, belief systems, emotions and how a person is making sense of the plot of one's life. It is receptively designed for the dialogue partner. The sharing of this "narrative can be a potent force in mediating disruption" (Becker, 1997, p. 25). When helping mediate disruption, healing occurs.

Chaplains are healers then through being participants in a patient's story. I admired Keith for the person he was. I grieved his functional decline and mourned his death. Because Keith had died, I, in my research role, contacted Keith's wife seeking permission to write about him. This permission seeking process became an opportunity for member checking (Braun & Clarke, 2013) regarding the details about Keith's life and illness. This qualitative research process provides a voice for the research participants confirming accuracy in representation. As a vocation that seeks to honor the voice of patients, member checking is consistent with this virtue. Like most qualitative research, the case I had originally written about Keith was deidentified. When seeking permission from Keith's family, they granted it if I changed the case to reflect his real name, true parts of his narrative, and his values and belief systems.

Keith's family added that writing a case honored him if it contributed to knowledge as they said he loved being a teacher in his professional role. Chaplaincy case study research contributes new learning for the field and will remain a personal experience. Personal because the nature of chaplaincy work involves dialogue in seeking to understand the patient's experience (phenomenology) as patients interpretively share stories (narrative hermeneutic) about what their illness experiences mean for them. The personal nature of composing chaplaincy case study research is evident in Fitchett's (2011) first four components for a "good" (p. 12) case study. When chaplains make a difference through their care, they become case study researchers when making a point (1) about their unique outcome(s). They write their cases (2) for one another as well as colleagues of other professions to help them understand chaplaincy care. In writing the background (3), chaplain researchers need to not only write about the patients within their care, but about themselves as a part of it. Last, a sense of the relationship (4) shared between patient and chaplain contributes to an understanding of the narrative, the dialogue, and the way in which a patient personally influences a chaplaincy researcher.

Chaplains interpret narratively through the experiences revealed in the stories heard and the relationships that emerge as a result. Only so much can be written about the nature of someone's life amid illness and the chaplain researcher's privileged involvement in it. In the end, writing a case is a humbling endeavor and inevitably, incomplete. In his epilogue to *Memory, History, and Forgetting* (2004, p. 506), Ricoeur writes:

Under history, memory and forgetting.
Under memory and forgetting, life.
But writing a life is another story.
Incompletion.

References

Anderson, H., & Foley, E. (1998). *Mighty stories, dangerous rituals: Weaving together the human and the divine*. Minneapolis: Fortress Press.

Becker, G. (1997). *Disrupted lives: How people create meaning in a chaotic world*. Berkeley: University of California Press.

Braun, V., & Clarke, V. (2013). *Successful qualitative research: A practical guide for beginners*. Los Angeles: Sage.

Buber, M. (1970). *I and thou*. Translated by Walter Kaufmann. New York: Touchstone.

Cassell, E. (2004). *The nature of suffering and the goals of medicine* (2nd ed.). Oxford: Oxford University Press.

Ferrell, B. R., Twaddle, M. L., Melnick, A., & Meier, D. E. (2018). National consensus project clinical practice guidelines for quality palliative care guidelines. *Journal of palliative medicine, 21*(12), 1684-1689.

Fitchett, G. (2011). Making our case(s). *Journal of health care chaplaincy, 17*(1-2), 3-18.

Frank, A. W. (2012). *Letting stories breathe: A socio-narratology*. Chicago: University of Chicago Press.

Frank, A. W. (2013). *The wounded storyteller: Body, illness, and ethics* (2nd ed.). Chicago: University of Chicago Press.

Furtak, R. A. (2005). *Wisdom in love: Kierkegaard and the ancient quest for emotional integrity*. Notre Dame: University of Notre Dame Press.

Gadamer, H. G., Weinsheimer, J., & Marshall, D. G. (2004). *Truth and method* (2nd ed.). London: Bloomsbury Academic.

Galchutt, P. (2020). "It was an easy choice. I'm not ready to die." – Keith, a 59-year-old living with Stage IV bladder cancer. In M. J. Wirpsa & K. Pugliese (Eds.), *Chaplains as Partners in Medical Decision Making: Case Studies in Healthcare Chaplaincy*. London: Jessica Kingsley (in press).

Hawkins, A. H. (1999). *Reconstructing illness: Studies in pathography*. West LaFayette: Purdue University Press.

Lee, B. M., Curlin, F. A., & Choi, P. J. (2017). Documenting presence: A descriptive study of chaplain notes in the intensive care unit. *Palliative & supportive care, 15*(2), 190-196.

Lincoln, Y. S., & Guba, E. G. (1985). *Naturalistic inquiry*. Newbury Park: Sage Publications.

MacIntyre, A. (2007). *After virtue* (3rd ed.). Notre Dame: University of Notre Dame Press.

Mattingly, C. (1998). *Healing dramas and clinical plots: The narrative structure of experience*. Cambridge: Cambridge University Press.

Mattingly, C., & Garro, L. C. (Eds.) (2000). *Narrative and the cultural construction of illness and healing*. Berkeley: University of California Press.

Meretoja, H. (2018). *The ethics of storytelling: Narrative hermeneutics, history, and the possible*. Oxford: Oxford University Press.

Nolan, S. (2019). Lifting the Lid on Chaplaincy: A First Look at Findings from Chaplains' Case Study Research. *Journal of Health Care Chaplaincy, 2*, 1-23.

Pargament, K. I. (2001). *The psychology of religion and coping: Theory, research, practice*. New York: Guilford Press.

Polkinghorne, D. E. (1988). *Narrative knowing and the human sciences*. Albany: State University of New York Press.

Puchalski, C. M., Vitillo, R., Hull, S. K., & Reller, N. (2014). Improving the spiritual dimension of whole person care: reaching national and international consensus. *Journal of Palliative Medicine, 17*(6), 642-656.

Ricoeur, P. (2008). *From text to action: Essays in hermeneutics, II*. London: Bloomsbury Publishing.

Ricoeur, P. (2004). *Memory, history, forgetting*. Chicago: University of Chicago Press.

Riessman, C. K. (2008). *Narrative methods for the human sciences*. Thousand Oaks: Sage Publications.

Schneider, P. (2003). *Writing alone and with others*. Oxford: Oxford University Press.

Smith, J. A., Flowers, P., & Larkin, M. (2009). *Interpretative phenomenological analysis: Theory, method and research*. London: Sage.

Strauss, D. (2010). *Half a life*. New York: Penguin Random House.

Chapter 12.

With an Open Mind for the Unexpected[23]
Prison Chaplaincy: a Case Study.

Reijer J. de Vries, Marja Went, Martin van Hemert, Soerish Jaggan, Geerhard Kloppenburg

Introduction

Prison chaplaincy in the Netherlands is in several respects quite diverse. We name but three aspects: religious diversity among the chaplains, different services as their tasks and various pastoral approaches in the way they work. In the research community of the Case Studies Project we try to do justice to this diversity in order to give as reliable as possible a picture of chaplaincy in the context of custodial institutions. The research community is composed of Roman-Catholic, Protestant, Hindu and Buddhist prison chaplains, men as well as women.[24] Besides their religious diversity, they also have different theological preferences and pastoral specializations. In their case studies they try to cover the breadth of their work in only one of the services provided, namely individual conversation and counseling. In this paper, the Roman-Catholic chaplain presents a case study on unexpected meetings, using a specific pastoral method and inspired by a specific spirituality.

In what follows, we first mention some characteristics of prison chaplaincy in the Dutch context as background of the case study. Then the case study, which is typical in two ways (Walton & Körver, 2017, p. 261), will be presented. It is paradigmatic in relation to the approach of the chaplain, because she daily has all kinds of short, one-off meetings, with prisoners as well as staff. It is representative, too, with regard to those prisoners who

23 The case study was presented at the 2019 case studies research conference by Marja Went. The presentation by Martin van Hemert, Soerish Jaggan, Geerhard Kloppenburg on the second day concerned the Dutch context of Prison Chaplaincy, in particular denominational working. They are members of the Research Community of Prison Chaplains, together with Ron Colin, Jacqueline van Heel, Jan Kraaijeveld (until 2019-04-08), Arjeh Heintz (until 2019-02-18) and Bart van den Bosse (from 2018-10-08). Reijer J. de Vries, as supervisor of this community, authored this contribution, using the two presentations. The presenters and the other members commented on the draft.

24 A Jewish chaplain was a member of the community for almost two years. Despite multiple requests, participation by Muslim or Humanist chaplains has regrettably not been realized.

do not, as is the standard procedure, write a note to request a visit from the chaplain. We conclude that discussing this kind of case studies in the research community leads to consensus on the importance of this way of working in prison chaplaincy, for several reasons, as well as to a learning process of which four preliminary results will be mentioned.

Dutch context

According to the rules of the Dutch Custodial Institutions Act (1998), article 41.1: "A prisoner has the right to freely practice and live his religion or belief, individually or in community with others," and 41.2: "The director shall ensure that sufficient spiritual care is available in the institution, that is as much as possible in line with the prisoner's religion or philosophy of life."[25] In order to make this work, seven commissioning authorities from the seven so-called "recognized" denominations endorse prison chaplains to provide spiritual care to prisoners. In total, about 150 chaplains are working in the custodial institutions, commissioned by those seven denominations. The proportion is based on a preference poll among prisoners and is since 2018 determined as follows, in descending order: Islam (36%), Roman-Catholicism (26%), Protestantism (15%), Humanism (12,5%), Judaism (2,3%), Buddhism (2,3%), Hinduism (1,9%). Under the umbrella of the protestant denomination Eastern Orthodox chaplains (3,5%) are also "recognized" as a denomination (Inview Veldwerk, 2017). The chaplains are commissioned by their denomination, but appointed and paid by the government. In this way church and state are separated but work together on equal footing (dual and equal).

Working according to denomination means that the choice of the denomination by the prisoner is decisive. This choice implies that all spiritual care services have to be received from the chosen denomination ("integral working"), although the policy allows exceptions. Seven services are distinguished, including three main tasks: individual conversation and counseling, discussion groups (sometimes about the Bible or the Quran), and religious services (including prayer services, reflection meetings, etc.). The other four tasks are: intake, ambulatory presence, special meetings (related to an incident, for example a suicide, a broader religious or social theme or special religious celebrations) and assistance in crisis situations. The case study that is presented here concerns the service of ambulatory presence.

---

25 Overheid.nl, *Penitentiaire beginselenwet*, chapter VIII. Cf. https://wetten.overheid.nl/ BWBR0009709/2019-01-01#HoofdstukVIII (retrieved February 3, 2020; translation by the authors)

According to the presenting prison chaplains, working denominationally offers added value as well as frictions. The advantages include:
- Prisoners receive support from their own (religious/cultural)
  background;
- University training programs have been developed for the different
  denominations;
- There are explicit relations with society, with religious and world view
  organizations (churches, mosques, etcetera) and with persons, particular volunteers who cooperate with the prison chaplains;
- "Exemplary" cooperation between chaplains of different denominations counteracts prejudices and conflicts among prisoners.

Frictions are mentioned as well. According to some chaplains the principle of working integrally, i.e. denominationally, is at odds with post-
modern "multi-religious belonging" and does not always fit the spiritual
needs of the prisoners. Another problem concerns the chaplains of the
smaller denominations who are unable to provide all services. On the
other hand, if needed, referral to other denominations is possible.

Ambulatory presence: an experience

In the research community, Marja Went presented a case study on unexpected meetings while walking on the corridor. Because such meetings
are incidental, short and diverse, Went mentioned eight cases. For that
purpose, she had to adapt the format of the Case Studies Project. She
combined the cases with reflection on her pastoral approach and her theological sources. As a Roman-Catholic prison chaplain she feels inspired by
three sources: the presence approach, her Christian background and Biblical stories, and womanist theology. Reflections on those three sources
will be connected below to discussions in the research community.

First, an experience will be presented which is representative for the
chaplain's presence approach: a conversation about a painting. After a visit on the unit, the chaplain walks back to her office. In the corridor close
to her office she sees a man, Robert, about 28 years old. She knows him a
little, because he always attends the church service. He tells the chaplain
about a painting. He shows it to her and tells her that he made it for the
final meeting in the Alpha Group. It is just a few moments before the
group will start and he would like to have a copy of his painting.

He says to the chaplain: "This is my life." He tells about things in the
painting and relates them to his life: the cross, a motorcycle, tattoos, dark
pieces on the road. He asks the chaplain if she understands the painting.
She responds that it is impressive and that it is great that in one picture he
is able to show and tell about his life. The chaplain sees his face opening

up and concludes that he feels relieved. Together they walk to the copying machine and make a copy. The chaplain wishes him a good meeting. Sunday, after the church service, he tells the pastor about the meeting and how they liked his painting. In the following reflection, the chaplain's considerations will be pointed out.

Presence approach

Can we call helping someone to make a copy call chaplaincy care? Is it important for the chaplain to do that kind of thing in a prison? And why is a chaplain doing it? Are such meetings typical for the work of a chaplain, alongside individual counseling?

When chaplains walk on a prison unit (in Dutch: "walking the ring"), a number of unexpected meetings and exchanges occur. That also is an aspect of their work. For both Marja Went and the other chaplains in the research community, it is important to take time for persons they meet unexpectedly, prisoners as well as workers in the prison.

As a chaplain Went feels inspired by the presence approach (Baart, 2001). The presence approach entails being open and unhurried for the other person, presence not being the opposite of absence, but the opposite of intervention.[26] There is no planned meeting, no specific question, no specific purpose for the conversation. It is about proximity and dignity. Starting point is what concerns the other person, what he/she wants to share: some experiences in prison, a meeting with the family, going to court, a good or bad message he/she got. It is about what is important for him/her at the moment, worries or happiness, such as a copy of a painting. According to the presence approach, the conversation is not only about problems and solutions, but about the whole of life. People are not just seen as "victims" who need advice and counseling. In the encounters there is also room for the happiness and strength of people. The most important thing is that people can feel seen and heard. Therefore, this kind of chaplaincy starts with an open mind, making oneself available, to see and hear the other person. Chaplaincy is not only successful when a concrete problem has been solved. It is about relationship and respect.

As is shown in the encounter, in this approach the chaplain is moving to the other. That is literally so: *to* the unit, the kitchen or the corridor; but also, mentally: *moving to* what is concerning the other. The chaplain and the other person are open to meeting each other and looking at each other. Sometimes the chaplain takes the initiative for a conversation,

---

26 This does not mean that intervention is excluded, but interventions should always be embedded in relational involvement.

sometimes the prisoner. In the research community there was a shared conviction that in prison this way of working is important, not only to see and hear the other person, but also to make connections between people: between prisoners as in this experience, between a prisoner and her family, or a prisoner and a guard, or between the guard and the chaplain, as the following experiences will show.

Why important and when possible?

Now the second question is: what makes this kind of presence so important for chaplains as well as prisoners? And what are the conditions for making it happen? After mentioning another experience, some reflections by the research community will be discussed.

Sometimes people ask a question because they know the chaplain is Christian (or more specifically Roman-Catholic), for example, after the Sunday service. Although chaplain Went works on the units with men during the week, on Sundays she also leads a service with female prisoners. She does not know the women very well, having only short talks during coffee and tea after the service. On that occasion, one of the women approaches the chaplain and says that on the next Thursday she will be free. After being in prison for four months, she will be going directly to Poland, to her family and children. She asks the chaplain to pray for her and to ask for God's blessing. The chaplain asks what she wants prayer for. She requests prayer for all the women who have to stay in prison, that they will be okay; for a safe journey, but particularly for her children who missed her too much; and that in her own country the family will have a good future together. The chaplain prays for the women in the prison and asks in the prayer for a blessing for the woman and her children. Afterwards she wishes her all the best and a safe journey.

In the research community the conditions of this kind of unexpected meetings were discussed. First, the chaplain's attitude is important: being open and available in order to see and to hear people. On the other hand, limitations of the presence approach are mentioned. One's own agenda can be such a limitation. Sometimes the chaplain really has to head to an appointment, or one needs to speak to somebody right away because (due to the daily schedule) there will not be another opportunity that day. Another limitation is the chaplain's receptivity. The chaplain may have just had a serious talk with someone else and may not have the inner space for another encounter. And sometimes a man or woman just asks things that have to be referred to a colleague or another worker in prison.

Another condition is the trust that prison chaplains receive from prisoners. Prisoners know that chaplains will not talk to others about what a prisoner tells him or her. Whereas psychologists or guards have to report, the chaplains can be a person, or create a place, where prisoners can talk freely, without a special (therapeutic or other) goal. And they know that what they tell the chaplain will remain confidential. Besides, the chaplains are well-known because of the Sunday services and the brief conversations afterwards in which one can ask for a Bible, a rosary or a visit. And chaplains regularly walk on the corridor. It also helps that the chaplains do not wear uniforms like many other workers in the prison do. The research community assumes that all that enhances different types of talks.

The theological foundation of these encounters is important as well. Chaplain Went is inspired by the story of Exodus in the Bible: people depart from slavery and travel to the Promised Land. But the journey takes a very long time. For forty years the people wanders in the dessert and does not know in the meantime when or if they will ever reach the Promised Land. They are worried; they complain; they ask God where He is. But in the struggling and in the surviving, God gives them manna, every day again, only manna for this day in order to regain their trust that also the next day God will provide care, enough manna to keep on going, to survive. Went sees many similarities with life in prison, where the struggle is like being in the desert of life. Prisoners do not know when or if they will reach the Promised Land. Chaplains can help them see and realize what might be the manna God gives them for the present day.

Struggles in life

There is not always a happy ending or a solution, sometimes there is no promised land to be seen. Another two unexpected meetings show how a womanist theology works as a source for chaplain Went.

When the chaplain enters a unit, a Moroccan man greets her immediately. He seems very, very confused. His movements and expressions are restless, and he regularly looks in different directions. He seems to be about 25 years old. "Are you coming to visit me?," he asks. "Maybe," the chaplain replies, "but I don't think we know each other yet." The chaplain says that she works in the prison as a chaplain from the Catholic Church. She mentions her name. His name is Mohamed. He says that it is too hot today. It is hard for him. They have a short talk about how he is dealing with the situation. And after a while he shakes her hand and says: "Thanks for the talk."

During the many following times when the chaplain visits the unit, Mohamed comes to greet her with: "Are you coming to visit me?" or "How nice to see you again." And every time conversation continues with brief exchanges about the present day, the weather, how he is doing, what the program will be for him, etcetera. Each time he is the one who decides when it is enough, thanking her for the conversations and her time.

Another experience concerns Rick, a Dutch single male, aged 37. Over a longer period, the chaplain has already had conversations with him. When the chaplain enters the unit a guard, Peter, tells her that Rick is not feeling well. The chaplain is surprised because two days ago he was not feeling bad. But now he feels depressed. The chaplain says that she has time to visit him and the guard happily agrees. Rick is worried about whether or not he can go to a mental hospital. He really wants to go to a place like that, to get more help when he leaves prison, because it is too difficult for him to do things alone. The institute of forensic psychology works on a report on him for court. Rick hopes that the psychologist will also recommend going to a clinic. Therefore, he wants to make a phone call and ask if the psychologist has already sent his report to Rick's lawyer and to court.

The chaplain and Rick walk back to the unit and ask the guard Peter if it possible to make a phone call. That is okay and they are allowed to sit in the consultation room. Rick has a package of papers all put together in different plastic bags and it takes some time to unpack and to find the paper with the telephone number. The chaplain remarks that it is really well packed. Rick answers that in this way he can see that nobody is inspecting his papers. He gives the telephone number to Peter who makes the connection. While Rick is calling, he wants the chaplain to listen and the chaplain hears that the psychologist indeed will advise that Rick be sent to a mental hospital and that he will visit him tomorrow to speak about the report and his advice. Rick feels really relieved and tells the chaplain that he is happy that she came today. The chaplain says that it is only because the guard Peter told her that he was not feeling well. Rick is surprised that the guard noticed. When they return to the guard, Rick and the chaplain tell him about the visit the next day and that Rick feels relieved. The chaplain tells the guard that he made that possible and that she told Rick that, too. The guard seems to be surprised. Afterwards, the chaplain sees that Rick contacts Peter more easily, although Rick usually does not readily trust people. She concludes that there seems to be a better connection between Rick and Peter, but also between Peter and the chaplain.

Responding to the questions asked by the members of the research community, chaplain Went explained how womanist theology provides a resource for her work. In prison she sees that life sometimes is difficult and full of struggles, especially on the units with prisoners who have serious psychological problems. For some people life is simply a matter of struggle for survival, but that it is still important for them to be seen and to be heard. And to see and to mention where people find the strength to survive. Or to stay at someone's side to help finding this strength.

Womanist theology starts with the experiences and stories of black women and the complexity of strength, forces and opposing forces in their lives (Williams, 2013). Although they hope to find freedom (literally or mentally), they realize that this is not always possible. Some womanist theologians feel inspired by the story of Hagar in the Bible. She flees to the desert and there she meets God. It is a God who gives her new strength to survive and a new vision, a new promise that she will not be alone.

In prison, too, people sometimes have been deeply hurt physically or mentally, as a result of illness, drugs or other experiences. People return again and again to prison or a mental hospital. Womanist theology taught the chaplain that one has to fight for freedom, for the happy end, but that sometimes that is not directly attainable. In the meantime, it is important not to be alone, to stay together and to strengthen each other. In womanist theology not being alone means being together with other people who stay with you, but also and in particular, together with God. As a chaplain, Went seeks to communicate implicitly the understanding that, if God is not present as a liberating God, God will be present as a God who helps one to survive and to improve quality of life. Even if one feels alone, it is with God on one's side.

Conclusion

In the research community case studies such as the one presented by chaplain Went are discussed. So far, these discussions have led to at least two conclusions. First, the experiences with unexpected meetings are only a small part of chaplaincy care in prison. However, there is consensus in the research community that this manner of working as a prison chaplain is important for several reasons.

- As the cases show, in those brief encounters people can feel seen and heard as human beings and not just as prisoners. As one prisoner mentioned: "In these last two weeks, this is the second normal conversation I have had";
- Being present with an open mind, the chaplain is not directly focused on problems and solutions. The Moroccan man just needed someone to talk to. Although she can offer some support with regard to specific questions (of Robert, or the Polish woman), she does not solve problems;

- The case of Rick shows that in this approach, chaplaincy care is not only successful when there is a happy end, but that care is also important for the sake of not being alone in surviving and being able to improve quality of life;
- In these encounters (such as with Rick), people who sometimes seem to be invisible or who will never ask questions can become visible;
- Connections can be made between people, with guards and other workers, with family, or maybe with oneself or with God;
- By being present with an open mind, the chaplain offers prisoners the opportunity to share what they are concerned about. Sometimes there is so much aggression or anger, that a short exchange can help bring de-escalation. That opens up a space to talk without violence.

Last but not least, many chaplains like these unexpected meetings. It makes invisible people visible. Suddenly the chaplain sees unexpected things in a person. This helps to see the little things that are also there. And sometimes, in the harsh world of a prison, there are beautiful little gifts to be received. From a religious perspective, that helps the chaplain to see where God is at work. And maybe the other can see things in such a way too.

According to Van Hemert, Jaggan and Kloppenburg in their contribution to the conference, a second conclusion concerns the learning outcomes of the discussions in the research community. They mentioned four preliminary results:

- Reflection on the identity of the chaplains, or on their various identities, raises several issues. Is a chaplain primarily a representative of his/her own tradition or a spiritual caregiver in general? And should one be called a chaplain or pastor/pundit/rabbi/etcetera? There is ongoing discussion on how the fact that prison chaplains work with an endorsement from their sending agency influences the way they work;
- Discussions in the research community promote learning about each other's background as chaplains of different denominations and about different concepts of the responsibilities of prison chaplains. A rebound effect is the growing awareness of one's own background. For example, the fact that the Hindu chaplain felt responsible for family members of the detainee and contacted them, was almost shocking to other members of the case study group. An open question for the research project is whether these denominational backgrounds influence the choice of the case studies?;
- There is a growing awareness of one's own manner of working, stimulated by the use of a strict format as well as by the interdenominational

composition of the research community. The question for the professional group is how this growing awareness enhances professionalization;
- As prison chaplains the group members become more aware of the unique features of prison chaplaincy in comparison with chaplaincy in other fields: providing sanctuary and not reporting confidential matters to others. And working on a denominational basis means that in many contacts religious or worldview background plays a significant role, although at the same time there is an openness towards all prisoners. Because ambulatory work (as in the case study of Went) and group work are essential for prison chaplaincy, the question arises whether the format of the Case Studies Project allows adequately enough for the uniqueness of prison chaplaincy.

Halfway through the duration of the Case Studies Project these questions are only preliminary and in the research community the need for further discussion is felt and expressed.

Chapter 13.

Is MacDonald's Freedom?

Tjeerd van der Meer

For young people in residential or confined youth care one of the core values of our open Dutch society, freedom, is, to say the least, a challenge. As a chaplain I provide time and a place to wrestle with their current situation, personal history and values. What does freedom mean when you are confined? What does freedom mean when you are addicted to drugs? This article presents two case studies that, each in its respective way, challenge our society's fundamental value of freedom. It will present some dilemmas and show what spirituality can offer young people to deal with these dilemmas.

Ralph, 15 years (confined youth care)

I knew Ralph for about a year before we sat down and talked. He suddenly said: "I would also like to go to MacDonald's with you." I responded by planning an appointment in my diary. When allowed, I take young people to places outside the institution, for instance for a walk in the woods or a talk in a restaurant, of which MacDonald's is their favorite. Ralph did not express a particular question about life, but he really wanted to get away from the group. I consider it part of my expertise to take them out into society and treat them as free individuals and, when necessary, help them express their questions about life.

In Ralph's case I start in with the general questions on how his day had been up to now; who were the members of his family; where he had been living; and what had been the cause of him being put in confined youth care. He does not seem very talkative. Nevertheless, he tells about his divorced parents, his two brothers and little sister, his grandma that cooks deliciously and his memories of warm family gatherings. When I ask him more about his mother and father, he explains that because of the divorce he and his younger brother and sister have moved around a lot and never stayed in one place for more than a few months. It resulted in many different homes and many different schools.

By telling these stories about his life, he gives the impression that he does not want to talk about any particular questions or dilemmas of life. He simply answers the questions. He does not start talking when I wait

for him to start. He is more or less "on hold," which is parallel to him waiting to move on to his next "home" now his treatment has ended. Because
he does not want to discuss his past any further (he explicitly tells me so),
we explore his dreams and future. He wants to be a Navy Seal. He is even
working for that dream by taking swimming exams. To add to his interest
in the navy, I talk to him about naval history.

In these interactions, Ralph and I can be silent for a while together,
which does not seem to bother him. The silences seem to function as a
moment of peace and space. He does not feel a need to start talking, but
does make eye contact, looks around and continues to do what he does
(enjoying his burger). Twice, in subsequent contacts, we take a walk in the
woods nearby. The silence then functions as a space to notice different
things about life. For example, I once pointed out the singing of a bird
and the rustling of leaves in the wind to him. He said, "Hush, let me hear...
Yes, I hear that too!"

Ralph says he finds it difficult to talk and that he is insecure about
what he is saying. He seems to be locked up in himself and (not surprisingly) he is not very confident that he can influence the world he has to
face. For instance, he looks down and talks quietly about taking swimming exams. For me, the goal of the contact shifts from helping him to express his questions on life to drawing Ralph out of his posture of waiting
and to focusing his attention on the beauty, instead of on the fear, of life.
By using my own interests (walking, nature, history) and by taking him out
into the "real world," I encouraged him to broaden the scope of his vision
and to aim at what he desires.

Two shocking events change our conversations. The first is the death
of his grandmother that makes him very sad. Sadness, however, is not an
easy emotion for Ralph to live with. He is almost unable to express it.
He would rather get angry. By encouraging him to talk about his (happy)
memories of his grandmother, saying that it is safe to express what he
thinks and that his feelings are of the utmost importance, it becomes possible for him to also express words of grief and to admit that he is missing
his grandmother.

The second shocking event is a cerebral hemorrhage of his father. His
father lives a three-hour drive away and Ralph has not seen him for a long
time when that happens. Only recently has he reconnected with his father
by talking to him over the phone. Ralph visits his father the day after the
incident. His father is a lot better then, but Ralph is worried and shocked
(as I can see in the expression on his face). He keeps talking to me about
this incident each time we see each other, whether I ask about it or not.

These two events trigger Ralph to express his feelings. Maybe for the first time there is a time and a place in which someone listens to what he wants to express. The counseling makes him aware of the different feelings he has: anger and grief, worries, shock and happiness and make him confident enough to take the initiative to express himself. Afterwards he reports the fact that he now can talk about things as the main result of our contact. He says: "I say and explain more to others. I talk about the things that worry me. Now, I speak out, whereas I kept it in me before."

What would have happened if I had not gone to MacDonald's with him because he did not express a particular question about life? Would he have found the freedom to express himself? More likely, he would have expressed his grief in anger. I think two factors contributed to his freedom. First, there was time, space, silence and genuine interest in Ralph that made him feel free to talk about anything. Second, the repetition of sitting at the same table, eating the same burger, drinking the same coke, talking about the same topics created predictability, confidence and courage to use his newfound freedom. Not long after I asked him to cooperate in the Case Studies Project, he moved to his next group. He was not only free to express himself, but also free of confined youth care.

Richard, 17 years (self-support training)

Richard has two sisters and a brother. His father is a driving instructor and his mother a traditional housewife. They adhere to a strict Christian lifestyle. He has had many fights with his father, that never seem to end. His sisters blame him for the fights, while his mother always tries to mediate. He does have a good relationship with his brother. He romps around with him and they like to spend time together. One of his grandparents died when Richard was five years old. That had a profound impact on him. He then felt anger with God for the first time. When I speak to Richard, his grandmother is quite ill, and she must be cared for in a nursing home. Richard visits her weekly and sees his grandfather there too. They are very important to him as a positive counterpart to the fights with his father, his anger with God and the strict religious context, although they belong to the same church.

At some point Richard started using drugs, which caused him to drop out of school. He went to a rehabilitation clinic because his parents wanted him to. He tried to fulfill all their wishes but felt that they were never satisfied and that he was not allowed to make his own choices. He felt like the black sheep of the family and wanted to get away to live his own life. With permission of his parents, he started to work on that perspective at a self-support training. His coach approached me with a request for counseling. He indicated that Richard gets stuck on what he wants. He has been raised in a family with strict values which he does not share; on the other hand, he is loyal to them.

When we (his coach, the therapist, Richard and I) speak with each other for the first time, it is clear that Richard wants to talk, wants to discover who he is and how he can manage the expectations of others, especially those of his parents. In the first conversation that Richard and I have together, he is fed up, tired and sometimes quite incomprehensible. He cannot even follow all of his own thoughts when I ask about things. It even makes him think of suicide, because everything seems so confusing. In the conversations that follow, Richard loves to talk. One question (What about your family?) is enough to get him talking.

Bit by bit I see the many elements that cause him to feel confused. At the age of five, his grandfather, with whom he felt at home, died. From early on he did not feel at home with his parents but felt more like the black sheep of the family. His not believing in God anymore, because of his anger, made him a black sheep even more. He fought with his father and sought relief in drugs. The restlessness in his head made him respond to the pressure of his family's expectations to make something of his life with passiveness and depression. That only increased the pressure he felt from his family. I respond by comparing his situation with the metaphor of a roundabout without an exit. Pointing that out acknowledges the confusion and Richard finds the image helpful.

In the conversations on his relation to his family, especially his father, I reverse the questions and ask, "What would you do, if you were your father?" and "How would your father respond if he fully understood your position?" The questions help Richard to discover what he is missing from his family. The death of his grandfather was clearly a major trauma that had not been talked about enough. When he talks about it, the anger is tangible. Richard likes to talk, but talking also makes him tired. His moods are sometimes cheerful, at other times gloomy. We speak every week for about an hour. After nine sessions, we end our weekly conversations and decide to see each other again after six weeks. In the last conversation we look at how far he has come. He is less confused and clearer about what he wants, though he is afraid of falling back into confusion and still uses drugs. He no longer has suicidal thoughts and his relationships with his family are better. He is able to talk to his father without fighting. When I one day met his father, he says: "You are the person that knows how to talk to my son." Richard's coach says she sees the positive effects that the conversations have had.

Challenges to freedom

From Richard's case study, it is clear that he is looking for freedom from the constraints his family has imposed upon him. The situation is very different from Ralph's case, in which family life and school were diffuse and chaotic, more fearful than free. Ralph was put within clear boundaries at the confined youth care and experienced a reliable environment. Richard was put in a self-supporting environment and developed his sense of will and identity. From that point of view, you could claim that they were treated well and at the right place. To a great extent I would agree. But saying only that would neglect the facts that Ralph was so suspicious of life that he could not express himself and that Richard was caught up in confusion and drug abuse. Basic freedoms of speech (in our society particularly valued) and of choice were effectively blocked for both young men, not by our systems, treatments or dealings with them, but by our lack of understanding of the convictions on freedom that young people cherish.

In our culture, we see many expressions of freedom in terms such as: "Feel free to do what you like," and "be who you are." Commercial products, like the Big Mac, are advertised as if they give a feeling of freedom. In rap songs freedom is cheered with angry lyrics and lots of nudity. In videogames, there is freedom in shooting down everyone, and in TV series, young people seek their way in life without the help of parents or other adults. These images of freedom communicate to our youth, who have to deal with reality in all its graveness, "You have to do it on your own," and "anger and money make you free." This first message is what Richard felt as a heavy load put upon his shoulders by his family. This second message was picked up by Ralph, who did not have another way of dealing with grief, for instance.

On top of that, many youngsters within (confined) youth care do not feel they can "be who they are" and "do what they want." The pedagogical staff asks them what they want to do with their life. They try to motivate them and help them discover who they are. However, at the same time they have to enforce restrictions upon their behavior and treat them in therapy for whom they are. I know from many stories in which that is experienced as a great discrepancy. The conclusion is often that the pedagogical staff ends up deliberately obstructing the freedom of the young person. When trained for self-support, many young people discover the large gap between the public images of freedom and the reality they have to face. They see that those images of freedom are a lie in themselves, or at best an unattainable dream. No one can have that kind of freedom without money, so you are subjected to expectations of others, parents, teachers or bosses (either criminal or not) to make money. That is not really freedom.

Those convictions about the world cannot change in treatment when that treatment is only focused on altering behavior and character. Such treatment does not erase suspicion but fosters it. Therefore, young people need adequate help in understanding themselves and the world. As a chaplain, with the knowledge of spiritual traditions and philosophy at the back of my head, I help them reflect on their convictions and beliefs about themselves and the world. It means talking through the questions that life is throwing at them: Who am I? What is freedom? Why is all this happening to me? Where am I going? It requires showing them how their beliefs, experiences and social environment interact. It also means showing them in what way those beliefs are helpful and in what way they are an obstacle. I search with them for alternative beliefs and for hope, courage and trust. Most important is helping them be convinced that they are worthwhile.

I explicitly talk about these things. However, talk is only talk. How can talk compete with a system that communicates, at best, half-truths about freedom? I practice what I preach by taking them away from their youth care residence into society. We walk and talk in the woods or sit and talk in restaurants as other people do. There they can find true attention to those probing questions of life and really be able to feel free because they are treated as free individuals who are a part of society. In Ralph's case, silence was essential; in Richard's case clearing his mind was the issue. So, is MacDonald's freedom? I would answer that it can be.

Chapter 14.

Agreement is Agreement? Moral Counseling in a Life-Threatening Dilemma

Monique van Hoof, Hanneke Muthert, Jacques Körver, Martin Walton[27]

The case study in this article shows step by step how moral counseling can be applied in the practice of chaplaincy. The reflection will clarify the content of and provide insight in the method used and provide a valuable glimpse into the kitchen of chaplaincy care.

In the framework of the Case Studies Project (Walton & Körver, 2017), that conducts research on good chaplaincy, the research community GGZ (mental healthcare) presents the following case as an example of moral counseling within the domain of mental healthcare. The case study describes a chaplain's counseling with a fifteen years old girl, Esther[28], who is struggling with the agreement that she made with a friend: when one of them would take her own life, the other would follow within a year. Now that the moment is approaching that a year has passed since her friend actually did kill herself, Esther feels a strong pressure to stick to her agreement. Her therapist signals that she does not know how to break through the agreement, and she suspects that the persistency is caused by a form of autism. Until now cognitive interventions seeking to make the client change her mind have been unsuccessful, and the year is almost over. The chaplain opts for moral counseling.[29] When, in difficult circumstances,

---

27 With thanks to the present research community Case Studies GGZ: Marie-José Bolhuis (GGZ NHN), Marianne Heimel (GGZ Rivierduinen), Ruud Jellema (GGZ WNB), Berthilde van Loosdrecht (Dimence), Arnoud van der Mheen (GGZ Drenthe), Irene Plaatsman-van der Wal (GGZ Lentis), Thea Sprangers (GGZ Breeburg) and Jacqueline Weeda-Hageman (GGZ Rivierduinen). This paper was published earlier in Dutch: Van Hoof, Muthert, Körver, & Walton (2019).

28 Esther is a pseudonym. Information has been anonymized as much as possible. The client has signed a statement of consent, in which she consents to the use of the case in research and publications.

29 The method used by the chaplain is inspired by moral counseling as developed by De Groot (2008). Because of the specific setting in mental healthcare, where it is not always possible to carry out an extensive examination of values, the chaplain has adapted the method as described above. The core is the examination of values with respect to the dilemma experienced by the client, in which various perspectives (client's and important others), are investigated. The content of the discussion is written down so the client can re-read it and can also consult with important others. In that way, the client can arrive at a well-considered choice.

clients have to make an important moral choice, with which they should be able to be at peace, also in the near future, then moral counseling is an appropriate approach. In addition, the chaplain is well-trained in it.

The counseling consisted of four sessions. In the first two sessions, moral counseling took place. The third session involved ritual guidance aimed at grieving and at reinforcing the road that the client has chosen. The last session was a winding up and aimed at the future. As moral counseling is our theme, the present description will concentrate on the first two sessions. Within them, the research community distinguishes nine interventions that make a crucial contribution. The therapist is present at both sessions.

First session

Esther and the chaplain meet in the therapist's room. After a brief introduction, the chaplain says that the therapist has told her that Esther is struggling with a difficult issue, but that she would like to hear the story straight from the horse's mouth. Esther stares at the floor and is wiggling her legs uneasily. Then she says very quietly, "Agreement is agreement. I think it's very important to stick to my agreements." She does not detail the content of the agreement. The chaplain remarks that she very much appreciates it when people stick to agreements. With this, she captures Esther's attention, who looks up, surprised. The therapist, too, sits up. The chaplain adds that life is much easier and more pleasant if people stick to their agreements. "If we didn't, it wouldn't have been possible to have this meeting today at this time. But sometimes agreements have to be reviewed because for all kinds of reasons you're unable or unwilling to stick to them." The chaplain deliberately does not directly pursue the problematic nature of Esther's agreement and her perseverance in this respect. *(Intervention 1. Creating space for the human value of making agreements as well as for the struggle that this can involve.)*

Next, the chaplain invites Esther to tell her something more about the agreement. Esther says, again in a low voice, that she made the agreement with her best friend that when one of them would take her own life, the other would do so too. The chaplain reacts by saying that it must be a very important friendship if together you agree to put your lives at stake. Esther starts crying and says that she misses her friend. The chaplain invites her to talk about her friendship. *(Intervention 2. The invitation to talk about this friendship provides a different perspective on the relationship between both girls than the one of a problematic agreement.)* Esther says that she had met her about two years ago in a care institution and that it clicked immediately between them. They had lots of fun. That experience had been new for Esther.

Prior to that time, she never had had friendships, she had often been bullied in school and she did not have a sense of belonging. She was lonely. The new friends did not want to lose what they had found in each other.

The chaplain asks what exactly it was that had got Esther to make this specific agreement. Esther says that she assumed that, when they would make this agreement, it would protect them against suicide, precisely because the other one's life would be at stake. The chaplain replies, "Your own life may sometimes make you feel that it's worthless, but your friend's life, you want to fight for that!" Esther looks the chaplain straight in the eyes and says in a clear voice, "Yes, that's how it is." "And," the chaplain continues, "for you, the agreement was not about dying together, but about being able to cope with life together." *(Intervention 3. The chaplain labels Esther's interpretation of the agreement as "being able to cope with life together" in friendship.)*

Esther starts wiggling again, says that she would like to stop. She wants to go back to the ward. The chaplain adds that she sees that her last remark has touched Esther. That Esther will miss her friend very much is what grieving is all about. *(Intervention 4. By acknowledging the loss, Esther will gradually be able to recognise and acknowledge her sorrow and her loss.)* Esther is crying softly. She looks at the chaplain and says that she wants to go to the ward. The chaplain agrees; it is enough for today. Respecting Esther's boundaries is important for the safety of the contact. The therapist brings Esther back to the ward. On her return, the therapist indicates that she is satisfied with the depth of the conversation. She sees a new perspective and she has the feeling that Esther might feel this too.

Second session

The second session takes place a week later; three days before the first anniversary of the date when Esther's friend took her own life. Upon entering, Esther huddles in a chair, her head down. She talks even more quietly than the first time. The chaplain asks her if she can say something about what is going on inside her. She shrugs and remains silent. After some time, the chaplain says that it must be a difficult week for her, with all the memories of the events of a year ago. Esther nods almost imperceptibly. Then the chaplain decides to structure the conversation. First, she briefly recapitulates the first conversation. She writes on the whiteboard, "Agreement is agreement. If one takes her own life, the other will do so too." Esther looks up. Below this, the chaplain writes what this agreement means to Esther, "The agreement is made to protect both of you against taking your own lives." She checks with Esther if what is written is correct. Esther nods. What the agreement exactly meant to her friend, Esther does not know. Her friend has always said, though, that she would kill herself when she would live on her own. Just before she did do that, she had gotten her own place to live. The last time that they saw each other, on the day before the suicide, Esther had said to her, "Don't make me sing!" That too was part of the agreement. If it actually would happen, Esther would sing a song at her friend's funeral service. (She could not sing at all and it would sound terribly off key.) The chaplain translates Esther's "Don't make me sing," as a cry for help, "Don't abandon me, I want to stay here, I think life is worth living." *(Intervention 5. By paraphrasing the request 'Don't make me sing!' at an existential level, Esther is being acknowledged in her deepest distress.)* Esther nods visibly, but her words are inaudible.

Then the chaplain asks why Esther thinks that life is worth living. She writes that down, too. Esther indicates that she has hopes for a better life. Moreover, she does not want to cause her family, and the friends whom she has acquired in the meantime, to experience the pain that she herself is feeling because of her friend's death. The chaplain labels this as love for and from the people around her. She also asks why Esther would want to die. Esther replies that she does not see any benefits and reasons why she should live. And she would want to die because of the agreement with her friend. *(Intervention 6. In this search the values regarding the agreement, and the issue of a life that is or is not worth living, are put side by side in an orderly way, inspired by De Groot's [2008] moral counseling method.)* Next, the chaplain asks Esther which choice she now makes, seeing all this together. Esther says that she would like to choose life, and she cries. After a silence, the chaplain says that Esther has had lots of difficulties in her past, and that the friendship with her friend must have been a breath of fresh air for her. That with that friendship her hopes for a better future had increased. *(Intervention 7. Here the way in which friendship is valuable to Esther is used to make a connection between the past and the future.)* Esther wants to go back to the ward. They say goodbye and Esther walks back with her therapist. The chaplain promises to bring photos of the whiteboard to the ward later in the day. *(Intervention 8: Through the photos, Esther tangibly receives her considerations as discussed together. This will reinforce her awareness that she is seen and heard in her choice.)*

In the afternoon the atmosphere on the ward is tense. The staff members act in a brusque manner and appear to feel disturbed in their work. The chaplain sits down quietly with Esther. She appears more relaxed than that morning and is glad to have the photos. They agree that the chaplain will come to see Esther on the day of the anniversary. She appreciates that. Finally, the chaplain has a chat with the therapist, among other things about the atmosphere. The therapist says that the team has had a difficult time. Recently there has been another suicide. A desire for control is the reason for the team to want to make firm agreements with Esther, in order to protect her (and themselves) against yet another suicide. The chaplain argues that, after their conversations, support and trust will be most helpful for Esther, by *holding*, co-experiencing the other person's emotions without interpreting or wanting to change them, all this in addition to protection (with "firm" and restrictive measures like not being allowed to go out and, if necessary, room searches). The therapist will discuss the matter in the team meeting. *(Intervention 9: Linking core values within the conversations with the chaplain, including safety and trust in Esthers own judgement and strength, with the daily reality on the ward where protection is central.)*

Reflection

With Esther the chaplain searches for space to examine the agreement, made by the client, regarding its value and meaning. To that end, she utilises Witvliet's (2003) thoughts. In his book *Het geheim van het lege midden* ("The secret of the empty center"), Witvliet examines the meaning of the biblical prohibition of images. The meaning and significance of this prohibition are, according to Witvliet, located in their protective function. In that way, the prohibition of images protects conceptual thinking against fixations that occur time and again, in order to create space for receptivity. That is related to Gadamer's (2015) philosophical hermeneutics, which considers understanding the other to be a fundamental human activity. Conversations that put "understanding" first and foremost, seek to unravel familiar frames of interpretation. In doing this, traditional meanings are made explicit and interpreted once again by all participants. In that way, an "empty space" contributes to the creation of new meanings and leads to new perspectives. With Esther, the perspective of friendship sheds a different light on "the agreement." The method of moral counseling requires an ongoing tuning in to what is presenting itself in the counseling.

In the second session, the examination of values (moral counseling) is intensified and concretely written out on the whiteboard. This structured way of working creates order in the various values that are important for the dilemma. That makes it easier to gain a clear view of all the thoughts and emotions that are part of it. By writing down everything, thoughts and emotions are briefly put outside the self. Considering one's own values from a distance in this way, also supports the development of a new perspective on the dilemma. Finally, because various perspectives (Esther's and her friend's) are also considered, space is created for revising the agreement that they once made together in the past, without having the feeling that she is abandoning her friend.

References

De Groot, J. (2008). Moral counseling voor de patiënt als pendant voor moreel beraad. *Tijdschrift voor Gezondheidszorg en Ethiek, 18*(4), 107-111.

Gadamer, H.-G. (2015). *Waarheid en methode. Inleiding in de filosofische hermeneutiek.* Nijmegen: Vantilt.

Van Hoof, M., Muthert, H., Körver, J., & Walton, M. N. (2019). Afspraak is afspraak: Moral counseling bij een levensbedreigend dilemma. *Tijdschrift Geestelijke Verzorging, 22*(94), 36-40.

Walton, M. & Körver, J. (2017). Dutch Case Studies Project in Chaplaincy Care: A Description and Theoretical Explanation of the Format and Procedures. *Health and Social Care Chaplaincy 5*(2), 257-280.

Witvliet, Th. (2003). *Het geheim van het lege midden.* Zoetermeer: Meinema.

Chapter 15.

You Can Remove a Person from the War, But Not the War from a Person

Gertjan Jorissen, Carmen Schuhmann, Theo Pleizier, Jacques Körver, Martin Walton[30]

The following case description touches on a painful chapter in the Netherlands' national history: the deployment of Dutch soldiers in the Dutch East Indies. The description deals with an army chaplain's home visit to Mr. Klaas[31], 89 years old and a veteran of World War II as well as of the Dutch East Indies. Just like many Dutch East Indies veterans, Mr. Klaas has PTSD related symptoms that only surfaced later in life. He has received extensive treatment, but eventually it became clear that the PTSD was untreatable. He has many residual complaints, including frequent nightmares. In the past, Mr. Klaas had contacted his own local pastor in order to be able to tell his story, but this came to nothing, according to Mr. Klaas because the pastor was not familiar with military lingo. The chaplain contacted Mr. Klaas at the request of the care coordinator of ABP (the pension fund from which Mr. Klaas receives a military disability pension). The care coordinator had sent an email in which he described Mr. Klaas as a veteran who could not be further treated, but who had an urgent need to talk about his past. However, he had no one in his environment who would be able to understand his story.

The chaplain is 57 years old and has been a chaplain for almost 30 years, initially in the Navy and the Marines, with whom he was regularly deployed, and since four years in veteran care. His involvement with veterans is nourished by his own experiences of being deployed. He knows what kind of impact deployment has, also on relatives and friends. In his work with veterans the chaplain uses, first and foremost because of the size of his field of activity, criteria for engaging or not engaging in conversations. For the "old generation veterans" (WW II, Dutch East Indies, Korea), one criterion is that the conversations should touch on the "deeper

---

30 This paper was previously published in Dutch: Körver, Jorissen, Schuhmann, Pleizier, & Walton (2019).

31 Mr. Klaas is a pseudonym for the veteran, who has filled in an informed consent form for the use of the anonymised case for publication. The fragments of the conversations come from the verbatim reports that the chaplain wrote from memory after the conversations.

layers" of moral damage, working through matters and meaning making. (For low-threshold conversations there are trained prevention workers in the care for veterans.) The chaplain has specifically emphasized this "depth component" in the first conversation with Mr. Klaas. They agree that feelings of loneliness, guilt and shame, etcetcetera, will not be avoided in the conversations, but that Mr. Klaas himself always can determine when and how he will raise his painful experiences, without the chaplain "digging" for them. Subsequently, the chaplain visits Mr. Klaas in principle every four weeks, the focus of the first couple of conversations being to gain his trust.

In the present case description, the conversation during the seventh home visit is central. In this conversation, several painful episodes in Mr. Klaas' life are raised explicitly. First, through a casual question from the chaplain about Mr. Klaas' exact age, his difficult childhood emerges, in particular his problematic relationship with his mother:

> Mr. Klaas: Ninety years ago, I still was inside the woman who put me into the world.
> Ch (Chaplain): Your mother...
> Mr. Klaas: That was no mother.
> Ch: No?
> Mr. Klaas: No, she was a bitch.
> Ch: You talked a bit about it last time.
> Mr. Klaas: She was a rotter.
> Ch: And why...?

Mr. Klaas then talks about his mother's physical and mental violence towards him and his younger brother and about his parents' violence towards each other. The chaplain comments that it was no "loving nest" in which Mr. Klaas was born. Mr. Klaas acknowledges this and a little later he goes on talking about the theme of "love," which turns out to be a bridge to talking about his relationship with his wife and, via a description of the impact of his war past on this relationship, also about his war trauma:

> Mr. Klaas: My dad had a difficult life with her too. And he was so crazy, so unbelievably crazy about her. And when I think back on that, he didn't know what love was. And it has left me with quite some problems. Because you tell me, what *is* love actually? Yes, when you're crazy about someone. I was crazy about my wife, but with her I didn't know what love was either.

Ch: And yet you always talk very lovingly about your wife, with loads of love.

Mr. Klaas: Yes, my wife, she *was* love. She has had to swallow so much from me. She was such a good girl. I've never laid a finger on her, but I've done wrong to her mentally. I've been a rotter to her. That's what I heard later in [name of a treatment center he has been in].

Ch: To go a whole step further now: you've been diagnosed with PTSD quite late in life. But did you know at that time that something was wrong with you?

Mr. Klaas: I just had tropical madness.

Ch: And that made you react towards your wife the way you did.

When, after this, Mr. Klaas's complaints and treatment are mentioned in the conversation, he comments that, prior to his treatment, he "always has had to do everything on his own." He did not talk about his war experiences, not with his wife, nor later with his children:

Mr. Klaas: But about the Indies... not a word!

Ch: Never talked about it.

Mr. Klaas: I was the ideal husband and that's how it had to stay. And for the children I was the ideal dad. It's only now that I'm starting to tell them a teeny little bit.

Ch: But you already did have nightmares. Were you able to explain that to her?

Mr. Klaas: I always just said that it was OK. I didn't know how to explain it. At the moment itself you don't experience it all that much. You think it's normal. Just like shooting someone is very normal, too. These are separate things.

Ch: Didn't it make you very lonely not to be able to share all of this?

Mr. Klaas: Yes, terribly, that's exactly the right word! And yet I wasn't. You also have the feeling that you're being led. You're walking there, but you could as well have been walking somewhere else. And then maybe that would have been the end of you. I've been spared after all. But so, did I do all these things? I can't explain it.

Ch: You clearly feel the need to talk about it now.

Mr. Klaas: Yes, with you. From soldier to soldier. You're not an ordinary reverend.

In this fragment, for the first time in the conversation Mr. Klaas touches on the question how to interpret the war actions carried out by himself. He does this rather indirectly; he doesn't name concrete, personal experiences but talks in rather general terms and indicates that he is unable to explain "it." The ambivalence in Mr. Klaas' story is striking, "you thought it was normal," yet obviously at the same time that's not what he thinks, "so did I do all these things?" In the description of his role as a husband he is ambivalent too: "I've been a rotter to her" in the previous fragment (and the same designation that he uses for his mother in the first fragment) versus "I was the ideal husband" in the present fragment.

The chaplain's way of working in this conversation can be described as gently moving with the story and carefully considering every time what to react to and what not. For instance, he consciously opts to let pass, for the time being, the question of responsibility for other people's deaths during the war. In these considerations, the chaplain uses, among other things, his knowledge of processing strategies and problems around traumas. With the words "loving" and "lonely" he twice proffers "existential language" and in doing so he makes a movement towards what he calls the "deeper layer," in particular the layer of working through the war experiences. When Mr. Klaas talks about "love" as something unfathomable (on the one hand, with his wife "he didn't know what love was," and on the other hand, "his wife *was* love"), this appears to open a way towards talking about events that are difficult to fathom – "separate things" – in his war past. Mr. Klaas labels the term loneliness as "exactly the right word," after which he gives a religious charge to that loneliness, in that way downplaying it. He was lonely and "yet he wasn't." From this religious perspective, he appears to be able to look warily at painful moral questions around his war past. What the chaplain expressly does not do is to proclaim value judgements regarding the narrative, or to keep asking about the ambivalences in it. When Mr. Klaas's religiosity, as a committed member of the Protestant Church in the Netherlands, surfaces – "you're being led," "I've been spared" – the chaplain does not capitalise on it in a "missionary" way. Yet at the same time, the chaplain is regarded by Mr. Klaas as a church official. Mr. Klaas addresses him as "padre" and is able to introduce religious language fairly indirectly, in the knowledge that this will be understood.

Most of the chaplain's interventions in the conversation as a whole are "small" questions or remarks, close to the narrative, encouraging Mr. Klaas to tell more about his life or to nuance what he has told. This is typical of the chaplain's biographical way of working, in which stimulating the telling and re-telling of the life story, including painful episodes, stands central. During a large part of his life, Mr. Klaas did not speak about his painful past. When eventually he did, it was in the setting of trauma treatment, often painful for him. The chaplain understands the problems in Mr. Klaas's life story not primarily through the "massive" diagnosis of PTSD, but rather through the relatively new theory of "moral injury." This theory provides a different and broader explanatory model for the problems with which veterans are struggling when returning home: the moral impact of war results in a loss of trust in the world and in themselves. According to the chaplain, in order to regain trust mildness is crucial. Hence, the aim of the guidance is not only that the life story can be told, including painful episodes, but also that it will be told with mildness and gentleness towards oneself and others. In this conversation, the latter aim can be seen, e.g. when the chaplain labels "the woman who brought him into the world" as mother; when, reacting to Mr. Klaas's assertion that with his wife "he didn't know what love was," he counters that he always talks about his wife with lots of love; or when, after Mr. Klaas's harsh self-reproaches about the negative impact of his problems on his wife, he interprets them in terms of PTSD. Within this conversation, these interventions do not seem to have the effect of a milder perspective. The chaplain does not press the issue when Mr. Klaas does not react to the encouragement to be milder.

A result of the guidance that is visible in this conversation, though, is that Mr. Klaas, albeit still somewhat indirectly, enunciates moral questions about his war past outside of a treatment setting. This appears to be related to a second outcome: Mr. Klaas talks about painful events in his life without physically tensing up. In previous conversations, moments of tensing up regularly occurred, and Mr. Klaas was unable or unwilling to go on talking. In the conversations, Mr. Klaas regularly reports that they give him strength. These outcomes obtain more (and sometimes: only) meaning in light of the accompaniment process as a whole. They do not seem completely explainable through the interventions within one specific conversation, but only in the context of the prior contacts, including the building of trust in the first couple of conversations. The later conversations, too, turned out to provide more significance to the outcomes mentioned above. A few conversations after the one described here, Mr. Klaas tells the chaplain in detail about his personal war experiences and his own actions in the Dutch East Indies.

The fact that the chaplain is a representative of the military as well as of religious life is a condition for these outcomes. A second condition is the time that the chaplain takes, the fidelity with which he visits every couple of weeks. It is the chaplain's experience that a minimum of ten conversations is needed for the life story to come up. Stories around events about which silence has been kept for decades, and that are colored by guilt and shame, are not readily told. The present case description shows the kind of specific and time-intensive attention demanded in the accompaniment of the rapidly shrinking (because of their age) group of "elderly veterans."

References

Jorissen, G., Schuhmann, C., Pleizier, T., Körver, J., & Walton, M. N. (2019). Je kunt een mens uit de oorlog halen, maar de oorlog niet uit een mens. *Handelingen. Tijdschrift voor Praktische Theologie, 46*(2), 33-37.

IV.   Case Studies Research and Professionalism

Chapter 16.

What Does Participation in the Case Studies Project Mean for One's Professionalism?

Preliminary Findings and Topics

Jacqueline Weeda, Hanneke Muthert

Introduction

In the previous chapters the general outline of the Dutch Case Studies Project (CSP) has been clearly introduced. Along with specific research goals of the project as a whole, such as an increase in knowledge on good spiritual care practices as agreed upon by professionals, the project also stimulates the research literacy of the participating chaplains. An interesting question therefore is, what do they learn? How do they reflect on the research process in which they are involved? What do they recognize as significant for their own professional practice? In this contribution one of the members of the research community mental health care elaborates on her experiences over the last two years. She has participated in the project from the very beginning. After introducing her research community, she describes a number of active ingredients that so far seem to be constitutive, followed by some critical issues that have been brought up. In conclusion she reflects on the question what it means to her as a professional to participate in the CSP.

The research community mental health care

In 2016 we started with ten chaplains from the field of mental health care: one man and nine women. We did not know each other beforehand. We have different worldviews. Some of us are affiliated with religious or humanistic institutions (Protestant, Roman-Catholic, Humanist or Buddhist); others are not. During the first two years two women left, and one new male member joined the group. A senior researcher chairs our meetings and monitors the process.

Three times a year we have full-day meetings. Depending on the scheme we discuss one or two new cases, following the case studies format (Walton & Körver, 2017). In addition, we discuss the second version of one or two cases with adaptations from prior discussions. To support the process of writing a good final version, one of the chaplains undertakes the task of writing a meticulous report of the discussions.

Now that we have been working for more than two years, we have all written one case study and some of us have already delivered a second case. After collecting the first ten cases, we started to look more selectively for what is still missing in our compilation. What kinds of cases do we need to provide a comprehensive picture of our work: chaplaincy in mental health care? As the case study format focuses on direct client contacts, we are limited to writing on those activities.

In retrospect, we experience that the quality of our writings and discussions has significantly improved. In the beginning there was a tentative scanning of each other's work caused, on the one hand, by hesitance on the part of the submitter to disclose one's views on what one considers to be an example of a good practice and, on the other hand, (the anticipation of) critical responses by other members. That has since been replaced by an atmosphere of connectedness, cheerfulness and trust. That enables us to ask critical questions in a respectful manner. It is that attitude that makes me consider my participation in the CSP really enjoyable. The discussions are critical but meaningful. By sharing we come closer to the topics we (dis)agree upon.

Active ingredients
In the following section I will present some of the common themes and experiences that seem to me to be important in the cases.

The absence of judgment
In their evaluations, clients recognize and appreciate the non-judgmental nature of chaplaincy counseling. For example, when a chaplain assisted in writing down the story of a young woman, Franka, the script enabled her to look at herself from a new perspective. That hard-copied story of her own life offered Franka a comprehensive form of what she experienced as meaningful. After sharing it with her caregivers, she felt more accepted in her hobby of playing with dolls and her need to be on her own for a couple of hours a day. It also became clear what Franka appreciated in the attitudes of her caregivers and what not.

Taking someone under one's wing
Clients often need to wait. They may be on a waiting list for treatment, or they may wait to be transferred to another department. Those pauses ask for patience and perseverance, but one often feels like one's life is on hold. Cases show that chaplains take some of these waiting clients under their wings. For example: one of the cases is about a man who waited for several months to be enrolled in behavioral therapy. The chaplain told the

research group that she invited this particular client, who was experiencing serious difficulties in bridging that period alone, to meet regularly. It turned out that several colleagues recognized this practice. The observation that we share this habit came to me as a surprise, especially since it is not strictly a part of our tasks. Such observations contribute to a feeling of connection between us as members of the research community.

Appropriate rituals and imaginative forms

Spiritual caregivers are creative in the design and use of appropriate rituals and playful forms. For example, they turn to music when difficult or ambivalent subjects like death are confronted, but words are not easily found. One chaplain unleashed a balloon with a message for a deceased girlfriend on the anniversary of her death. In another situation the chaplain suggested to a client to draw an animal that the client admired, an image that ultimately supported him to assume a renewed and longed for identity. In one case, the chaplain used a "close reading" of the client's paintings. By talking about his own work, the client arrived at a better understanding of what was meaningful to him. Chaplains employ sources from art, literature, poetry and nature for various purposes. The core common aspect seems to be the appropriateness of these interventions, in which timing and attunement to the conversation partner are crucial.

How to endure difficult behavior

Clients can be quite sad or cynical; they may express their despair or show their anger. Chaplains seldom ask clients to behave differently, but instead they try to stay with the client and remain calm. By doing so, chaplains demonstrate how to endure such behavior. Cases seem to indicate that clients like all human beings need live examples of people who are able to cope with or endure pain or sadness. Chaplains seem to be able to function as identification figures in these circumstances.

Critical issues

Besides fruitful, enjoyable and constructive ingredients of chaplaincy in mental health care, we also encounter critical issues in our discussions. I will list five important issues here.

Distance and proximity

Chaplains invest in relations and proximity, thereby coming close to the client's essential concerns. Cases show that chaplains meticulously follow their clients' thinking and acting, asking questions that help others to understand themselves better. A critical issue that puzzles us is: what is the specific value and significance of proximity? Is it in itself an active ingredient, or is it a "facilitator" through which other active ingredients can have an effect, such as asking the right questions, or being non-judgmental? What kind of personal traits or gender characteristics support proximity constructively and which ones do the opposite? We hope that new cases will shed some light on these questions.

To change or not to change?

There is a tension between, on the one hand, the notion that as a matter of principle chaplains do not set such clearly defined goals the way treatment plans do, while on the other hand chaplains do hope for meaningful changes and are convinced that their practices do make a difference. Cases in our group do, in fact, show examples of changed behavior and emotions. How can we speak fruitfully about the tension? Different aspects come to the fore.

The research format asks the researcher to note concrete results or effects of the interventions in a specific case and also asks the researcher to define what the chaplain was aiming at. Our group members were not used to that type of reflection, but by practicing it, we made progress. Cases mention changes in relation to one's life story, self-perception and meaningful sources or ideas. Concrete signs are, for example, described as: feeling less sad; a sense of being seen or heard; and expression of pleasure, pride, or liberation. Examples of goals aimed at are: finding words to express what is hidden inside, or strengthening one's own self by allowing space for oneself.

A critical issue is whether the intervention of the chaplain can also be defined as successful if the intended goal is not achieved. It might for example be that during the process other goals arise that are more important. But there is also another issue at stake. The chaplain makes an effort to connect with the other person and to look carefully for what is needed. Are those efforts good in themselves? (Kolen & Vosman, 2019). Sometimes results are felt, but are hardly visible. A related topic concerns the question whether we are able to describe conclusively *what* has changed. Sometimes we have the impression that we are close to the right description of something, but that we just cannot grasp exactly what has made the intervention valuable.

Describing the effects and the intended goals is also challenging for another reason. We work in a mental health care environment in which evidence-based treatment is the dominant perspective. However, our cases show that it is often difficult to translate our aims and achievements into the unambiguous language of objective evidence. Chaplains also show some reluctance in this respect. They insist on the narrative character of their work, that, like the making and finding of meaning, is considered to be a uniquely subjective process (Boertien, 2017). However, we keep trying to express ourselves as unambiguously as possible because we acknowledge the importance of doing so.

Body of knowledge

We play with the metaphor of our "body of knowledge" (Muthert, Van Hoof et al., 2019). By that I mean the sum of knowledge, skills, wisdom and experience as a professional. We agree upon the idea that such a concept is helpful in reflecting on our cases, but we have several critical questions. What is the impact of such a body of knowledge on the interaction with a client? Is there a significant overlap between the bodies of knowledge of various chaplains? Should there be a demonstrable overlap? We are not sure yet. Future cases and comparisons might shed a light on this.

A related topic concerns the multitude of perspectives. After the initial introductory phase of getting to know the client and finding out what is needed, chaplains proceed with appropriate guidance by drawing eclectically from a multitude of perspectives. Cases show interesting varieties. Quite often awareness of specific theories seems to be absent during the concrete, performed interventions. Such action can be linked to the body of knowledge in the sense that the chaplain unconsciously, but competently acts with a set of knowledge, wisdom, skills and experience. Other examples show deliberate choices at the very moment of interaction. The critical issue in all this is: does it make a difference for the quality of the counseling if theories are used consciously or not? So far, we do not know, but we enjoy reflecting further on the body of knowledge.

Storytelling

The narrative characteristic of chaplaincy is widely recognized, and all research members have been trained in narrative counseling. That explains perhaps why in our first year of participation we experienced doubt with regard to the research method itself, whether the CSP format could fully acknowledge the narrative character of the profession. We do understand that a format is necessary for the sake of comparison and the identification of fruitful interventions. In the meantime, we have experienced that it takes time to improve our case descriptions so that the narrative character of the work is better taken into account. However, the format may exclude constructive ingredients as well. This remark brings us to the last topic.

What escapes our attention?

Our cases show clients who benefited from spiritual guidance in various ways. To support these findings, we can catalogue active ingredients and critical issues. Nevertheless, we share the feeling that we are not always able to adequately put into words what actually happened. At the same time, we feel more or less attached to the specifically inexpressible aspect of our work. It will be a challenge to get closer to ineffabilities in the near future. At the least we do apply quite a lot of words to this topic.

For me the ineffability has to do with an openness to the unexpected, things beyond control, protocol or methods. Perhaps this attitude is related to attunement (Stanghellini, 2004). If both chaplains and clients show their attuning capabilities, it explains the chaplains' modesty about their own interventions. We strongly recognize a "facilitator role."

What does participation in the CSP offer me as a professional?

I list a number of aspects.

- I experience recognition as a professional in the group. We recognize the good in each other's professional behavior. This stands in contrast with the start of the project's, when our different backgrounds and resources appeared as a challenge to conversation;
- I feel strengthened by my participation in the CSP. In my daily work I feel supported by the fact that we experience some common ground;
- Participation in the CSP develops for me a critical attitude towards my work. I more often question what I used to take for granted. Due to my participation I am more aware of the ultimate question about my presence and my work: what is it all about in the end?;
- I am challenged to relate concrete actions and interventions to my theoretical sources. By doing so, I move towards more awareness of our professional knowledge;
- I am challenged to express more clearly the possibilities that the spiritual caregiver has in relation to recovery, the dominant perspective in mental health institutions;
- I feel encouraged to position my profession in relation to other healthcare providers;
- Participation in the CSP provides insight into arguments that can be used on an institutional level to continue to employ chaplains in the future;
- Participation in the CSP brings both excitement and modesty about who we are and what we do.

Conclusion

In short, participation in the Case Studies Project contributes to professionalization. Chaplains put into words what they do in order to have an impact. Our research group shows that chaplains are interested in improving their client's situations, but that these goals are usually not fixed in advance. With our skills in connecting with the language and experiences of the client we are very well equipped to establish relationships in difficult circumstances. Such open and attentive conversation allows the client from the beginning to bring to the table what really matters. The chaplain then joins in with appropriate interventions by employing a rich and imaginative toolbox. Some of the tools seem to be present in all cases, but there are also differences in equipment. Although we make progress in our descriptions of concrete effects, our process also shows our difficulties in clearly linking specific fruitful ingredients with exact outcomes.

There is no doubt that chaplains need to make their work visible in order to clarify how they contribute to and support people's recovery processes. That is important with respect to our patients, our health care colleagues and the institutions we work for. Therefore, we are very motivated to move forward as research chaplains.[32]

References

Boertien, D. (2017). Neergeslagen in taal en observatie. Pleidooi voor vrijheid en spiritualiteit buiten de diagnostiek om. *Tijdschrift voor Gezondheidszorg en Ethiek, 27*(1), 15-21.

Kolen, M., & Vosman, F. (2019). Getuigen van het echte leven. Een zorgethische reflectie op geestelijke verzorging in tijden van transcendentie. *Tijdschrift voor Geestelijke Verzorging, 22*(94), 12-20.

Muthert, H., van Hoof, M., Walton, M., & Körver, J. (2019). Valuing one's holding to a suicide appointment. Embodied moral counseling in a Dutch case study of chapaincy in mental health care. *Tidsskrift for Praktisk Teologi, 36*(2), 81-89.

Stanghellini, G. (2004). *Disembodied spirits and deanimated bodies. The psychopathology of common sense.* Oxford: Oxford University Press.

Walton, M., & Körver, J. (2017). Dutch Case Studies Project in Chaplaincy Care: A description and theoretical explanation of the format and procedures. *Health and Social Care Chaplaincy, 5*(2), 257-280.

---

32 We are grateful for the input of the research group mental health care of the Dutch Case Studies Project: Marie-José Bolhuis, Monique van Hoof, Ruud Jellema, Berthilde van Loosdrecht, Arnoud van der Mheen, Irene Plaatsman-van der Wal and Thea Sprangers.

Chapter 17.

Interdisciplinary Work in Chaplaincy Care

Loes Berkhout

For two years I have been involved in the Case Studies Project (CSP). Participating in the project has encouraged me, once again, to reflect on the characteristic nature of chaplaincy. In this contribution, I want to report on this. More than 25 years ago I became a qualified psychologist. After about 15 years of working as a psychologist in mental healthcare, I thought that I had a fairly good picture of what a conversation with a client should look like. But as my career in that profession progressed, I discovered that psychological talking therapies were not the solution for all the problems brought up by the people with whom I was speaking. In those moments when we spoke about existential issues, about spiritual pain or the fear of death, in particular when – as often in my case – it was about the approaching end of life of a child, the language that I had learned failed to come up to the mark. In those situations, there was no need for formulating a (DSM) diagnosis, no need for a syndrome that had to be treated, and a term like "evidence based" was not at all relevant. At such moments I felt a need for a different language, for symbolism or rituals. Because of that need I eventually undertook a study of theology. Since graduating as a theologian, I am working as a chaplain in an academic hospital, initially with children as well as with adults, but since a few years exclusively with children and their parents.

One of the most important areas in which chaplains are working is care, in the broadest sense of the word. Alongside chaplains, in all branches of care other professionals are active who have conversations with clients, residents or patients, namely, psychologists, coaches and social workers. Hence, demarcating the profession's individual character is important. For what kind of question (for help) can you call upon which professional? What differentiates a conversation with a chaplain from a conversation with a professional from another, related professional group? An important distinction is situated in the language that is used. The theme of language, and in particular the question if there is a language that is specific for the chaplain, received a lot of attention in my training as a chaplain.

Of course, language is not the only aspect differentiating the conversation with a chaplain from a conversation with another professional like a psychologist or a social worker. The chaplain's position in a conversation is also different from that of professionals from related professions. That position likewise received much attention in the training. On the one hand the position of the conversation partners in relation to each other, on the other hand the role of the chaplain's endorsement.

When I started to work as a chaplain, the kinship between psychology and chaplaincy was cause of role confusion. The confusion was twofold. First of all, I was troubled by an internal confusion. In my head I was often reflecting on conversations that I had had. Was my approach or my use of language not too therapeutic? Was a conversation in which there was no talk of meaning making at all, but that had a rather practical character, appropriate in my role as a chaplain? Would I myself actively have to raise the issue of faith and/or worldview?

Secondly, in my work environment the role of the chaplain often was not clear at all. My work sometimes was made difficult by images like "that patient is not a Christian, hence you don't have to see them" or "that gentleman has such a large network, he doesn't need a chat." I also noticed it in the questions by colleagues from different disciplines. They felt a need for a kind of manual regarding whom to approach for what type of conversation.

Case Studies Project
In the past 10 years, differences between the various people-oriented professions have become much clearer to me, but when two years ago the Case Studies Project started, it seemed a good moment to plunge deeper into the matter. Participating in the Case Studies Project has provided me the opportunity to shadow colleagues' conversations and to evaluate those conversations together from various perspectives, on the basis of the important question: What is "happening" in this conversation? Before we started, I hoped and expected that reflecting together based on a fixed structure would yield new insights, more clarity about my role (are my conversations perhaps often still therapeutic?), and knowledge of relevant literature. In this contribution, I want to outline the development that I have undergone, illuminating a number of aspects:
- Themes in conversations (what belongs to the domain of the chaplain?);
- The chaplain's endorsement and its effect on conversations;
- Position of the conversation partners in relation to each other;
- Language.

Themes

In our training we were taught that the chaplain's conversations are usually about meaning making and worldview. Meaning making is a normal part of daily life, at various levels and from various perspectives: having a zest for life; dealing with the questions about meaning that accompany life (such as: why am I living; what is the purpose of my life; where will I go after this life; and will I see my loved ones again?), or meaning making with regard to coping. Furthermore, we were taught that conversations with a chaplain often happen in the context of experiences of contingency. Scherer-Rath describes contingency as follows:

> An experience of contingency is the experience of a dearth of possibilities of interpreting the situation with which one is confronted in accordance with the lines of one's own life story. Because of this, people are no longer able to attribute meaning to an event, because it exceeds the powers of imagination. (Scherer-Rath, 2013, p. 185)

I know from experience that several of the themes mentioned here are also being dealt with in conversations with the psychologist and the social worker. They too, for example, state that they are specialized in coping and managing bereavement and experiences of loss. Moreover, the conversations with a psychologist or social worker likewise often take place at life's tilting moments, moments after which life will always look different. In psychology such tilting moments are called moments of a contrast experience. So, what makes the conversation with the chaplain different?

At the start of the Case Studies Project, I thought that I knew that the difference is not situated in the theme, but rather in the approach. Where the psychologist and the social worker formulate a treatment plan and step by step work towards a goal or solution with their client, the chaplain does not formulate a treatment plan but rather moves sensitively with what presents itself in the conversation.

What I've discovered not to be there

In conversations in the case study group it became fairly quickly clear that the chaplain's apparently "aimless" presence actually is not aimless at all. All of the chaplains in our research group agreed that they were there (were present) in order to share experiences and pain, to make things more manageable for the clients by letting them talk, to alleviate loneliness, to generate peace and quiet in chaotic and stressful situations. It became obvious that many of the group members (just like I myself) regularly offer advice. We also all consult with other colleagues (treatment providers) and we write notes in electronic patient files. That does not harmonise with the image of the conversation partner who is equal to the patient. But that is an image that we as chaplains cherish: professionals who enter a conversation at a completely equal level and who, without having their own agenda for the conversation, move sensitively with everything that the other person raises.

In the conversations of our research group, I noticed that a striking difference between the conversations of psychologists and social workers on the one hand and chaplains on the other hand, was the lack of a clear contract phase in the chaplains' conversations. Where the treatment provider spends much time in clarifying the relationship as well as the goals and expectations and the trajectory to be followed, chaplains appear to have hardly any contract phase. After a brief positioning, almost all conversations move quickly to the content level. Often, but by no means always, to a deeper layer.

Vignette

The following is taken from a conversation with the mother of "Bram," a two-year-old and one of twins. The family recently moved from the village where both parents come from. Now they are – again - in the hospital.

Chaplain: "So then you didn't sleep here in the hospital with Bram?"

Mother: "Yes, we were there! (She laughs. Meanwhile Bram defiantly throws all sorts of things on the floor.) And then Bram became short of breath again. Oxygen dipped to 92. The community nurse had told the nurses here. And they didn't do anything with it. 'Cause in the protocol you only start optiflowing [a method of administering oxygen] when the oxygen dips to 89 or lower. But Bram's already having a very hard time. And when he dips that far, he's not going to be okay. Then he's working terribly hard. Then you see that he's suffering. And I don't want him to suffer extra. He's having enough of a hard time already. And with all these hospital admissions, his quality of life is not high, we think that's unbearable..."

Endorsement and its effect in conversations

As said above, I had been taught that chaplains do not formulate a (treatment) goal but position themselves as neutral conversation partners. That role has an influence on their position in the relationship. The relationship of a treatment provider (like a psychologist or a social worker) with a patient is one-sided and hence unequal by nature. As a chaplain, one would present oneself more as a person, and hence the relationship with the chaplain would be more one between equals.

Since my training I have become aware of the special role that a chaplain has in a conversation. In all people-oriented professions the personal aspect plays a part alongside the professional aspect. For a therapy to "work," there has to be a "click" with a client. Conversation partners can enter into a conversation with each other after the first introduction because they have a feeling as if they know each other already for much longer. Put differently: There has to be a positive interpersonal experience. That mysterious click has to do with factors like vulnerability, closeness and resonance. But also, with the feeling that the other person provides a safe place. De Moor describes aspects that are important in the interpersonal experience in a conversation between a client and a professional in a people-oriented profession. "What emerged as most important ingredients of this interpersonal experience were: The therapists' warmth, their respect, interest, understanding, and integrity" (De Moor, 1987, p. 72). The "click" or positive interpersonal experience is necessary for a good conversation with a chaplain too. In the conversation with a chaplain, however, alongside this shared dimension still another one plays a part, a dimension that is connected with the profession's endorsed character. With or without a religious connection, the chaplain represents the transcendent in the conversation.

In our research group it became clear time and again that the degree of equality in conversations was a bit disappointing. All of us are part of the care organisation for which we work. And that in itself implies a certain degree of inequality. What *does* harmonise with the acquired image, and what surfaced in many conversations, is the endorsed role that we fulfil.

In the group I have learned how important this endorsed role still is. We heard an impressive example in our most recent meeting. The chaplain who brought the case had introduced himself to an (African) patient as a chaplain. He had had a good conversation. When at the end of the conversation he asked if he could be of any more help to the patient, and then (perhaps unconsciously) called himself a pastor, the tone and the nature of the conversation changed on the spot. The patient "bounced up." He raised a completely different theme (his faith and trust) than the previous matter. A totally different dimension entered the conversation, one that was very important to the patient.

From the conversations in the research group it becomes clear time and again that attributing this endorsed role is an issue not only for patients, but also for colleagues in the care institution. Even though I myself do not always think that this role is that conspicuous, it very much is for my conversation partners. Since I have become aware of this, I more often position myself as an endorsed official. For example, I make religious and existential themes a subject of discussion more often. Maybe that is why nowadays, more often than previously, I am asked to explain religious (and associated cultural) standpoints and phrases.

The positions of the conversation partners

Chaplains in a hospital often have conversations at a patient's bedside. Of course, that is not always, nor by definition, the case. Sometimes we talk with family members apart from the patient. I work in a paediatric hospital. It is normal for me to have babies placed in my lap, play peekaboo with toddlers, tell eight-years-olds about Easter, all while I am in a conversation with their parents. In our case study group, all of us are working in a hospital. There are quite some similarities in the settings and in the ways in which patients are referred to us.

In the past two years I have become very aware of the fact that I am working in – even for chaplaincy – an unusual setting, where parents and children are frequently together present in the conversation. All the other supportive services in the hospital have a primary focus: the child or the parents. That fits their respective roles as treatment provider. As a chaplain I can also have that focus sometimes, e.g. when parents talk about their fear for their child's death or about ethical choices, but often I am just sitting with the parents with their child. Sometimes other relatives and grandparents are present as well. At the start of the case study research I had my questions about this. Is that appropriate? Is that actually chaplaincy? But through reflections in the group I have started to feel freer in this respect. It certainly does fit with the position of a chaplain and with a more horizontal relationship. Moreover, it also fits with family-centered care (which is increasingly the norm in hospitals). Where the family is an equal conversation partner, the child belongs there, too. Sometimes this causes conversations to proceed "untidily," in a way corresponding with a family's "normal" functioning. Similarly, in the conversation with Bram's mother:

It is a muddled conversation (three times a nurse enters, once the doctor, meanwhile Bram is also there (in bed, is fed in part through a feeding-tube), and we play with a ball and with other things than can drop with a lot of noise. I let the mother talk.

Language

A remarkable phenomenon in the research group is the use of language; everyone regularly uses images and metaphors in order to introduce depth into the conversation and to make effable that which is almost ineffable. I, too, did it regularly, but since I am part of the case studies group, I am much more aware of it and I am using metaphors in a more purposeful way. An example is the following case of a female patient who is on the ICU after a trachea operation and who is unable to talk.

> The chaplain asks her how she used to fill her days. The patient communicates with the chaplain about her daily schedules (they kept her going), her caring for others, and her singing. She also sang in a choir. She reckons that that's going to be difficult now. Even a little sip of fluid almost makes her suffocate. There is a little blue bird on her bedside table. The chaplain comments on it. "It's a present from a friend, it can 'sing'" (by pressing a button). The patient shows it to the chaplain, who responds: "So now the bird is singing on your behalf?" The patient nods and starts laughing. The patient uses the image a couple of times herself.

Another remarkable aspect of the way in which language is used is with regard to the terms that are typical for the profession. When in one of the meetings I used the term "fear of death," the members of the research group gave me a quizzical look. A term that is very common among behavioural scientists, but obviously was not understood to fit in the chaplain's terminology. I have learned that even two professions that are very close in various areas, can use clearly different terms. You have to take that into consideration, for otherwise you may well run the risk of not understanding each other.

What profit has participation brought me?

Participating in the case studies group has offered me new insights into specific features of the conversations held by chaplains and more clarity about the specific individual character of the chaplain's role. In conversations I have become more aware of my endorsed role and of how, for the other person, that role can represent the transcendent. I am also less afraid of fleshing out my role in a therapeutic way. In the group we also discuss a whole raft of relevant and applicable literature, often from neighbouring professional domains (e.g. philosophy), which I experience as an enrichment.

References

De Moor, W., (1987). *De psychotherapeutische interventie: De probleemidentificatiefase.* Deventer: Van Loghum Slaterus.

Scherer-Rath, M. (2013). Ervaring van contingentie en spirituele zorg. *Psyche en Geloof,* *24*(3), 184-195.

Chapter 18.

Towards a Distinct Professional Identity

What Chaplains Have Learned in Flanders Case Study Research

Lindsy Desmet

In Flanders, little research has been conducted on what chaplains do, how they do it and what it leads to (Dillen, Vanderheijden, & Vandenhoeck, 2018). Although there is an increasing need to formulate the contribution of chaplains in health care, written reports on interventions and outcomes are not common in this research field. In order to present the activities of chaplains, there is a need for research on the interventions and outcomes of spiritual care. In other words, if chaplains want to demonstrate the added value of their work, they need to report and substantiate their spiritual care. At this moment Flemish chaplains describe their work by charting, in personal reflection or supervision. These reflections are mostly personally related instead of professionally substantiated and focus on the personal experiences and processes during an encounter with a patient instead of focusing on the interventions of the chaplain and outcomes of the patient.

Lindsy Desmet and Frieda Boeykens, both researching chaplains, wanted to meet the need for a more structured representation of chaplains' activities and their contribution in health care. Based on the book of George Fitchett and Steve Nolan (Fitchett & Nolan, 2015) and on the research project of Martin Walton and Jacques Körver conducted in The Netherlands (Walton & Körver, 2017), a small research community of four hospital chaplains started to reflect on four case studies in 2017. The research project was led by Desmet as researcher, Boeykens as process supervisor in the research community and Anne Vandenhoeck as project coordinator. It was set up as Desmet's master thesis at the Faculty of Theology and Religious Studies at the Catholic University of Leuven (Desmet, 2017), and led to two articles in this book, the current chapter and chapter 19. This article discusses the research community from a research perspective and the importance of formulating interventions and outcomes towards others (e.g. colleagues, policy makers). The article by Boeykens (chapter 19) reports on the learning processes of chaplains during the case study research community.

Research design

In our research, three research questions were raised. First, what is the added value of a research community and the use of case studies in the context of a growing professionalization of the chaplain's profession? Second, if the research community is helpful, what interventions and outcomes can be derived from the case studies? Third, in what way can the case studies reflections contribute to the daily activities of the chaplains? The master thesis consists of two parts. The first part of the thesis is a literature review on the paradigm shifts in health care institutions, how those shifts challenge the role of the chaplain and how case study research could contribute to professionalization. The case study project in the research community is described in the second part of the thesis and summarized in the two articles in this book.

The purpose of the research community was fourfold. First, the research community provided a method to enable chaplains to formulate the interventions and outcomes of their work. The case study method was chosen because of its proximity to chaplains' daily functioning. Second, we wanted to empower chaplains to formulate interventions and outcomes by discussing their case studies. Third, the research community sought to achieve a more professional identity of the chaplain substantiated by formulated interventions and outcomes. Finally, by integrating their professional identity, the chaplains of the research community articulated what they do and what the effect is on patients and communicate with colleagues, family members, patients, policy makers and other chaplains. Various catholic chaplains in hospitals in Flanders were asked to participate in the research community. Four chaplains were chosen, based on diversity in region, age, gender and number of years of experience. They were between 26 and 54 years old and at the time, they had worked as chaplains between two and eighteen years. One of them works in a university hospital, the others in three different general hospitals. During two sessions, four case studies were discussed by the four chaplains. The discussions were led by Boeykens and analyzed by Desmet, based on the protocol of Walton and Körver. The discussions of the four case studies in the research community were recorded and written down by Desmet with the aim of enabling the chaplains to make a summary report of their case study. The report reflects on the role of the chaplains in the case study, the intervention of the chaplains, why the chaplains choose this intervention and the outcome of the intervention according to the chaplains. Based on these summaries and the recorded discussions, Desmet distillated seven common interventions and outcomes. This is illustrated by anonymized quotes of the case studies further on in this article. In the following section the background of the case studies is described. For each case study the patient (and family) is shortly characterized, followed by the reason the chaplain is involved in the case study, the intervention of the chaplain and its effect on the patient. The outcome of the intervention has in all instances been assessed from the chaplain's point of view.

The 83-year-old patient in the first case study has been admitted to the hospital several times and knows the chaplain very well. The man is married and one of his sons has died. At the moment of the case study, the patient is recovering from surgery. The first request for support comes from the geriatrician who feels powerless because of the patient's difficult recovery. While the man himself is too depressed to ask for help, the doctor asks the chaplain to provide spiritual care. During the different encounters with the chaplain, the chaplain recognizes the depressive symptoms of the patient and through reading books together, the chaplain taps into the resources of the patient. By building a durable relationship with the patient, the chaplain sees that the patient finds peace and his melancholy is replaced by a positive attitude.

The second case study is about a sevenfold encounter between the chaplain and a thirty-year-old man who is divorced and has a son and daughter. The patient prays a lot. The chaplain is a priest who does not know the patient beforehand. As in the first case study, it is the doctor who asks for a chaplain. The doctor thinks that taking care of the patient's spiritual well-being will benefit the recovery. The chaplain communicates with the patient in two ways. First, the chaplain uses open and direct questions to let the patient focus on the important things in life. Second, the chaplain enhances the patients' spiritual process by taking time to bless the patient. In this way the chaplain aids the patient in reflecting on his spiritual experiences. According to the chaplain, this enabled the patient to regain his self-esteem.

In the third case study the chaplain does not know much about the patient. The patient is dying, and a chaplain is urgently requested by the daughter of the patient. The daughter is restless and does not know if she needs to contact her brother. The daughter asks for a ritual and the presence of the chaplain for her mother. The chaplain listens to the life story of the family and integrates the story into a ritual. The patient dies after the ritual. By connecting the patient with the family and with God through the ritual, the chaplain observes that the daughter is able to reflect on her life so far.

In the fourth case study the son of the patient is told that his father will die within the next few days as the patient's condition has unexpectedly deteriorated and the patient is unconscious. Because of the nervousness of the son, the nurse calls for a chaplain, since she is afraid that the situation will escalate. The chaplain starts a conversation with the son who asks for a ritual and a reconciliation with God for his father. The chaplain tries to explore the deeper need of the son through a conversation and a ritual and acknowledges his powerlessness. The chaplain observes that the son of the patient calms down and is able to express his feelings towards his father.

Reporting interventions and outcomes towards others

As shown above, in three out of four case studies the chaplain is called by the health care team. Because of the referrals by the health care providers, it is important to report the interventions and outcomes of the visits to the team. In that way the team can gain a better idea of what the chaplain has done and the following referral will be based on that interdisciplinary work. In the case studies the health care team consulted the chaplain because of two reasons. In the first and fourth case study the chaplain is called because team members experienced their own limitations and powerlessness during the recovery of a patient. They see how the medical part of the recovery is complementary with spiritual and psychological parts and include a chaplain in the recovery process of a patient. We illustrate the reasons for interdisciplinary work in both case studies:

> Case study 1: The geriatrician notices that the rehabilitation of the patient is not going well. The health care team observes that different therapies have already been tried but did not work. The doctor shares his concerns with the team and tells them that the patient needs more than just medical care. The geriatrician asks the chaplain to visit to see if he could support the man in his recovery.
> Case study 4: The chaplain receives a phone call from the head nurse asking for assistance for a man who has just received the news that his father will soon die. The man is very nervous, and the nurse is afraid that the situation will escalate.

Another reason to refer to a chaplain is shown in the second case study. The team consults the chaplain because it has observed that the patient's spirituality has been helpful during his recovery.

> Case study 2: The chaplain is called by the team to visit the patient because the doctor has observed the patient's religious side. Although the patient is confused, the doctor wants the chaplain to explore the spiritual dimension.

During the research community meetings, the three chaplains indicate that they rarely or never inform the health care teams about what they do, even though the referral comes from those teams. They talk about their encounters with patients in an informal way, but the interventions of the chaplain and the outcomes for the patients and their families are rarely officially communicated to the entire team. Only the chaplain from the third case study, where one of the family members asked for a chaplain, gave feedback of the encounter to the team. The reason for not briefing the team is because the chaplains do not know how to formulate interventions and outcomes. One of the reasons for the chaplains to participate in the research community was to be able to express what they do and what it leads to. That is needed if they want the health care team to continue calling for a chaplain. The more other caregivers know what exactly the chaplain contributes to their care, the more they will integrate spiritual care and refer to the chaplain.

Interventions and outcomes

In the final meeting of the research community the chaplains formulated interventions and outcomes based on their summary report. Thereafter, Desmet formulated seven interventions with their related outcomes, based on the case studies, the recorded research community discussions and the summary report of the chaplains. Each intervention and outcome, based on the chaplain's interpretation, is illustrated by the case studies. Further research is needed to know if the chaplain-reported outcomes are similar to the patient-reported outcomes. What follows is a short description of the seven interventions and outcomes.

Patient-centered use of time

In the first intervention the chaplains adjust to the time the patients need from them. To quote one of the chaplains: "The chaplain visits the patient each week. In total, it involves seven visits over a period of one and a half months in total. The chaplain makes time according to the needs of the patient. The chaplain estimates how much time is needed, but the patient decides how much time he wants to spend with the chaplain." The chaplain emphasizes that the use of time is often overlooked but is an essential part of spiritual care. In addition, when a patient is in the hospital for a long time, the chaplain keeps visiting the patient even when he or she did not ask for it. According to the chaplain, this patient-centered use of time has the following result: "The patient experiences the value of long term trust relationships enabling him to enter into similar relationships with other people where there is equal room to share what is on the person's mind."

Connecting, connection and connectedness

In the case studies the chaplains connect, are a connection and facilitate connectedness between patients and their family, patients and God, the situation of the patients and their life and between the patients and other caregivers. One of the chaplains indicates that "the chaplain is the connection between the patient and his girlfriend who does not understand his needs. The chaplain tries to articulate the man's needs by repeating what he says and explaining it to her." This intervention of the chaplain is grounded in the multi-directed partiality of Ivan Boszormenyi-Nagy (1986) in which the chaplain is involved with the various parties in the patient's life, even if they are not present at that moment or are deceased. The chaplain describes the effect of this connectedness as follows: "By giving the man the chance to express his feelings towards his girlfriend, the patient feels acknowledged in who he is. He feels loved and relieved."

Acknowledging powerlessness

Chaplains are often called when the health care team feels powerless in stressful situations. The four chaplains acknowledge the powerlessness felt by the patient, the family and the team and try to connect with those emotions at that moment. "Through questions and acknowledgment, the chaplain goes along with the powerlessness of the son of the patient. The chaplain recognizes and accepts that the son feels like everything is unpredictable and cannot be solved at this moment." While the feeling of powerlessness is common to everyone providing and receiving care, it is the chaplain who puts it into words. The effect of this intervention, formulated by the chaplain, is the return of peace in these precarious moments: "The son is reassured. The son acknowledges his anxiety and tries to cope with it. The situation did not escalate but has brought the man new insights."

Broadening life stories

The chaplains broaden the patients' life in two ways. First, the chaplains walk with the patients' powerlessness and brokenness and then the chaplains try to bring in new perspectives, possibilities for the future. One of the characterizing aspects of their spiritual care is that they start off by acknowledging what the patient has lost before moving on to the future. An example from one of the case studies: "The chaplain who is a priest fulfills, through the sacrament of reconciliation, the desire of the patient to open a new perspective and thereby receive the forgiveness of God." As a result of this intervention, the patient restarts activities, brings in new ideas and undertakes new actions. He is able to think about his past, present and future. The chaplain articulates that "the patient develops a positive attitude towards the future, reconciles himself with the past and feels peace in his life."

Praying

Praying with the patient or family occurs in all four case studies. Praying is used in different contexts: to complete a conversation, as part of a ritual, to be able to say goodbye to something or someone or to get forgiveness of God. The content of the prayer is always adapted to the story and the needs of the patient. For example: "In prayer, the chaplain pays attention to who the woman has been throughout her life and expresses the difficulties that the woman is facing." Through praying, the chaplain wants to share faith, create a moment of connection and empower the patient. This causes, according to the chaplain, that "the patient has been able to find the words to describe his situation and to put the difficulties into words, which strengthens him and makes him feel relieved while sensing a renewed connection with God." The chaplains observe that praying with the patient and his or her family also has an effect on the family. One chaplain articulates that "the family is able to express their feelings, regrets and concerns to the patient. The family feels relieved and is grateful to experience faith together."

Facilitating grief

Chaplains notice that the loss of good health brings forth experiences of loss from the past, which cause an obstruction in the recovery process of patients. Facilitating grief means that the chaplain acknowledges loss and looks for resources of the patient to cope with this grief. For example: "The chaplain helps the patient to handle his loss of independence by asking the patient what helped him to cope with the loss of his son a few years ago and taps into it again." The outcome of facilitating grief by the chaplain is that the rehabilitation process can continue and is strengthened by the motivation of the patient. The chaplain notices that "the health care team reports that the patient is no longer bedridden and plays an active role in the health care decisions. The patient is motivated to go to the physiotherapist."

Formulating identity

At the beginning of the encounter, the chaplains introduce themselves and note that this already influences how the chaplains will affect the patient. While it is not necessary to have the same cultural or religious background, representing a spiritual identity affects the outcomes. One of the chaplains reports that "the chaplain represents the close proximity of God, but the chaplain also represents himself as human being. The identity of the chaplain determines the direction of the conversation." When the chaplain evokes spirituality and religiosity, the patient is inspired to look at his or her own faith or spirituality. From the chaplain's point of view, the transparent identity of the chaplain ensures that "the patient has found someone with whom he can share his spirituality, which creates safety in a bond of trust."

Conclusion

This research is the first case study research project in Flanders in the context of professionalization of chaplains and should be read as a pilot project. The interventions and outcomes in this case study project cannot be generalized but may be included as a starting point for further research. The formulated interventions and outcomes should be retested in a larger case study project. In addition, it must be examined how case study research can contribute to formulating outcomes. Each outcome in this project is formulated from the point of view of the chaplain, but there is no evidence that the patient would acknowledge these outcomes. It is unclear if these outcomes are the observed or desired outcomes of the chaplain or the actual outcomes of the patient. Further outcome research is needed to know how patients would formulate the effect of the intervention of the chaplain. In line with this, it must be investigated whether other health care providers such as psychologists or social workers also have this effect on patients or if this is unique to the profession of chaplains.

While chaplains formulated interventions and effects, they discovered that intervention and outcome language does not harm their unique identity of being a chaplain. On the contrary, it emphasizes their specific way of working with patients and their family. The case study research community was initiated in order to reflect and discuss on formulating the core of chaplains' contributions in function of better care for patients and their family. Besides better care for patients, the project developed a common language that expresses spiritual care in a way that is understandable for others, such as policy makers and the health care team. One of the chaplains said: "The research community helped me to express my work to the health care team. I feel more convinced about the changes that spiritual care can make." This article formulated seven interventions of chaplains in the case studies: patient-centered use of time, the role of connecting, connection and connectedness, broadening life stories, praying, acknowledging powerlessness, facilitating grief and formulating identity.

Even though the formulated outcomes are limited, and the underlying processes of these interventions lack clarity, the research group has created awareness among the chaplains for the sake of integrating this method into their own practice as a way to profile their identity.

References

Boszormenyi-Nagy, I., & Krasner, B. (1986). *Between give and take: A clinical guide to contextual therapy*. New York: Brunner/Mazel.

Desmet, L. (2017). *Meten en meetellen. Een empirisch onderzoek naar interventies en outcomes van pastores in algemene/universitaire ziekenhuizen aan de hand van casestudy's en onderzoeksgroepen* (Unpublished master thesis). Leuven: KU Leuven Faculteit Theologie en Religiewetenschappen.

Dillen, A., Vanderheijden, E., & Vandenhoeck A. (2018). "Wat doe jij hier eigenlijk?" Resultaten van empirisch onderzoek naar de tijdsbesteding van Vlaamse ziekenhuispastores. *Collationes. Vlaams Tijdschrift voor Theologie en Pastoraal, 48*(2), 163-190.

Fitchett, G., & Nolan, S. (Eds.) (2015). *Spiritual Care in Practice: Case Studies in Healthcare Chaplaincy*. London: Jessica Kingsley Publishers.

Walton, M., & Körver, J. (2017). Dutch Case Studies Project in Chaplaincy Care: A Description and Theoretical Explanation of the Format and Procedures. *Health and Social Care Chaplaincy, 5*(2), 257-280.

Chapter 19.

What Are Chaplains Learning by Producing Case Studies?

Frieda Boeykens

Since 2015, several initiatives in Flanders turned the attention of health care chaplains to chaplaincy research. For example, chaplaincy research regularly appeared as a theme in the annual conferences of the Flemish professional health care chaplains' association and was covered in several issues of the association's professional journal. A nice highlight in this growing attention was the invitation addressed to the chaplains to attend the launch of ERICH, the European Research Institute for Chaplains in Health Care in June 2017 in Leuven. When Lindsy Desmet launched a call in 2017 for a case study research group, it became clear that chaplains were also interested in actually participating in research. Four chaplains were selected for the project that was led by Desmet as researcher, by me as moderator and by Anne Vandenhoeck as project coordinator (Desmet, 2017). The project was set up to meet the need for research on interventions and outcomes of spiritual care and to empower chaplains in discovering, formulating and communicating their interventions and outcomes. Two articles in this book are a result of the research project. For more details about research goals, questions, outline and results, I refer to the contribution by Desmet in this volume (chapter 18), which focuses on the project from a research perspective. I will report from a perspective of guiding a new kind of learning process, a challenging one for all those involved.

Chaplains in Flanders are familiar with reflecting on cases in the context of individual or group pastoral supervision. For the participating chaplains it was the first time, however, to work with cases in the context of a case study research project. New for them was to step into a, somewhat uncomfortable, research role, conducting their own research in a systematic manner from a meta-position. For myself, as a hospital chaplain and pastoral supervisor, it was the first time I led group discussions and guided a process with a specific research outline towards a clear result: a written and commented case that provides insight into the chaplains' own interventions and outcomes. Together with the chaplains, I had to make the transfer from the familiar context of pastoral supervision to the unknown context of chaplaincy research.

What was exactly new for the participants in the research context? To answer that question the first section compares reflecting on a case in pastoral supervision and in case study research. How did the chaplains and I, as a moderator, deal with the new research context? What challenges did this new context bring with it? What did the chaplains have to learn and what did that require in terms of guiding their learning process? The second section focuses on four specific challenges we encountered in discovering and applying the new research role. The last section deals with the question what the participants have actually learned by working in a research modus. What were the learning outcomes?

Case study in pastoral supervision versus case study research

How does reflecting on cases in the context of pastoral supervision relate to conducting research with the case study method? There are similarities and differences between both methods that are not absolute but relate to each other on a continuum.

Both methods work with written preparation and processing and with further deepening of insight through conversation and discussions. Both methods require the participants to have skills in selecting, querying, researching, writing, dialoguing and reflecting. Both methods ask for an ability to step into a meta-position. In both methods, one works with a magnifying glass: a case is magnified and viewed from all sides and angles. In addition, in both methods a facilitator is designated: a supervisor for the supervision and a discussion moderator for the case study research. Both have in common that they increase the language skills of the chaplain. Through pastoral supervision and case study research, chaplains develop the communicative ability to explain to themselves and others what they do, why they do it and what they are achieving by doing so.

Pastoral supervision aims to initiate personal experiential learning in professional practice as a contribution to the development of the professional expertise and identity of the chaplain. The personal learning process of the supervisees is central. The participants reflect on a process in which they learn to become a chaplain in a particular context. The learning process is driven by the questions that the supervisees ask of themselves: what do I want to learn in supervision; what do I want to learn from a case? In the investigation of the case, the inner world of the supervisees has a high degree of relevance for their learning process. The language used to express this inner world is first person language. The interventions of the group members stimulate that personal reflecting process. The meta-position helps the supervisees to look at their experience from a helicopter view and to integrate several perspectives. The process itself is more central to supervision than the outcome of the process. The act of reflecting is more important than the reflection itself.

In the research group, the chaplain departs from that person-oriented track to focus on what transcends the person and is specific to the profession. The challenges and the needs of the profession are what drive the research process, more than the personal questions and doubts of the participants. Those questions and needs are reflected in the research format used. There is a strong focus on the outside world: the chaplains' interventions and the outcomes. Those are submitted to discussion and critical thinking in the group. A new role is introduced: the chaplain as a researcher. The request, to write and discuss in the third person language, as in the model of the Dutch research project (Walton & Körver, 2017), aims to contribute to that more generalizing level. The meta-position is strongly connected with the role of researcher and the professional. Unlike supervision, the research group is more focused on achieving a result: a written and commented case that can deliver data to be analyzed and interpreted. There is a strong focus on connecting with theoretical and conceptual frameworks. By doing so, the research group contributes to the development of the profession, whereas in pastoral supervision the chaplain is introduced into or becomes more integrated within that same profession.

Challenges

Dealing with the new research context, we encountered four challenges in guiding the learning process of the chaplains. First of all, in our research project we worked with a systematic approach to collect, discuss, analyze and interpret data out of the presented cases, based on the format presented by Walton and Körver (2017). As a moderator it was my responsibility to keep the group discussions in line with the format and to keep an eye on the timing. In order to guarantee the meta-position of the research I had to make sure the group discussion would not lead to a consultation between colleagues or group supervision. It was also a matter of safeguarding a certain discourse. Chaplains are used to telling stories. When they start telling, however, the conversation can quickly start to meander, as did happen in the group. One subject brought up another. In addition, by telling their stories, they were opening up about their daily practices and exposing their vulnerability. Personal questions, uncertainties and doubts were shared and put forward for advice. It was then my task to ensure that the focus of the group discussions was kept within the research boundaries. I had to encourage the participants to gather information which could be used to respond to the actual research questions. The chaplains had to learn to integrate a more informative discourse, alongside the narrative discourse they were already familiar with. The interplay between meandering between stories on the one hand and keeping the right focus on the research goals on the other is not possible without creating a safe conversational climate. So, I had to keep an eye on the uniqueness of each chaplain and the equal treatment of the cases. I had to find a balance between maintaining and letting go of the conversational outline and between the task of the group and the person of the chaplain.

Second, the most challenging task for the participants was to write and talk in third person language, as indicated in the original format. The writing in third person went quite well but speaking and discussing in third person was enormously difficult. It caused great inconvenience for the participating chaplains. In the end we did not manage to continue using the third person position, either in speaking or in writing. I still question whether I should have consistently insisted on maintaining the third person in the description and analysis of the cases and in the group discussions. Is the use of third person language necessary throughout the whole process to foster the meta-position?

When I look to my own experience as a hospital chaplain, I notice that I chart in patient files in third person language. By doing so I create for myself a space of conscious reflecting, carefully formulating interventions and outcomes, choosing a language that is understandable for the other involved healthcare disciplines. Reflecting on this personal experience and regarding one of the main research goals of the case study project, namely to enhance the ability of hospital chaplains to explain their interventions and outcomes towards other health care disciplines, it seems now legitimate to maintain the third person position, certainly for the final reports the chaplains are supposed to write about their case in the research project.

A third challenge we met was to foster a discussion culture in the group. Was it due to our Flemish nature or pastoral culture that there was a trend to dialogue in harmony and seek consensus rather than confrontation? The participants encouraged and admired each other, taking care of each other in a pastoral way. That was good for a welcoming and affirming atmosphere but made it hard work for me to enhance critical questioning. In this regard I have to mention the importance of time and group dynamics in this kind of learning processes. Establishing such a critical culture in a new group requires time. In a short process of four meetings, each of them limited in duration, the shortage of time was an impeding factor. Also, the question is whether the chaplains had a clear view of the goals of the project. Was it because the goals were not clear enough that they returned almost automatically to the familiar pastoral supervision context? I wonder if the opening ritual in the Dutch research project, in which chaplains introduced themselves as researchers, could help in establishing a clearer view on the goals.

A final challenge for the group was a lack of theoretical frameworks in the written cases and the group discussions. There was clearly need for more theoretical input to gain more depth in the discussions. Spontaneously, the participating chaplains remained submerged in their practice, not demonstrating sufficient theory-inspired, critical reflection. Most of the time the interventions were limited, and a lot of outcomes were labeled vaguely as "something": "something changed in his behavior when I left the room." The chaplains had to be encouraged to formulate their interventions and outcomes more precisely. Theoretical frameworks can deliver a language to do just that, a language that goes beyond a personal level and is common to the profession of the chaplain. As a moderator, I took it as a task to introduce various concepts and models to enable and discuss different interpretations of the practice. In order to enhance such theoretically inspired reflection, the project needs more elaborate description of the researcher role as someone who can elaborate on theory and relevant literature to stimulate the transfer from practice into praxis.

Learning outcomes
Taking into account the small scale of this research project and the associated challenges, the chaplains experienced what it is to grow into a new research role. They certainly still have a way to go if they wish to integrate this role in their chaplaincy. Nevertheless, the research group has encouraged the participating chaplains:

1) To take a closer look at one's own professional practices, to select one representative case, to then observe oneself but also others within that case, to describe and name one's own actions and outcomes and above all to take the time. They have learned that working in a more methodological and systematic way can change their perceptions of the case. It can also help them to take a more critical approach to their own professional practices.

2) To employ a common vocabulary, unique to the profession of a chaplain. Personal questions, uncertainties and vulnerabilities were kept out of the focus. Instead the focus was brought to bear on what is meant by spiritual care in a particular case study and what kind of spiritual care has

been offered with what results. During the research process the chaplains were trained in formulating what the chaplain did and what the outcomes were. By using the case studies, chaplains became aware of what they do and how they can communicate in a specific profession bound language, understandable for other disciplines.

3) To become aware of personal conceptual frameworks and become acquainted with new conceptual frameworks. The participants learned about the existence of their personal conceptual frameworks. That realization grew throughout the group discussions. Furthermore, they learned to conceptualize interventions and outcomes in spiritual care in more clearly defined terms. The frameworks supported the naming of interventions and outcomes.

4) The methodology of our case study introduced the chaplains to a specific view on professionalism. According to Ruijters and Simons (2015) a professional is someone who, by choice, dedicates him- or herself to the service of clients. That act of dedication is expressed in a competent and upright manner, using relevant knowledge and experience. By doing this, he or she uses and actively contributes to a community of professionals that continually develops the field (p. 87).

What stands out in the definition is the following: professionalism is the consequence of a choice. It requires a specific way of working (Ruijters & Simons, 2015, p. 86). What sets a professional apart is the drive to consistency in the following respects:
- To do the best for people, for the organization one works for, and for society;
- To act with integrity in unique situations;
- To actively connect theory and its developments to practice;
- To assess one's own practice;
- To contribute to the development of the field and other field experts;
- To focus on deliberate self-development (Ruijters & Simon, 2015, p. 86).

In addition, I would also mention the use of a profession bound language that can express relevant knowledge and experience.

What is intriguing about this perspective on professionalism is the integration of individual and collective components. Professional growth contributes on the one hand to personal development, on the other hand to the development of the field and of colleagues. One shares one's accumulated specialist knowledge, experience and language. By specialist the authors mean a personal expertise that grows from one's own interests in a combination of experiences, reflections and theoretical knowledge (Ruijters & Simon, 2015, p. 89).

That is what happened in a systematic manner in this case study research team, working with the specific practices of the chaplains and at the same time on a more generalized level. That is exactly the sort of learning outcome the chaplains gained from the research: taking their stories to a meta-level that incorporates their own practices and personal stories and at the same time transcends them.

Conclusion

Participating in this small-scale research project the chaplains became acquainted with a rewarding and promising method for working with case studies. They experienced how close the method is to their daily practice and reflection. New for them was the meta-position of the researcher and the systematic way of collecting, discussing, analyzing and interpreting data out of their stories in a common vocabulary. By producing case studies in that way chaplains became aware of what they did and achieved and of how they could communicate their contribution in interventions and outcomes. As Desmet points out in her contribution in chapter 18, this project should be read as a pilot project. Not only the results should be retested in a larger case study project, but also the interventions of the moderator to encourage the chaplains to step in the researcher role. As such, the case study method provided them with an accessible, but challenging tool to do research. Within the context of healthcare, demanding a much more evidence-based way of working, this increases the professional status of the chaplaincy.

References

Desmet, L. (2017). *Meten en meetellen. Een empirisch onderzoek naar interventies en outcomes van pastores in algemene/universitaire ziekenhuizen aan de hand van casestudy's en onderzoeksgroepen* (Unpublished master thesis). Leuven: KU Leuven Faculteit Theologie en Religiewetenschappen.

Ruijters, M. C. P., & Simons, P. R.-J. (2015). Professionaliteit. In M. C. P. Ruijters (Ed.), *Je binnenste buiten. Over professionele identiteit in organisaties* (pp. 59-98). Deventer: Vakmedianet.

Walton, M., & Körver, J. (2017). Dutch Case Studies Project in Chaplaincy Care: A Description and Theoretical Explanation of the Format and Procedures. *Health and Social Care Chaplaincy, 5*(2), 257-280.

Chapter 20.

'Oneself as Another'

Combining the Roles of Chaplain and Researcher in the Dutch Case Studies Project

Niels den Toom

Imagine that you connect two wires, the first is the role of researcher, the second the role of chaplain. What will you get: light or a short-circuit? Attitudes regarding research and chaplaincy raise primarily responses for and against the combination. Some experience it as impossible to have a twofold relation with a client of emphatic chaplain and detached researcher (Nolan, 2018). Others emphasize that their research has changed them (Grossoehme, 2011), enlivened their practice (Kelly, 2014) and that both roles are mutually fruitful (Van der Leer, 2016).

In this chapter, I want to deepen the understanding on chaplaincy and research by reflecting on experiences of chaplains that are active as co-researchers in the Dutch Case Studies Project (CSP). To do so, I start with an introduction on the relation between chaplaincy and research that uncovers the gap that I would like to fill. Subsequently, I typify and elaborate on four ways of characterizing the relation between chaplain and researcher on basis of interviews with the chaplain-researchers. Finally, I look back on the insights and outlooks this chapter offers.

Research as part of the methodical competency

In the growing attention for research on chaplaincy, a "research-literate" profession is advocated (Fitchett, Tartaglia, Dodd-McCue, & Murphy, 2012; Murphy & Fitchett, 2010). It sets the ideal that chaplains keep up to date with the best available academic knowledge regarding their profession, in addition to the already strong developed (self) reflection. Although not all chaplains have to conduct research, the "Standards of Practice" (APC, 2009 [revised 2015]) of the American *Association of Professional Chaplains* stimulates involvement in research (they call it "research literacy") on three levels (Fitchett, Tartaglia, Dodd-McCue, & Murphy, 2012). It is about the ability to understand published research and apply it where it seems appropriate (1), to contribute to a research project that is carried out by other disciplines (2) and the capacity to be a lead investigator (3). The Dutch "Standards of Practice" (VGVZ, 2015, p. 13) mentions "the ability to use the results of research and to participate in research."

This is part of the methodological competence of chaplains, which in its turn is part of the process-oriented competences of chaplains. The latter refers to "the professional, organizational and academic contexts in which the chaplain works" (VGVZ, 2015, p. 12). While the emphasis on the importance of research is described primarily in terms of improvement and legitimization of the profession as a collective, it is interesting to look at the experiences of individual chaplains as well, inasmuch as an increasing number of chaplains are themselves doing research.

The scientist-practitioner

Hutschemaekers (2010) offers a model (see figure 1) in which he depicts the ideal-typical relation between practice and research for the practitioner. The position of *scientist-practitioner* is the point of focus in his model.

Figure 1: model of the "scientist-practitioner" (Hutschemaekers, 2010).

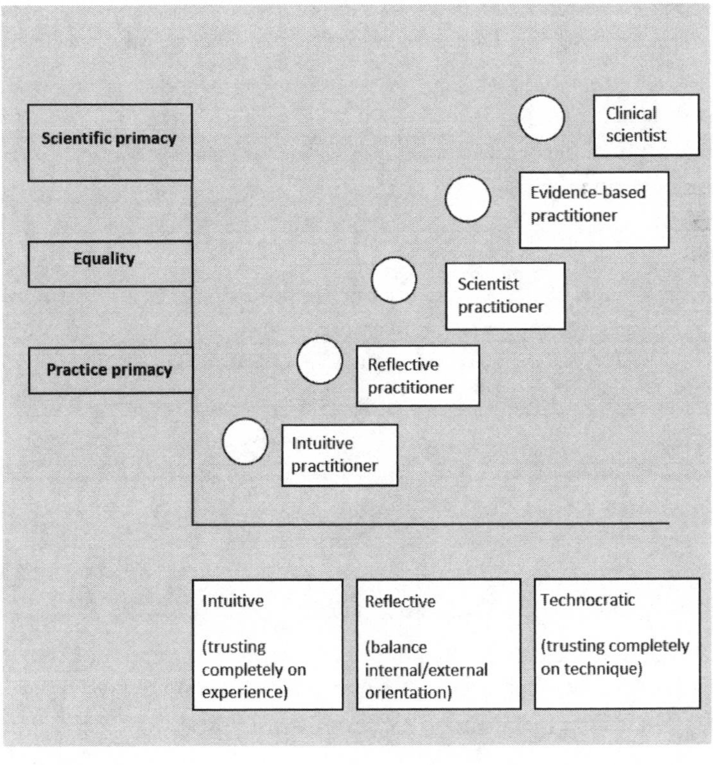

He typifies this position as one that accords to research and practice the same value in which the practitioners reflect both on their intuition (internally) and on their clinical knowledge (technique). What remains out of sight in this ideal-typical model, is the dynamics between both roles. Do they reinforce each other, are they at odds, or are both things true? To answer this question the Dutch Case Studies Project is analyzed.

The Case Studies Project as case

The interaction between both roles becomes even more interesting when chaplains study their own practice, as they are doing in the CSP. In this project, that lasts for four years, over fifty chaplains from diverse fields study their own practices. They describe and collectively discuss their work in case studies to arrive at descriptions of good practices. In the so-called research communities, a set format is followed for description and analysis. Every research community consists of eight to twelve chaplains from different denominations and one or two scholars that lead the gatherings. The working fields of hospital, military, prisons, nursing homes, mental health care and mixed care (primary care, youth care, etc.) are represented.

When the project started in the Fall of 2016, a sort of ritual was performed. The chaplains present were asked to rise and introduce themselves to their neighbors as follows: "Hello, I am [name] and I am a researcher." Without doubt, it caused some hilarity, but it marked the moment, that from then on, they received a new role: chaplain-researcher.

Method

In a first round of qualitative, semi-structured interviews with eight of the participants, spread over all six research communities, I addressed the experiences with regard to the combination of both roles.[33] In my analysis, I focused on how the chaplains describe and experience the relation between these roles, using open coding (Evers, 2015). This led to four characterizations of the relation between chaplain and researcher: *resemblance, difference, tension* and *reinforcement.*

Resemblance

When I asked the chaplains how they experience the combination of being a researcher and a chaplain, the answers were compelling. Five of the eight chaplains responded: "A researcher, who calls me a researcher? I don't feel like that!" That made me wonder: what might be the reason that

---

33 The primary questions on the subject were: "How do you experience your participation in the CSP?," and, "How do you experience the combination of being a researcher and a chaplain?"

most of them do not directly identify themselves as a researcher? And how can we best understand this relation?

Ivan tells us,

> I do not regard myself as a researcher ... As a chaplain I am researching as well. I am searching for what it means for you and my conversation partner if you say things. What values are behind that and what theories enter into this or which context? ... So the difference between chaplain and researcher is a very thin line to me. (Ivan)[34]

Just like Ivan, other chaplains felt that there is a resemblance between their role as a chaplain and as a researcher. The searching of the chaplain to understand the situation of the other person seems to many chaplains to be similar to the task of research in seeking to understand what chaplaincy is and does. In fact, in Dutch you can use the same word (*onderzoek*) for "to research" and "to search for, to inquire, to look into." It is interesting to note that the chaplain-researchers who more strongly drew a distinction between the two roles, used a different word for "research."

One of the reasons that the researching chaplains might not without hesitation identify with the role of the researcher, is that they experience their researching role in line with that of chaplain. Hutschemaekers' model (figure 1) provided different ways in which research can relate to practice. Though differences between the positions is only one of degree, the suggestion of the model seems to be that practice and research are two separate, alien activities, that somehow have to be combined. The double meaning of "to research," however, shows that they bear similar characteristics.

That similarity is in accordance with the position of the practical theologian Richard Osmer (2008), who describes a concept of practical theology that bridges academy and ministry. He sees the same interpretative tasks for both the academic researcher and for the practitioner. Both need to follow the steps of his four questions: What is going on? Why is this going on? What ought to be going on? How might we respond? In the interviews primarily the first two steps can be recognized. The third and fourth step ostensibly appear solely in a single question in the format (Walton & Körver, 2017) that is followed by the research communities. One could wonder whether all these four steps are taken into account in the CSP, but my point is that in both contexts the same researching cycle is followed.

---

34   The names (pseudonyms) between brackets refer to the respondents.

Moreover, the chaplains mentioned that interest or curiosity is needed for both the chaplain and the researcher in order to provide chaplaincy care or to do research. Like Nolan writes:

> Research is about finding answers to interesting questions. To that extent, everyone is a "researcher" ... What distinguishes professional or academic research ... is the requirement that the process of finding out "stuff" follows a robust and logical methodology, so that other researchers can check that what has been found out is credible and valid. (Nolan, 2018, p. 12)

In other words, the chaplain and researcher experience similarity between the practices of research and of chaplaincy, albeit in a different manner. The difference is explored in the following section.

Difference

Though most chaplains emphasized the resemblance, they nevertheless mentioned differences between both roles. One of the major differences they mentioned was the chaplain-researcher's attitude towards the case of one's colleague. The members of a research community discuss the case study of an accompaniment process on the basis of a format. The discussion is not so much about evaluation of what could have been done otherwise but focusses on the goals, interventions and outcomes that come to the fore in a case. The chaplain-researchers experienced it as a challenge to put aside their values and convictions with regard to the case. It seems surprising that they mention this as a difference, in view of the strong influence of Rogers' non-judgmental "unconditional positive regard" (Rogers, 1967) in chaplaincy. A non-judging attitude with respect to clients, however, seems to come easier than a non-judging attitude towards colleagues with regard to their profession.

> You have to put aside your own prejudices if you read it [the case, NdT] ... You have to give the one who contributes the case actually the chance to make clear how everything went. And that is not easy for me. (Eline)

A research attitude demands that you want to do justice to the studied object or subject. Since the researchers all have their convictions, values and beliefs with regard to what good chaplaincy is, those views can easily intertwine with their research attitude. Although one cannot erase the chaplaincy part from oneself, it demands some form of self-discipline to focus on how the accompaniment process of the chaplain actually was and not how it could have been otherwise.

> I mean, I had to learn that, like eh, what is exactly active in the method of this particular chaplain. That is something different than what I would have done in this situation, but that is not what it is about. (Maaike)

The chaplain-researchers experience this shift of focus as a process of struggle and of finding out how to discuss the cases in an appropriate manner. They searched for an attitude that was both open and critical, but in such a way that the involved chaplain did not feel roasted. That attitude did not come naturally to the chaplain-researchers but demanded a certain development in the research community.

This open, critical mode was also referred to as getting beyond the obvious or that what is perceived as obvious. Quinten stated: "I wanted exactly in this scientific research ... to get rid of the obvious." In order to do that, it is important to "see with detail what is going on in such a [accompaniment, NdT] process, without passing judgement on why someone acts in that way." As a researcher one tries to look from the outside in, setting aside one's own involvement to the project and viewing oneself from a distance.

Third-person perspective

One of the methodical features of the CSP that proved to be helpful to stimulate the research focus, was the use of the third-person perspective. The chaplains do not write their case in the first person, as "I," but in the third person, as "the chaplain." Even more, this is not only the case in the written case study, but in the plenary discussion in the research community they also refer to "the chaplain." This causes some hilarity now and then. "On the one hand it is of course very artificial, but it is a useful tool to create some distance ... it is not so much about the chaplain, but rather about what happens there in the intervention" (Simone).

The third-person perspective is sometimes treated with suspicion, as if it would ensure objectivity (cf. Nolan, 2018). However, the third-person perspective need not be interpreted as a means of attaining objectivity, but rather as a way of focusing on the research object (what happens in the intervention). The depersonalization, even if it is partial, that occurs by use of the third-person perspective can stimulate a focus on the actions and outcomes, instead of the person who is performing those actions. Obviously, the chaplains' values were involved in their actions. For that reason, their involvement should be explicitly reflected upon, without the need for the first-person perspective. In this context, I do not advocate one of the perspectives, but rather illustrate how the use of the third person can work.

A second advantage is that the third-person perspective enhances openness and critical thinking. For Maaike it "neutralizes" the case "so that you can analyze it better," at least in reading it. Yet, the analysis is not uncritical, because the use of the third person neutralizes emotions as well. "You can tell without empathy what you think about it ... you can just ask a question" (Maaike). Moreover, it helps to receive critical comments: "You can, perhaps, detach your mind and feelings for a while" (Eline).

The use of a set format

A second feature of the CSP's method is describing the case according to a set format. Dutch literature on chaplaincy shows a certain ambivalence when it comes to working with goals and methods in chaplaincy (cf. Jorna, 2005; Mackor, 2007; Molenaar & Top, 2004), since it would be at the expense of openness for both the client and the transcendent. I expected therefore that the use of a set format would be in contrast to the chaplains' way of working. Although the (chaplain-)researchers had to become accustomed to working with a format, a process that caused some critical experiences in the research communities, most of them did not feel a tension between the format and an open attitude. Despite some critical remarks with regard to the content of the format, the working with a set format was experienced as useful guideline, pleasant, and structured. Thus, the format leaves sufficient space for the highly valued attitude of openness. Like Anna responds: "Yes, I have a format in my mind, isn't it! I am open, but..."

The role of theory

The chaplains pointed out that it was not only necessary to describe what they did (step one of Osmer), but that reflection was demanded as well (step two of Osmer). The latter proved to be more complicated than they initially thought. Simplifying a complex reality is not easy at all. Even more, the project appeals to the work experience of the chaplains and makes critical connections to existing theories. The chaplain-researchers explicated, for example, what they had learned previously or reflected with the help of literature that was suggested by the research community leaders. "You analyze it more and ground it in theories, where I would usually stay in intuition, in eh experience" (Maaike). Although some chaplains are more interested in this connection to literature than others, this aspect points to a distinguishing feature of research which is to transcend mere experience and connect it to theories.

Tension

Above, some moments were indicated in which the relation between researcher and chaplain became critical. In those instances, there is a tension between the role of chaplain and that of researcher. I elaborate on three concrete tensions that arose in the interviews.

First, the personal involvement of the chaplain-researcher can lead to feelings of being criticized, personally and professionally. It remains a delicate balance between discussing someone's work and the person who performs the work. In some of the research communities this has led to the introduction of a first round of positive feedback, before starting the rather critical inquiry. Here, the roles of chaplain and researcher influence each other, both consciously and unconsciously.

Second, although the format might be experienced as useful despite struggling with it, is the experiences with the format are sometimes more critical. Some chaplains feel that there are normative concepts behind the format. In addition, not all concepts of chaplaincy seem to fit in. Another chaplain expresses that the use of a format in itself is contrary to the principles of chaplaincy. "It *has* to [emphasis added] be put in a format ... So, the less attractive side ... the rules! And I think that we as chaplains are just not like that." A certain incongruence is experienced when it comes to putting a complex story into a set model, implicating that the model does not do justice to the client's story.

Third, the method can raise ethical questions. Most of the research is done out of the client's sight. However, the use of an informed consent form to gain permission to use the case, is felt to intervene in the chaplain's practice. Although the chaplains underscore the importance of the use of informed consent, a certain tension arises as well. Simone tells of her client, reading the case: "Something happens in the relation and in the interventions." "Yes, it was once more a complete intervention, all kinds of things were touched upon again ... In this case it turned out well, but I can imagine that it could turn out very uncomfortable sometimes." This makes some chaplains hesitate to write a case about some accompaniment processes. They feel that it could possibly injure someone. Or, the chaplains think that it affects the relation with the client negatively, since the chaplain has a hidden agenda as a researcher. One chaplain even argues that you therefore cannot be a chaplain and researcher at the same time (cf. Nolan, 2018). It is interesting to see that the values of the chaplain with regard to the profession prevail over the values of research and that the role of the chaplain in a way limits the role of the researcher.

Reinforcing potential

One can also imagine that the two roles reinforce each other. The interviews provided concrete examples that confirm this assumption. However, at the present point in my research it is only possible to speak of the "reinforcing potential" of both roles. The curiosity to find out how, why and to what ends chaplains act, provides the chaplains insight into the profession as a whole and into their particular practice. The use of the third-person perspective is helpful in this respect. One of the chaplains witnessed, "Sometimes I get the feeling that it is like my fellow case-study-colleagues are joining me on the gallery, while I have a conversation with someone" (Ivan). And when the case is finally written, they learn to "see themselves from a distance" (Marijn) as if they were someone else. They learn to see themselves as another (Ricoeur, 1990), due to which they notice other things. Participation in research offers chaplains the possibility to relate to themselves and their practice in a different way and is in that way a potentially rich learning tool. Here, chaplaincy as a "research-informed profession" has an additional meaning. It is not so much the academic knowledge *from outside*, that influences the chaplains. Doing research itself evokes an opportunity for the transformation of practice.

Insight and outlook

I have shown that the relation between research and chaplaincy is much more nuanced and dynamic than is usually argued on basis of *a priori* convictions for or against research. Doing research is accordant with chaplaincy but differs at some points as well. That can raise tensions. At those moments, it is part of the chaplain's professionalism to discern if the research intervention is appropriate with regard to the profession's values. Finally, it became apparent that research does not offer mere knowledge *from outside* but involves the possibility of transformation *from within* as well.

Research appears to be not only part of the methodological competence with regard to the profession, but is, according to the chaplains, close to the heart of the profession. This raises additional questions. Is research only similar to the hermeneutical aspects of chaplaincy, or just as close to the spiritual content of the profession as well? Further elucidation is needed to discover whether research by professionals who are committed to a world view leads to insights or wisdom with regard to that world view. In what light do they see light? And what role do theological or philosophical reflections play? All this arouses curiosity and is an incitement to continue the present study. I conclude, therefore, with my thanks to the participants in this study for their contribution.

References

APC (2009 [revised 2015]). Standards of Practice for Professional Chaplains. *Plain Views,* *6*(2).

Evers, J. C. (2015). *Kwalitatieve analyse: kunst én kunde.* Amsterdam: Boom Lemma uitgevers.

Fitchett, G., Tartaglia, A., Dodd-McCue, D., & Murphy, P. (2012). Educating Chaplains for Research Literacy: Results of a National Survey of Clinical Pastoral Education Residency Programs. *Journal of Pastoral Care & Counseling: Advancing theory and professional practice through scholarly and reflective publications, 66*(1), 1-12.

Grossoehme, D. H. (2011). Research as Chaplaincy Intervention. *Journal of Health Care Chaplaincy, 17*(3-4), 97-99.

Hutschemaekers, G. (2010). De psycholoog als scientist-practitioner. In R. Kessels, G. Hutschemaekers & D. Beckers (Eds.), *Psychologie en praktijk* (pp. 15-42). Amsterdam: Boom.

Jorna, T. (2005). De geestelijke dimensie in de geestelijke verzorging. Kritische noties bij Bouwers competenties van het vak. *Tijdschrift Geestelijke Verzorging, 8*(34), 36-46.

Kelly, E. (2014). Introduction - Invitation and Rationale: Why is it necessary to research chaplaincy care practices? In G. E. Myers & S. Roberts (Eds.), *An Invitation to Chaplaincy Research: Entering the Process* (pp. i-xi). HealthCare Chaplaincy Network.

Mackor, A. R. (2007). Standaardisering en ambtelijke binding. Lopen de idealen van geestelijk verzorgers gevaar? In J. Kole & D. De Ruyter (Eds.), *Werkzame idealen. Ethische reflecties op professionaliteit* (pp. 89-103). Assen: Van Gorcum.

Molenaar, B., & Top, M. (2004). De VGVZ: een diagnose... *Tijdschrift Geestelijke Verzorging, 7*(30), 39-46.

Nolan, S. (2018). Introduction - Autoethnography in Chaplain Case Study Research. In G. Fitchett & S. Nolan (Eds.), *Case studies in spiritual care. Healthcare chaplaincy assessments, interventions and outcomes* (pp. 11-30). London: Jessica Kingsley Publishers.

Ricoeur, P. (1990). *Soi-même comme un autre.* Paris: Éditions du Seuil.

Rogers, C. R. (1967). *The Therapeutic relationship and its impact. A study of psychotherapy with schizophrenics.* Madison: University of Wisconsin Press.

Van der Leer, N. (2016). De geestelijk verzorger als onderzoeker. De integratie van zingeving en spiritualiteit in de zorg en de rol van de geestelijk verzorger. *Tijdschrift Geestelijke Verzorging, 19*(84), 42-47.

VGVZ (2015). *Beroepsstandaard geestelijk verzorger.* Amsterdam: VGVZ.

Chapter 21.

Epilogue

Developing the case

Jacques Körver, Renske Kruizinga, Niels den Toom, Martin Walton

Introduction

Out of the variety of contributions to this conference volume we select a few key issues for concluding remarks. The remarks, however, are not conclusions but questions and issues for further research. We reiterate the comment in the introduction that we are well aware of the building stage in which case study research in chaplaincy care finds itself and into which this volume offers several different doors. We comment on three areas of concern: methodology, characterizations of chaplaincy care and the professionalization of chaplaincy.

Methodological notes

Research agenda

Chaplaincy is in development, in practice and in theory. Research into chaplaincy has also made a great leap forward over the past few decades. Fitchett (chapter 2) and Körver (chapter 3) show that empirical research into the goals and target groups, interventions and effects of chaplaincy has increased in breadth and depth worldwide. The diversity of research methods (qualitative, quantitative and mixed methods) has also grown. The professional group is clearly more positive about research than in the past, is more involved in it and shows a greater degree of research literacy (Snowden et al., 2017). There has been more cooperation between researchers from different institutes, also internationally. At the same time, it becomes clear that there is a great need for a research agenda that not only identifies the substantive priorities in the research, but also the good practices in methodology (Damen, Delaney, & Fitchett, 2018; Damen, Schuhmann, Lensvelt-Mulders, & Leget, 2019). Such a research agenda can ensure that financial and human resources can be used more effectively, that individual researchers and institutes are called to account for their specific expertise, and that the emancipation of chaplaincy in relation to other professions and in relation to subsidy providers is strengthened. At present, research is still too fragmented. This is in part unavoidable, precisely because the diversity of fields of work, religious and philosophical backgrounds, cultural contexts, existential themes and target groups represents the richness and broad bandwidth of chaplaincy. Moreover, the research is of varying methodological quality and too often there is a lack of clarity about the concepts used, the intended objectives and the forms of guidance or interventions used. The definition and focus of chaplaincy also need to be more clearly defined.

Case studies and the level of evidence

Case study research has the potential to be a connecting factor in international chaplaincy research. It is precisely the meticulous mapping of what chaplains do (interventions), what they aim for implicitly or explicitly (intentions), which theoretical orientations they use to map out their path, and what effects can be observed or reported, that offers the opportunity to make active elements and good practices visible. This exploratory effort also has an emancipatory effect on those directly involved (chaplains, researchers, stakeholders) and on the profession of chaplaincy. These precise probes and descriptions can then serve to initiate follow-up research. That need not necessarily be randomized controlled trials. The field of chaplaincy should remain aware of the specific nature of its research object, which to a large extent requires other research methods than those that are prevalent, for example, in the medical or social scientific research traditions. It is precisely the emphasis on the complex subjects of meaning and world view (which, according to the professional standard of the Dutch association of chaplains, are the central objectives of chaplaincy) that require pre-eminently qualitative and mixed methods research (Flyvbjerg, 2006; Creswell & Plano-Clark, 2011; Gijsberts, 2015).

In his contribution based on the effectiveness ladder, Veerman (chapter 4) makes clear that interventions can be developed step by step. Qualitative and naturalistic case studies (chapter 10) are excellently suited for making active elements in the interventions explicit, including the underlying theoretical basis, eventually leading to the status of "promising." Subsequently, the use of quantitative case studies (N=1-studies, without or with control, without or with follow-up) can lead to higher levels of evidence. It is, therefore, always necessary to consider the degree of evidence required, the context in which the intervention (or elements of it) will be used, the priority of any research in relation to the further development of chaplaincy, and who the stakeholders are. In this approach, evidence-based practice will thus be developed on the basis of practice-based evidence. Insight into the goals, interventions and effects of chaplaincy will be developed in close proximity to the practice of chaplains, serving step by step to clarify, deepen and broaden the profession and providing insights to better guide, profile and position the practice of chaplaincy.

Methodological questions

These latter steps already anticipate the next phase of the research with the help of case studies. However, before these next steps can be taken, a number of conditions must be met. These relate to issues such as sampling and comparison of case studies (chapter 8). The choice of a case study is always made by the chaplain. It needs to be clear what motives played a role in the selection, and what arguments are later linked to the choice during reflection. Can a reasonable representativeness with regard to target groups, methods and themes in the relevant field of chaplaincy be achieved gradually by comparing case studies with each other? Can, on the basis of such comparison, "active elements" be identified that can be further investigated with a view to the development of plausible or effective interventions? Against the background of these questions, it is also important to consider how the contribution of the chaplains themselves can be valued in this type of research. With the help of the participation ladder, Jacobs (chapter 5) offers a matrix with which the narrative contribution of the chaplains can be characterized and the significance of the collaboration between the researchers and the chaplains can subsequently be indicated. These questions and issues reflect the weak spots in the current research based on case studies: the subjective choice for a case study, the reporting by the chaplain himself and not by an independent researcher, and the fact that the perspective of the client is less present despite the member check. This requires case study research into chaplaincy to learn from and become more in line with research within other disciplines that have a longer research tradition in this type of research (Stake, 2005; Thomas, 2011; Smith, 2012; Yin, 2014; Tate et al., 2016; Forrester, 2017).

An important issue for the next steps in the case study research is from what perspective and on the basis of which research questions case studies are compared with each other. A number of contributions in this publication already provide some very interesting suggestions in this respect. For example, Braakhuis (chapter 9) recommends that the relationship between basic relational attitudes and concrete purposefulness in the actions of chaplains should be investigated with the help of case studies. In the literature on chaplaincy she discovered that the basic relational attitude receives almost exclusive emphasis and that specific goals related to the expertise of the chaplain are in danger of being neglected. Is that also the case in practice? The research project described by Höfler and Roser

(chapter 10) takes on another fascinating perspective. In this German research project case studies are examined from the point of view of the extent to which the spirituality of the chaplain itself influences the effects of
chaplaincy. And elsewhere, Wirpsa et al. (2019) have described how case
study research is helpful in clarifying the contribution that chaplains can
make to shared decision making in healthcare. Whatever the focus, the
three challenges formulated by Schuhmann and Pleizier (chapter 8) need
to be addressed. What counts as data? How does sampling take place?
And what are the methodological strategies?

A final, more methodical point concerns the quality of the case studies. Good (qualitative) research depends, after all, on good data. The use
of a detailed format for the description of a case study and for the reflection on the case study in the research community lift the data to a more
intersubjective plausibility. Further research should clarify whether the
use of the third person in the description and reflection contributes to
this plausibility. The Dutch Case Studies Project has good experience
with the third person perspective, but it is questioned by others. The approach to case studies from a naturalistic perspective (chapter 6) focuses
on the complex layers of meaning in which the chaplain is involved, on
the interpersonal construction of meaning and on the inescapable inter-
wovenness of the researched and the researcher. The plausibility of the
case studies is also supported by the continuous efforts of the member
check at a double level: in the relationship between chaplain and client
and in the relationship between chaplain and researcher. All these points
deserve more attention and research. These are points that have gradually
appeared on the agenda while conducting the research and that can further clarify this form of research, make it methodologically stronger and
offer researchers more and better tools.

What do we learn from case studies about the core of the profession of chaplains?

Case studies analyzed

As case study research in chaplaincy is relatively new and the Dutch project is still underway, we cannot yet present definitive conclusions on
what we learn from case studies. Hopefully in the coming years we will be
able to provide a clearer picture of what it is that chaplains do, for what
reasons and to what ends. At the case study research conference in 2019,
discussion arose as to how chaplains' interventions should be positioned
in relation to other therapeutic interventions. The discussion was initiated by Steve Nolan's claim that chaplaincy care is a highly specialized

form of psychological therapy (chapter 7). In this concluding chapter we want to examine that claim by looking at case studies gathered in this book (chapters 12, 13, 14 and 15).

Chaplaincy as a religious practice

Nolan states that to date the theoretical assumption is that chaplaincy is essentially a religious practice. In the Netherlands, where a relatively large number of humanistic and non-religious affiliated chaplains are working in different fields, that assumption is not so evident (Liefbroer & Berghuijs, 2019). In view of the international literature, however, we have to agree with Nolan that literature thus far suggests a religious tradition for chaplains. That is likely due to the fact that the field of humanistic and non-religious affiliated chaplaincy is relatively new (Schuhmann & Damen, 2018; Savage, 2018) and not so much rooted in the international debate as is, for instance, the Christian foundation of chaplaincy is. In society, at least in Dutch society, the overall image of chaplaincy being a religious practice is not shared by all. The picture is more diverse. It would be helpful, as Nolan suggests, if more case studies were published that provide insight into the practice of non-religious affiliated or humanistic chaplains.

Chaplaincy as a specialized form of psychotherapy

A more important remark we want to make concerns Nolan's description of five common factors in chaplaincy that also apply to psychotherapy. Nolan identifies five common factors: making assessments, building rapport, active listening, intentionally use of self and challenge, and demonstrating unconditional positive regard and empathy. Indeed, these factors may be shared between the two professions. However, we believe that under the surface these factors are employed differently by chaplains due to their unique role, expertise and professional identity.

In the case study described by chaplain Jorissen (chapter 15), we can see that the unique position of a chaplain working in the military context is quite significant. This is characteristically paraphrased by the client, a war veteran who never spoke about his experiences, when he replies on the need to talk about his military past: "Yes, with you. From soldier to soldier. You are no ordinary pastor." This statement summarizes the position of a military chaplain who is part of the military, including having his own rank, and at the same time a representative of a certain religious background. This position opens a shared frame of reference that facilitates talking on complex issues such as moral injury.

Another example is shown in the case (chapter 12), in which chaplain Went is approached by one of the women in prison who tells her she will be released from prison on the following Thursday. The woman asks the chaplain to pray for her and asks for God's blessing. This example shows that the focus of chaplaincy is ultimately different from psychotherapy. Religious aspects cannot be applied as "special factors" or as an extra curriculum but are fundamental to the position of a chaplain. Being rooted in a certain religion or life view is central to the professional identity of a chaplain and not something that can be turned on or off when necessary. A chaplain can and may always be addressed on to the basis of affiliation with a certain life view.

In comparison with the other case studies gathered in this book, the case studies presented by Van der Meer (chapter 13) exemplify more similarities with psychotherapy. Especially when looking at the "outcome" of Van der Meer's interventions. A youngster named Ralph summarizes the main result of their contact: "I say and explain more to others. I talk about the things that worry me. Now, I speak out, whereas I kept it in me before." Hearing this, one would not specifically ascribe these words to a chaplain's intervention. The chaplain, however, does not describes his intervention in terms of psychotherapeutic methods, but rather as methods underlining the uniqueness of chaplaincy. "There was time, space, silence, genuine interest and repetition creating predictability, confidence and courage." The second case reported by Van der Meer immediately addresses the client's anger with God. Knowledge of how religion works in people's life belongs to the specific task of a chaplain. That knowledge is not an additional element to psychotherapy, but a much more rooted source from which chaplains can draw. On a more critical note: there is, of course, a discrepancy between how chaplaincy ideally differs from psychotherapy and to what extent this is the case in practice. We find in many cases also religious themes that could be addressed but were not.

The case study of chaplain Van Hoof about Esther (chapter 14), sheds new light on our discussion. In this case study a therapist calls in the help of a chaplain to change the clients thinking patterns, as cognitive interventions have thus far not been successful. The chaplain works with a moral counseling approach as it concerns a case of a life-threatening dilemma in which an agreement is made between two teenage girls. The agreement means that if one of them committed suicide, the other would follow within a year. At the first consultation between Esther and the chaplain the therapist is also present. Afterwards, the therapist expresses appreciation of the depth of the conversation. The chaplain explores values that are important to Esther and links those core values, including safety and trust in Esther's own judgment and strength, to daily reality on the treatment ward. Because the therapy team has a desire for control and want to protect Esther and the team from another suicide, the team tries to make firm agreements with her. The chaplain advises that Esther would be helped above all by support and trust and with the help of holding, experiencing the emotions of the others without interpreting or wanting to change them. The chaplain's insight, derived from exploring the life-threatening dilemma on values and meaning, shows the additional impact chaplaincy can have alongside (other forms of) psychotherapy.

Examining and exposing the special impact of chaplaincy care, not instead of but in addition to other therapies, better reveals the value of chaplaincy than emphasizing what chaplaincy has in common with psychotherapy. Furthermore, it can be asked whether the latter approach does sufficient justice to the case studies that demonstrate a fundamental different field of work in terms of underlying theories, the focus on values and meaning in life and the impact of being affiliated to a certain life view. More importantly, chaplains' interventions may lead to other outcomes for the client. At this point we have only indications of this, but not enough results to generalize and substantiate this claim. Hopefully, research in the field of chaplaincy such as our Dutch Case Studies Project can help us further in understanding what chaplains do and to what outcomes that may lead.

How does case study research contribute to chaplains' professionalism?

Case study research and professionalization
Several chapters in this book are written from the perspective of professionalization of chaplaincy and address the question how involvement in case study research affects the professionalism of chaplaincy and chaplains. Den Toom (chapter 20) pointed out that literature already indicates that the relation between research and chaplaincy can be fruitful for the chaplain's professionalism. Here, this indication is crystallized in the witnesses of chaplain-researchers. It is not only so that case study research evolves in the wake of the quest for professionalization of chaplaincy, but also that the willingness of chaplains to participate in a research project can also be seen as part of a personal professionalization process. It is, therefore, difficult to distinguish between what can be ascribed to participation in case study research and what is the fruit of an already active professionalization process.

What complicates the matter even more is that one cannot speak of case study research univocally, as case study research is conducted in many ways. Some reflect individually on an accompaniment process (Galchutt, chapter 11), whereas others reflect on the case studies of both themselves and others in a research community for a relatively short (Boeykens, chapter 19; Desmet, chapter 18) or longer (Weeda, chapter 16; Berkhout, chapter 17; Den Toom, chapter 20) period according to a set format. Obviously, the various approaches result in different learning processes. This being said, we glean from the chapters what is indicated to be the contribution of case study research to the professionalism of the chaplains.

Researching chaplains

As Den Toom argues, being involved with research is increasingly considered to be part of chaplains' professionalism. He describes the resemblances between both roles and the possible differences and tensions. Boeykens, Desmet and Galchutt support the resemblances as they report that the case study method is in line with the way chaplains work, in which the central role of hermeneutics is emphasized. Galchutt, who conducted the research individually, reports a higher degree of resemblance between chaplaincy and case study research. In the case where chaplains worked according to a format and from a third-person perspective a degree of alienation takes place as well, resulting in uncomfortable feelings (e.g. due to translating a narrative into a formatted case study). The main difficulty seems to be in finding language that is precise enough to describe goals, interventions and results and in conceiving of the profession accordingly. Long term involvement seems to make writing and discussing go more easily (Weeda).

Professionalization of chaplaincy

Case study research can be seen as a part of professionalization at two levels. It contributes, first of all, to the profession as a whole, and secondly, to the development of the individual professional. The argument for case studies is generally made in favor of the profession as a whole (Fitchett, 2011; Walton & Körver, 2017). It is interesting to see that various authors stress the significance of case study research to describe what chaplains do (goals, interventions and results), adding to the professional body of knowledge, and to make the case for chaplaincy. Thereby, case study research is used as advocacy of or argument for the added value of chaplaincy. Weeda, Desmet, Boeykens and Berkhout all formulate the value of case studies in terms of adding to the *exchange value* (Van der Krogt, 1981) of chaplaincy among other professions. Boeykens and Desmet refer to this as "professional identity," implying that chaplains know *what* they do and with what *effects*. They report that a certain common language emerged in the Flemish research community that helps in sharing information with other professionals. The contribution to the advocacy of chaplaincy is in line with what Den Toom observes in the professional standard of chaplaincy in the Netherlands (VGVZ, 2015), i.e. that research improves communication in organizations with other professionals.

However, one could ask critically, if the focus on strengthening the argument of the added value of chaplaincy does not hinder the researchers from seeing what is really going on. This is especially the case inasmuch as the goals, interventions and effects are reported by the chaplains themselves. In other words, does case study research reveal new insights or does it mainly reproduce the values and desirable outcomes of which chaplains are already convinced? Desmet, for example, notices that is hard to assess whether the described outcomes are observed or just desired. In addition, Den Toom shows that when the values of research and chaplaincy seem to contradict each other, chaplains let the assumed values of their profession prevail. This raises the question, how case studies might not only make the values and claims of chaplaincy more tangible, but also criticize existing, and perhaps distorted, images of chaplaincy.

Berkhout and Weeda report that they experienced that their existing images (e.g. learned during their initial education) were challenged. Berkhout explicitly mentions that her image of the fully equal, non-intervening chaplain was altered. The chaplains of the research community turned out to have more goals, to chart more often and to advise more extensively than they thought they did. Weeda reports that she was encouraged to critically reflect on her goals (e.g. on proximity) and to relate her care to theories of chaplaincy and the surrounding context.

Professionalizing chaplains

Case study research thus contributes to the professionalization of chaplaincy, but how does it affect the professionalism of the participating chaplains? It becomes clear that it challenges the way chaplains think about their profession. In general, case study research evokes reflection on the nature and specific features of chaplaincy. It provides insight into the themes that are discussed, the methods employed, the way chaplaincy is embedded in the organization, etcetera. These insights result in a better articulation of goals, interventions and results and of the added values, all of which help chaplains to communicate about their profession to others (Berkhout, Boeykens, Desmet, and Weeda). Some report that they feel more recognized and that they are more confident about their professional identity. In addition, they are challenged to engage in theoretical reflection on their profession. Theoretical insights from the case studies occasionally lead to a change in behavior. As Berkhout reports, she positions herself more explicitly as an endorsed chaplain and addresses religious themes more directly. Furthermore, becoming conscious of the frequent use of metaphors in chaplaincy, enables her to use metaphors in a more intentional way. Here we see that doing case study research reinforces chaplains in their professional identity and challenges them to critically reflect on it at the same time. Consequently, they find more appropriate words to communicate with other professionals and to employ their interventions more consciously, resulting sometimes in modesty, but mainly in excitement about chaplaincy.

References

Creswell, J. W., & Plano-Clark, V. L. (2011). *Designing and conducting mixed methods research* (2 ed.). Los Angeles: Sage.

Damen, A., Delaney, A., & Fitchett, G. (2018). Research Priorities for Healthcare Chaplaincy. Views of U.S. chaplains. *Journal of Health Care Chaplaincy, 24*(2), 57-66.

Damen, A., Schuhmann, C., Lensvelt-Mulders, G., & Leget, C. (2019). Research Priorities for Health Care Chaplaincy in The Netherlands. A Delphi study among Dutch chaplains. *Journal of Health Care Chaplaincy*, in press.

Fitchett, G. (2011). Making our case(s). *Journal of Health Care Chaplaincy, 17*(1-2), 3-18.

Flyvbjerg, B. (2006). Five misunderstandings about case-study research. *Qualitative Inquiry, 12*(2), 219-245.

Forrester, J. (2017). *Thinking in cases*. Cambridge: Polity Press.

Gijsberts, M. J. H. E. (2015). *Spiritual care at the end of life in Dutch nursing homes. A mixed method study*. Amsterdam: Vrije Universiteit Amsterdam.

Liefbroer, A., & Berghuijs, J. (2019). Spiritual Care for Everyone? An Analysis of Personal and Organizational Differences in Perceptions of Religious Diversity Among Spiritual Caregivers. *Journal of Health Care Chaplaincy, 25*(3), 1-20.

Savage, D. (2018). *Non-religious Pastoral Care: A Practical Guide*. London: Routledge.

Schuhmann, C., & Damen, A. (2018). Representing the Good: Pastoral care in a secular age. *Pastoral psychology, 67*(4), 405-417.

Smith, J. D. (2012). Single-case experimental designs. A systematic review of published research and current standards. *Psychological Methods, 17*(4), 510-550.

Snowden, A., Fitchett, G., Grossoehme, D. H., Handzo, G., Kelly, E., ... Flannelly, K. J. (2017). International Study of Chaplains' Attitudes About Research. *Journal of Health Care Chaplaincy, 23*(1), 34-43.

Stake, R. E. (2005). Qualitative case studies. In N. K. Denzin & Y. S. Lincoln (Eds.), *The SAGE handbook of qualitative research* (3rd ed., pp. 443-466). Thousand Oaks: Sage.

Tate, R. L., Perdices, M., Rosenkoetter, U., Shadish, W., Vohra, S., ... Wilson, B. (2016). The Single-Case Reporting Guideline In Behavioural Interventions (SCRIBE) 2016 statement. *Archives of Scientific Psychology, 4*(1), 1-9.

Thomas, G. (2011). *How to do your case study? A guide for students & researchers.* London: Sage.

Van der Krogt, T. P. W. M. (1981). *Professionalisering en collectieve macht: een conceptueel kader.* 's-Gravenhage: Vuga.

VGVZ (2015). *Beroepsstandaard geestelijk verzorger.* Amsterdam: VGVZ.

Walton, M., & Körver, J. (2017). Dutch case studies project in chaplaincy care: A description and theoretical explanation of the format and procedures. *Health and Social Care Chaplaincy, 5*(2), 257-280.

Wirpsa, J. M., Johnson, E. R., Bieler, J., Boyken, L., Pugliese, K., ... Murphy, P. (2019). Interprofessional Models for Shared Decision Making: The Role of the Health Care Chaplain. *Journal of Health Care Chaplaincy, 25*(1), 20-44.

Yin, R. K. (2014). *Case study research. Design and methods* (5th ed.). Los Angeles: Sage.

Personal information authors

L. (Loes) Berkhout works as a healthcare chaplain at the UMCU Hospital, Utrecht, The Netherlands; l.berkhout@umcutrecht.nl.

F. (Frieda) Boeykens is pastoral supervisor at the Academic Center for Practical Theology of the Faculty of Theology and Religious Studies, KU Leuven, Belgium; frieda.boeykens@kuleuven.be.

M. (Myriam) Braakhuis works as a chaplain at the Salvation Army, Utrecht, The Netherlands. She worked for one year as a PhD candidate within the Case Studies Project; the article is a result of her literature study; myriam.braakhuis@legerdesheils.nl.

L. (Lindsy) Desmet is a PhD candidate at the Faculty of Theology and Religious Studies, KU Leuven, and former coordinator of the European Research Institute for Chaplaincy in Healthcare (ERICH), Belgium. Her PhD project is titled "Measuring the impact of spiritual care provided by hospital chaplains"; lindsy.desmet@kuleuven.be.

J. N. (Niels) den Toom is a PhD candidate at the Protestant Theological University, Groningen, The Netherlands. His PhD project is titled "Shaping Chaplaincy by Doing Research"; j.n.toom@pthu.nl.

R. J. (Reijer) de Vries is assistant professor of Practical Theology and Pastoral Care at the Protestant Theological University, Amsterdam and staff member at the University Center for Chaplaincy Studies (UCGV), The Netherlands; r.j.de.vries@pthu.nl.

G. (George) Fitchett is a Professor and the Director of Research in the Department of Religion, Health & Human Values at Rush University Medical Center, Chicago, United States. He is also the director of Transforming Chaplaincy; George_Fitchett@rush.edu.

P. (Paul) Galchutt works as a research staff chaplain at the M Health Fair-view, Minneapolis, United States. He is also active as convener for Trans-forming Chaplaincy's hospice-palliative spiritual care research network; pgalchu1@fairview.org.

N. (Nika) Höfler is a PhD candidate at the Chair for Practical Theology and Religious Education of the Westfälische Wilhelms-Universität Mün-ster, Germany; nika.hoefler@uni-muenster.de.

G. C. (Gaby) Jacobs is professor in Humanist Chaplaincy Studies for a Plu-ral Society, University of Humanistic Studies, Utrecht, The Netherlands; G.Jacobs@UvH.nl.

S. (Soerish) Jaggan works as a prison chaplain, Zaanstad, The Netherlands; s.jaggan@dji.minjus.nl.

G. M. (Gertjan) Jorissen is military chaplain, with special attention for the care of veterans, The Netherlands; gj.jorissen@mindef.nl.

G. (Geerhard) Kloppenburg works as a prison chaplain in Zaanstad and Lelystad, The Netherlands; ge.kloppenb@dji.minjus.nl.

J. W. G. (Jacques) Körver is associate professor of Practical Theology and Spiritual Care at Tilburg School of Catholic Theology and director of the University Center for Chaplaincy Studies (UCGV), Tilburg/Utrecht, The Netherlands; J.W.G.Korver@tilburguniversity.edu.

R. (Renske) Kruizinga is researcher/policy officer at the University Cen-ter for Chaplaincy Studies (UCGV), Tilburg/Utrecht, The Netherlands; R.Kruizinga@tilburguniversity.edu.

J. K. (Hanneke) Muthert is associate professor of Psychology of Religion & Spiritual Care at the Faculty of Theology and Religious Studies University of Groningen, The Netherlands; j.k.muthert@rug.nl. She also works as a chaplain: www.BijHannekegv.nl

S. (Steve) Nolan is chaplain at Princess Alice Hospice and visiting re-search fellow at the University of Winchester, United Kingdom; steveno-lan@PAH.org.uk.

T. T. J. (Theo) Pleizier is assistant professor of Practical Theology at the Protestant Theological University, Groningen, The Netherlands; t.t.j.pleizier@pthu.nl.

T. (Traugott) Roser holds the Chair for Practical Theology at the Westfälische Wilhelms-Universität Münster, Germany; traugott.roser@uni-muenster.de.

C. M. (Carmen) Schuhmann is assistant professor in Practical Humanistic Studies at the University of Humanistic Studies, Utrecht, The Netherlands; C.Schuhmann@UvH.nl.

M. J. (Martijn) Stoutjesdijk is a PhD candidate at Tilburg School of Catholic Theology and policy officer at the University Center for Chaplaincy Studies (UCGV), Tilburg/Utrecht, The Netherlands; M.J.Stoutjesdijk@ tilburguniversity.edu.

T. C. (Tjeerd) van der Meer is spiritual counselor at Jeugdhulp Friesland, The Netherlands; meer.tcvander@jeugdhulpfriesland.nl.

M. (Martin) van Hemert works as a prison chaplain, Zaanstad, The Netherlands; mvhemert@kpnplanet.nl.

M. (Monique) van Hoof works as a mental healthcare chaplain at GGZ OostBrabant, The Netherlands; mji.hoofvan@ggzoostbrabant.nl.

J. W. (Jan Willem) Veerman is professor emeritus of Special Child and Youth Care at Radboud University Nijmegen, The Netherlands, and former director of Praktikon, an organization for research in youth care and education; jw.veerman@pwo.ru.nl.

M. N. (Martin) Walton is professor emeritus of Spiritual Care and Chaplaincy Studies at the Protestant Theological University, Groningen, The Netherlands; mwalton@pthu.nl.

J. (Jacqueline) Weeda works as a healthcare chaplain at GGZ Rivierduinen, The Netherlands; j.weeda@rivierduinen.nl.

M. (Marja) Went works as a prison chaplain, The Netherlands; m.went@ kpnmail.nl.

Stakeholders Case Studies Project

The Dutch Case Studies Project is a collaborative research project with the following stakeholders:

- Agora; www.agora.nl
- Amsterdam UMC; www.amsterdamumc.nl
- Amphia Ziekenhuis; www.amphia.nl
- Antoni van Leeuwenziekenhuis; www.avl.nl
- AxionContinu; www.axioncontinu.nl
- Careyn De Vier Ambachten; www.careyn.nl
- Dichterbij; www.dichterbij.nl
- Dimence Groep; www.dimencegroep.nl
- Envida; www.envida.nl
- Erasmus MC; www.erasmusmc.nl
- GGZ Breburg; www.ggzbreburg.nl
- GGZ Oost Brabant; www.ggzoostbrabant.nl
- GGZ Rivierduinen; www.rivierduinen.nl
- GGZ-NHN; www.ggz-nhn.nl
- Isala Klinieken; www.isala.nl
- Jeugdhulp Friesland; www.jeugdhulpfriesland.nl
- Lentis; www.lentis.nl
- Liberein; www.liberein.nl
- Lunetzorg; www.lunetzorg.com
- Maasstadziekenhuis; www.maasstadziekenhuis.nl
- Martini Ziekenhuis; www.martiniziekenhuis.nl
- Máxima Medisch Centrum; www.mmc.nl
- Mediant GGZ; www.mediant.nl
- Diensten Geestelijke Verzorging Ministerie van Defensie; www.defensie.nl/onderwerpen/personeelszorg/geestelijke-verzorging
- Dienst Geestelijke Verzorging van de Dienst Justitiële Inrichtingen; www.dji.nl
- New Connective; www.newconnective.nl
- NPV; www.npvzorg.nl
- OLVG; www.olvg.nl
- Protestant Theological University; www.pthu.nl
- Reliëf; www.relief.nl

- Residentie Ruitersbos; www.ruitersbos.nl
- Rijnstate Ziekenhuis; www.rijnstate.nl
- Stichting Kwaliteitsregister Geestelijke Verzorging; www.skgv-register.nl
- St. Antonius Ziekenhuis; www.antoniusziekenhuis.nl
- St. Jansdal Ziekenhuis; www.stjansdal.nl
- Tergooi Ziekenhuis; www.tergooi.nl
- Tilburg School of Catholic Theology; www.tilburguniversity.edu/theology
- Universitair Medisch Centrum Utrecht; www.umcu.nl
- Vereniging van Geestelijk Verzorgers; www.vgvz.nl
- Vilans; www.vilans.nl
- Zorgspectrum Het Zand; www.hetzand.nl